London, Hub of the Industrial Revolution

The International Library of Historical Studies
Series ISBN 1 86064 079 6

The International Library of Historical Studies (ILHS) brings together the work of leading historians from universities in the English-speaking world and beyond. It constitutes a forum for original scholarship from the United Kingdom, continental Europe, the USA, the Commonwealth and the Developing World. The books are the fruit of original research and thinking and they contribute to the most advanced historiographical debate and are exhaustively assessed by the authors' academic peers. The Library consists of a numbered series, covers a wide subject range and is truly international in its geographical scope. It provides a unique and authoritative resource for libraries and scholars and for student reference.

Titles in the Series

London, Hub of the Industrial Revolution

A Revisionary History 1775–1825

DAVID BARNETT

Tauris Academic Studies
LONDON · NEW YORK

Published in 1998 by Tauris Academic Studies
an imprint of I.B.Tauris & Co Ltd,
Victoria House, Bloomsbury Square, London WC1B 4DZ
175 Fifth Avenue, New York NY 10010

In the United States of America and in Canada distributed by
St Martin's Press, 175 Fifth Avenue, New York NY 10010

A full CIP record for this book is available from the British Library
A full CIP record for this book is available from the Library of Congress

ISBN 1 86064 196 2

Library of Congress catalog card number: available

Set in Monotype Dante by Ewan Smith, London
Printed and bound in Great Britain by WBC Ltd, Bridgend

Contents

Tables

Preface

It has become a modern truism that information is power and that the technology and systems used to deliver that information are the keys to the exercise of that power. In practice, nothing like so simplistic a situation holds true. A career of over 30 years in two very different sectors of the British economy – energy and road transport – taught me many things. Among these was the crucial lesson that most people prefer to determine economic policy and make business decisions in the light of their prejudices, rather than in the light of objective fact. All too often dogma comes first; it is literally true that many people prefer not to be confused with the facts when they have already made up their minds. A major problem is that setting up objective information systems is difficult and costly. Another is that when they are set up they do not always give the answers people want to hear. It is not surprising, therefore, that in this field, as in many others, it is less often the case that the solution has been tried and found wanting and more often that it has been found difficult and not tried.

On a personal note, 36 years ago, after the privilege of working under the late Professor David Chambers at the University of Nottingham, I succumbed to the temptations of the business world and abandoned my academic ambitions. Thirty-one years later my business career came to a premature end and I was fortunate enough to meet up with a contemporary post-graduate student of David Chambers from the late 1950s and early 1960s, Stanley Chapman, now Professor of Business History at the University of Nottingham. I had never lost interest in economic and social history and he unerringly steered me to a PhD project which combined my interests in these subjects, my love of and fascination with London – I am a cockney born within the sound of Bow Bells – and my practical experience of both business information systems and business planning up to the level of chief executive. He was able to point me to a unique and virtually unused source of data in the London fire office records in the Guildhall Library. Without his advice, guidance and enthusiastic support neither the PhD I was awarded in July 1996 nor this book would have been possible.

I was moved to attempt a reconstruction of the economy of London during the Industrial Revolution, adhering to the strict rules of statistical evidence which I had seen so regularly ignored throughout my business career. This book is the result of that project, my attempt to construct a sound and objective database for the history and historians of the greatest city the world had ever seen, in part in the hope that historians will prove more receptive to 'facts', however inconvenient, than government and business.

More specifically, this book is based on my common-sense belief that London had to have been far more important during the Industrial Revolution than many historians believed and on the realisation that, however derided by the critics of economic planning in the late twentieth century, the techniques painfully evolved by modern economic statisticians can readily be applied to the huge volume of factual evidence surviving for London in the last quarter of the eighteenth century and the first quarter of the nineteenth.

Although acutely aware of the possibilities offered to businessman and historian alike by the computer, I am myself of the pre-computer generation. This book would have been impossible without the computer expertise of my son-in-law Jonathan Birkett. I could not have coped without the programs and systems he devised for me and his ever ready willingness to help and advise, especially when I reached what seemed to me to be a complete impasse. I am also grateful for the help of the staff of the Guildhall Library, and the many other libraries I used, over the many months during which I was gathering the mountains of data on which this book is based.

Finally, this book would never have been written without either the constant support of my family or the patience and understanding of my wife during the several years in which it took up so much of my time. It is my greatest pleasure to dedicate it to her.

Introduction

'The chief business of the American people is business' said President Calvin Coolidge speaking in New York in 1925. One hundred years earlier this could have been as well said of London. It was then that the poet Robert Southey marvelled of London, as he might a century later of New York:

> I happened to go into a pastrycook's shop one morning and inquired of the mistress why she kept her window open during the severe weather – which I observed most of the trade did. She told me, that were she to close it, her receipts would be lessened forty or fifty shillings a day – so many were the persons who took up buns or biscuits as they passed by and threw their pence in, not allowing themselves time to enter. Was there ever so indefatigable a people.[1]

Writing in 1994, Roy Porter expressed the view that London 'Between the two Elizabeths ... was to become the world's greatest city'.[2] If so, London in 1700, a century after the death of the first Elizabeth, was still just one of Europe's major cities, not particularly pre-eminent compared with, say, Paris or Amsterdam. However, within another hundred years, by the first quarter of the nineteenth century, London had become indisputably the largest city the world had ever seen. By 1831 it had a population in excess of one and a half million, greater than or equal to that of the capital cities of 8 of the 14 European Community nations in the 1990s.

Between the middle of the eighteenth century and the first quarter of the nineteenth, London not only more than doubled in size, it became the largest single business and industrial centre and market of the world's first modern industrial economy. The key period was the half century from 1775 to 1825. Just as the United States was to achieve an unparalleled growth in prosperity in the half century of political stability after the end of the Civil War, so the background to the Industrial Revolution in Britain was also one of political stability. Although more than half the period was dominated by far-flung wars on an almost world-wide scale – the American war of the 1770s and the far greater French revolutionary wars of 1793 to 1815 – and although there was some internal unrest, such as the Gordon Riots in the earlier part of the period and the Peterloo massacre in the latter part, it is nevertheless true that the half century from 1775 to 1825 was characterised by an essential political stability.

Yet, for most of the twentieth century, the view has been that the Industrial Revolution passed London by: that at best its contribution was modest and outside the industrial mainstream; at worst, it was characterised by gloom and decay. For Fernand Braudel, 'Not London but Manchester, Birmingham, Leeds, Glasgow and innumerable small proletarian towns launched the new era'.[3] Two of the foremost economic and social historians of the earlier part of the twentieth century, J. L. Hammond and Dorothy George, shared this view. For the former, the Industrial Revolution was like 'a storm that passed over London and broke elsewhere';[4] to the latter, less poetically, 'the direct results of what is called the Industrial Revolution were not conspicuous there'.[5] More recent historians have also shared this view. The index to T. S. Ashton's classic study *The Industrial Revolution 1760–1830*, published in 1948, has only one reference to London. Later still, in the 1970s, I. J. Prothero asserted, after discussing the impact of the Industrial Revolution elsewhere, that 'London was not revolutionized',[6] while G. S. Jones stressed the grave disadvantages suffered by the capital in comparison with those areas which relied on steam and coal so that 'the effect of the Industrial Revolution in London was to accentuate its "pre-industrial" characteristics'; such industry as there was made London 'predominantly a finishing centre'.[7] George Rudé, writing of Hanoverian London, expressed the view that 'London's eminence as a manufacturing centre was no more conspicuous than that of any other large north European capital, such as Paris [but] her position as an international port and a centre of trade was quite unique. It was, in fact, trade rather than manufacture that dominated her economy'.[8] Even in the 1990s, Leonard Schwartz characterised the eighteenth and early nineteenth centuries as a whole as marking a lull in the growth of London.[9]

Only in the last ten or fifteen years have historians begun to question the traditional view. Two of the most eminent to have done this in the 1990s are Martin Daunton and Roy Porter. The former has concluded that London in the period of the Industrial Revolution 'was the most important industrial centre in the country';[10] the latter that 'the capital hardly lagged in technology and innovation ... As late as 1850 London's manufacturing output was still unrivalled in Britain ... and the nation's industrial economy was profoundly dependent upon the capital's imports, transport and communications, wholesale and retail networks, finance skills and its service sector more generally'.[11] Pat Hudson, in discussing provincial concentrations of manufacturing activity, also talks of the 'role of London as a centre of production [representing a] parallel story of the industrial revolution'.[12] Nevertheless, if there is a new consensus that London was not sunk in decay or gloom, and that it did not pale in comparison with the relatively faster growing areas of the Midlands or north, there is little agreement among historians on what exactly the role of London was, and what provided its dynamic for growth. Thus, for example, Wrigley stresses that London assisted the process of industrialisation through stimulating the demand for coal,[13] Clive Lee argues that the important factor was the capital's early shift from industry into services,[14] Paul Johnson that it was the dynamism of flexible specialisation, most often based on the small firm, which enabled rapid response to the changing demands of the market,[15] and David Green that it was precisely the opposite factor, that is the key importance of larger businesses.[16] Fifty years ago, Ashton argued that it was trade rather than manufacturing which defined London's position in the wider economy[17] and, within the last ten years, Rubinstein, from his study of the distribution of millionaires and half-millionaires, concluded that it was import and export and financial services rather than manufacturing that caused their greatest concentration to be found in and around the metropolis.[18]

Of course all these factors, and others too, were important. However, this book argues that detailed study of London's economy as a whole in the key half century for the Industrial Revolution from 1775 to 1825 suggests that no single answer can possibly be credible. The fact is that London was the hub of the Industrial Revolution precisely because its economic infrastructure developed a dynamic of its own from the inter-relationship between all the factors for growth and did not rely on any one at the expense of any other. It was this inter-relationship which enabled the economy of London to optimise the advantages to be drawn from its enormous size.

It will be argued that by the end of the first quarter of the nineteenth century London had evolved into the world's first truly modern city. Contemporaries had perhaps a clearer view. Long before 1800 it had become the wonder of the world, not only for its sheer size, but for the complexity and sophistication of its industry and commerce. The Prussian Moritz reflected in awe: 'How great had seemed Berlin to me when first I saw it from the tower of St Mary's and looked down on it from the hill at Templehof, how insignificant it now seemed when I set it in my imagination against London.'[19] Nearer to home, Thomas De Quincey spoke in 1800 of 'this mighty wilderness, the city – no!, not the city, but the nation – of London'.[20] In our time, and describing the later seventeenth and early eighteenth centuries, Peter Earle called London 'A City Full of People'.[21] How much more so was it a century later when its population had more than doubled in size to over one and a half million, and how little likely is it that its ability to sustain such a population could be put down to only one factor.

This book seeks to describe in detail the industrial structure of the world's first modern industrial city of over a million people, centred in the world's first industrialised national economy. How did the economy of London change to encompass its enormous growth? What goods were required to satisfy the demands of such a population, and where were they produced? How far was it a market for the manufactures of others, and how far a major manufacturing centre in its own right? And how far had it moved from its earlier characterisation as a centre for luxury crafts and trades? Were finishing trades predominant? What services were required? How far had London already evolved a service economy, and what was its importance within the economy as a whole? What was its commercial topography? Put simply, what did a million and a half people actually do?

Not the least reason for the lack of consensus over the years on whether or not London played a significant role in the Industrial Revolution, and, if it did, what that role was, is the paucity of hard fact on which all of these opinions are based. Dorothy George's classic study of *London Life in the Eighteenth Century*, though never out of print, was first published as long ago as 1925. She based her chapter called 'The People and the Trades of London' on a detailed study of just three trades – watchmaking, silk and shoemaking – and brief passing references to another 22. No historian since has made systematic reference to significantly more London trades than this; most have done nothing as remotely comprehensive. Yet contemporary sources contain references to many hundreds of separately identifiable London trades and industries. Nearly 300 separate London trades were identified as early as 1747; a century later in 1843 George Dodd claimed that 'whoever were to attempt to classify all the trades and occupations of London ... would perhaps be somewhat startled to find it amount to something like thirteen or fourteen hundred'.[22]

The time is long overdue for a revision of London's industrial role in the last quarter of the eighteenth century and the first quarter of the nineteenth, based on hard factual evidence. All too often, historians have described a particular trade or an individual firm as 'typical' of this or that time or place. However, if there is no body of hard data as a bench-mark, it is difficult to see how any particular example can be regarded as objectively 'typical' of anything. This book seeks to provide a revision based on hard data, the unique source for which is the fire office registers held in the Guildhall Library in London, supplemented and complemented by a systematic use of the many contemporary London trade directories.

By far the most complete series of surviving fire policy registers is for the Sun Fire Office. The Guildhall Library holds 1262 volumes covering the period 1710 to 1863. For the Royal Exchange there are 173 volumes covering the periods 1753–59 and 1773–1883, and 160 Hand in Hand volumes survive for the period 1696–1865. There are also a few volumes from the 1820s for the Globe and London Assurance. Each volume records details of up to about 1800 individual policies, which suggests that over two and a half million policies may be recorded in all. This book utilises all extant policies for the 1820s; however, for the 1770s only the Sun registers are relevant since it had a virtual monopoly of industrial and commercial business for most of the eighteenth century.

The early history of the major fire offices and the methods they used are well documented by Cockerell and Green,[23] Clive Trebilcock,[24] D. T. Jenkins[25] and others.[26] A major issue for all of them is the extent to which late eighteenth- and early nineteenth-century policies valued accurately the property insured. Jenkins argues: 'There seems little reason to doubt the accuracy of most of the information ... There was little reason for proposers to falsify the basic information they supplied to the underwriters.' On the other hand 'there is uncertainty about the meaning and accuracy of the values cited in the policies [and] there is, at present, no unanimity about the extent to which the values specified for insurance purposes represent true values'.[27]

Only in very exceptional cases did fire offices themselves value the property proposed to them for insurance. The value of the risk was set by the proposer. In theory, the value reflected the replacement cost of property and payment of loss was made on this basis. Only when a claim was made were values checked, and even then only where large losses were involved. However, significant differences did sometimes arise between historic cost and replacement cost. Higher premium and duty charges would have discouraged overvaluation other than for deliberately fraudulent reasons, though no doubt this was as common in that age as in any other. However, fraud would have been particularly difficult in the case of fixed capital such as buildings or machinery. Overvaluation might also arise in cases of fluctuating stock, as for example with warehousemen or merchants. In practice, a kind of blanket cover was evolved and Jenkins argues: 'Generally one must assume that proposers ... would attempt to value their warehouse contents at a figure that represented the normal or usual value of the stock they held, or even perhaps at a maximum possible value.'[28]

Accidental undervaluation might also arise from a failure immediately to update additions to stocks in those businesses where new stocks were acquired very frequently. In this case, though, there is plentiful evidence that policies were altered meticulously as stock changes took place. Deliberate undervaluation might arise most commonly from a simple desire to minimise premiums and duty rates. In the case of buildings, undervaluation might arise from a belief that some part of the property would always be salvageable or that only the mortgage on the building need be covered. Deliberate undervaluation is likely to have applied least often to plant, equipment, stocks, utensils and goods which comprised much the greater part of the capital insured by most firms in this period.

Clive Trebilcock has argued forcefully that fire offices inhibited risks being insured to their true value.[29] Conversely, Cockerell and Green, and Dickson take the view that fire offices required maximisation of premiums and encouraged insurance to the full value of the risk.[30] However, Trebilcock is adamant that the Phoenix required clients to share their risk from its inception, that its underwriters ensured that this happened, and that this was usual practice with other fire offices. In other words, it was generally understood that the proposer always shared the risk to be insured.[31] Jenkins accepts that the late eighteenth and early nineteenth centuries were a period of evolution and change in underwriting principles, but argues in some detail that the evidence for Trebilcock's contention is both insubstantial and contradictory. He does allow that there are special problems arising from insured values of very large and/or hazardous property. All fire offices imposed risk limits on, and charged higher premiums for, property classified as 'hazardous' or 'doubly hazardous'. In the case of very large and valuable properties, these were accepted in some cases for full cover, though often at higher rates of premium. In other cases, cover was obtained from more than one fire office.[32] Throughout the period of this book, examples are to be found of businesses insuring with more than one fire office. Sometimes as many as five or six are referred to in a given policy. Thus, the Albion Flour Mill in Blackfriars was insured in 1786 for £41,000 by five fire offices, all of whom paid up in full when it was destroyed by fire in 1791.[33] Overall, Jenkins would seem to have the edge in concluding:

> for very large industrial property and that of a particularly hazardous nature, it would be safer to assume that insured values underestimate the total risk … Trebilcock's stricture that most industrial property is affected by this problem is too pessimistic, through its overestimate of the average size and value of industrial property in this period. Surely only relatively few types and numbers of large and hazardous industrial property would have had its insurance cover limited in this way.[34]

Certainly, this conclusion is borne out by the data on which this book is based. The average commercial capital insured was only £672 in the period 1769–77, and, more significantly, the median £200. For the period 1819–25, the equivalent average figure had risen to £1510, although the median was still only £320. In the earlier period, the proportion of businesses insuring a commercial capital valued at over

£1000 was 12.8 per cent; in the later it was still only 23.2 per cent. It is also instructive to consider the very recent research of Robin Pearson. He has shown that for the textile industries, the financial burden was small, with average insurance costs largely balanced by sums paid back in claims.[35] For all these reasons, it is assumed for the purposes of this book that the values shown in the policy registers for fixed and/or working capital are a valid guide to the size of the individual business concerned. Certainly, an important consideration suggested by Jenkins has the ring of pragmatic truth and may serve as a final word: 'Premium income seems to have been an important consideration ... Likewise commission was the important consideration for the agent. It was in his interests, financially, to encourage his client to insure fully even if the underwriters had reservations about such a practice.'[36]

Another key issue is the duration of the policy. Information given by the secretary to the Sun Fire Office to the Secretary of the Treasury in 1796 has often been quoted. The former said that it was the normal practice of policy-holders to renew each year and to change the actual scope of their policy every seven years, 'for it was supposed the Sun Fire-Office had 100,000 policies in force, & that the Office issue about 15,000 Annually, which multiplied by 7 gave 105,000'.[37] Jenkins also points out that some Royal Exchange policies are marked as running for this period[38] and most Hand in Hand polices were clearly marked with a seven-year duration. On the other hand, the minutes of the Sun Fire Office make it clear that the period of insurance could vary at the behest of the proposer and that discounts were available on premiums for those insuring for a period greater than a year. Policies stated that 'Persons may insure for more Years than One, and in such Cases there will be a Discount allowed of 5 per Cent per Annum ... for every Year except the First'.[39] Policies for periods shorter than a year were also not uncommon, most usually for three or six months. At the other extreme, the Sun agreed in 1822 to quote a premium rate for a fire policy for life.[40] In practice, policies might be taken out for almost any reasonable period.

In the past, comparatively little use has been made of the fire insurance records by economic and business historians; certainly, they have not been used in any systematic or comprehensive way. However, for this book there has been constructed a database containing the records of over 31,000 London businesses in over 1300 separate industries and trades for the periods 1769 to 1777 and 1819 to 1825, either end of the key half century of the Industrial Revolution.

Even at their simplest, fire insurance policies record the value of stock and/or goods and/or utensils. However, many also record the value of industrial and commercial buildings such as warehouses, workshops, counting houses, mill houses, shops, public houses, brew houses, sugar houses, engine houses, distilleries, wharves, sawpits, laboratories and manufactories. Sometimes shown are the values of wagons and coaches, steam engines, cranes, vats, shop fittings, tools, plant and machinery. On occasions the stock is described in detail: oil, coal, timber, cotton, flax, wool, sugar, tea, fruit, nuts, tallow, plate, precious stones and so on. In the building trades, values are often recorded for property under construction: houses, a church, a warehouse or some other commercial enterprise.

A database constructed from the money values of the period 1775–1825 makes it necessary to make at least some comparison with those of the 1990s. Such comparisons are notoriously difficult, especially given the wide differences between living standards and expectations at the personal level and in technology, industrial organisation and commercial practice at the level of the firm. Nevertheless, it is possible to suggest that insured capital in the period 1775–1825 must be multiplied by a factor of several hundred to give a comparison with the final years of the twentieth century. This is not to say that either period was stable in prices or costs – witness the fluctuations in commodity prices in the 1790s and in house prices in the 1980s – or that they rise equally for all elements in the economy. Even so, it is clear that the factor of comparison is not less than 200 and possibly as much as 300. If nothing else, this does enable us to say with reasonable confidence that any commercial capital risk insured for £50 in the period 1775–1825 equates to a five-figure sum in the 1990s, one insured for £500 with a six-figure sum and one insured for £5000 with a seven-figure valuation.

Of course, this begs the question of changes *over* the period 1775–1825. Many attempts have been made to compile historic indices of prices; none is totally satisfactory. Some suffer from restriction to one item, often in only one place, such as the famous series on the price of wheat at Winchester College from 1690 to 1817, others to limited and arbitrary periods of time. Nor do the compilations always agree on trends, and even when they do it is still the case that any period of fifty years is bound to show considerable and contradictory fluctuations. Not least is this true for a period of profound economic change like 1775–1825, during which there took place the greatest war the world had yet seen. This is not a criticism; the survival of reliable data from a period long before routine and systematic governmental compilation of economic statistics must be arbitrary. Fortunately, however, there does exist for the period 1661–1823 the Schumpeter–Gilboy index. Although compiled as long ago as 1938 it is a remarkable index of the price of consumer goods ranging from barley and wheat to cider and ale, butter and cheese, beef and pork, tea and sugar, candles, coal, broadcloth, felt hats, Brussels lace, Irish linen, leather backs and blue yarn stockings. It shows that prices were higher in the early 1820s than the 1770s. However, the conclusions to be drawn are far from clear-cut. Thus, for example, if an arbitrary comparison is made between 1823, the last year covered by the index, and fifty years earlier in 1773 very little change is apparent. The index was 119 in the earlier year and 128 in the later, an increase of only 7 per cent. At the turn of the century it was 212 and it rose to a wartime peak of 243 in 1813. What can be said is that throughout the early 1770s the index was rising, from 99 in 1769 to 119 in 1773 but that during the early 1820s it was falling rapidly, from 192 in 1819 to 128 in 1823. This impression is confirmed by the Gayer–Rostow–Schwartz index of British commodity prices. Although it does not start until 1790, it suggests that there was very little change between the 1770s and 1790s. Gayer–Rostow–Schwartz shows that prices were below 90 in the immediate pre-war period, rose to 169 by 1813 but then fell from 128 in 1819 to 100 in 1827 and to 95 in 1830.

The overall conclusion to be drawn is that prices were a little higher in the 1820s than the 1770s, but probably by less than 15 per cent. Schumpeter–Gilboy is 14 per cent higher for 1821–23 than for 1771–73 and Gayer–Rostow–Schwartz 13 per cent higher for 1820–22 than for 1790–92. In both cases prices were rising in the earlier period and falling in the later.[41] It is reasonable, therefore, to compare directly the values of capital insured in the periods 1769–77 and 1819–25. A rise of under 15 per cent must be compared with an increase in the average value of capital insured of 125 per cent.

The many propositions put forward by historians to explain the role of London in the Industrial Revolution and to account for its success can be tested using the database prepared for this book. It is argued that *all* contain a measure of truth. Perhaps the most important point about London is that it was characterised by all these factors simultaneously, and to an increasing degree throughout the period 1775–1825. It was precisely the complexity and diversity of its economy which was the key to its success.

. . . .
The Metropolis Defined

Geography

Defining the ever-growing outward sprawl of London has been a problem for every generation since at least Tudor times. Certainly this was a problem faced by those responsible for the first censuses. However, they did use the same definition for 'the metropolis' for each of the first four censuses of 1801 to 1831, and this is also used for this book. Included were the City within and without the walls, Westminster, Southwark, the out-parishes of Middlesex and Surrey within the London Bills of Mortality and the out-parishes of Middlesex without the Bills of Mortality. The out-parishes covered Aldgate, Bermondsey, Bethnal Green, Bloomsbury, Bow, Chelsea, Hackney, Holborn, Islington, Kensington, Lambeth, Limehouse, Mile End, Newington Butts, Paddington, Poplar, Rotherhithe, Saffron Hill and Hatton Garden, St James's, St Luke's, St Pancras, Shadwell, Shoreditch, Somers Town, Spitalfields, Stepney, the Strand, Wapping and Whitechapel.

Fortunately for the modern historian, these boundaries are virtually identical to those used by the best of the contemporary maps of London. This was William Faden's 1813 update of Richard Horwood's *Map of the Cities of London and Westminster*, originally published in 1799.[1] It covered an area some seven and a half miles across from east to west, just under three and a half miles from north to south, and of over 26 square miles. To the north, the boundary stretches from Regents Park through Somers Town, Islington, Hoxton, Bethnal Green and Globe Town to the River Lea at Bow. The western boundary stretches from Regents Park through Hyde Park and Kensington to the Thames at Chelsea. To the east, the boundary is the River Lea and the loop of the Thames to the east of the Isle of Dogs, while the southern boundary stretches from Vauxhall Bridge to the Royal Dock Yard at Deptford.

Population

Throughout the last quarter of the eighteenth century and the first quarter of the nineteenth, London's pre-eminence in the British economy was based to a considerable degree, as it had been since the seventeenth century, on its size, both in absolute terms and relative to other parts of the country. Dorothy George was quite mistaken in her belief that 'its share of the population of the country declined, its share of the urban population declined still more'.[2] The facts are quite different. Prior to the first Census of 1801 there are only best estimates of the population. However, it is unlikely that London's share of the population of England and Wales was very different in, say, the middle of the eighteenth century from the proportion of 9.7 per cent recorded in 1801. This actually increased to 9.9 per cent in 1811, to 10.2 per cent in 1821 and to 10.6 per cent in 1831. London's population, after barely changing since 1700, rose from about 676,000 in 1750 to 865,000 in 1801, an increase of 28 per cent in 50 years. In the next 30 years the increase was over 70 per cent, to nearly one and a half million in 1831. In that same period, the population of the remainder of England and Wales increased by under 55 per cent.

In 1801 London was over ten times the size of the next largest town, Liverpool with 82,000; by 1831 it was still seven and a half times Liverpool's size (202,000). Again, in 1801 London had equalled the populations of the next 28 largest towns put together; despite the rapid pace of industrialisation elsewhere, by 1831 it still equalled the next 16. In 1831 London still exceeded the populations of the other six towns in the kingdom with over 100,000 put together by well over half a million.

The most important factor is the huge absolute growth in the size of London. Between 1750 and 1831 its population grew by over 800,000. This did not happen at the same rate in all parts of the metropolis. By and large the older districts declined while the newer expanded rapidly. The population of the City itself was in decline. In 1700 it was estimated at 139,000; by 1750 it was probably under 90,000 and it fell further to 65,000 in 1801 and to 57,000 in 1831. By far the largest increases between 1801 and 1831 occurred in the districts to the north of the City, defined as Marylebone, St Pancras, Islington and Hackney. There, the population increased from 120,000 to nearly 300,000. By 1831, Marylebone alone had a population of over 122,000, equal to that of Leeds, while St Pancras with over 103,000 was the size of Bristol. The East End also saw a huge growth in population, from under 180,000 in 1801 to over 330,000 in 1831. Bethnal Green and Poplar trebled in size, Shoreditch and Stepney doubled. Much the same population explosion occurred south of the river. In total, the increase was from 137,000 to over 266,000: both Lambeth and Newington trebled in size. Closer to the City, Clerkenwell doubled its population and there were large increases in St Giles and Holborn. To the west and south-west, Kensington increased its population two and a half times to 53,000 in 1831 and even Chelsea expanded three-fold to over 32,000.[3]

Topography

It has been claimed with only a modest degree of exaggeration that 'In 1700 an observer who climbed the gallery around the dome of St Paul's would have been able to view London in its entirety', and that 'An insistent impression of London at this time would have been its rusticity'. Pastures and scattered farms extended from Lamb's Conduit Fields towards the villages of Highgate and Hampstead; Covent Garden and Leicester and Lincoln's Inn Fields had only small clusters of buildings standing in the midst of fields; and open countryside surrounded St James's and Hyde Parks. A century later the built-up area had more than doubled. By 1800 the panorama to be seen from St Paul's would have been urban to the furthest horizon and such fields as remained would have been marked out as building sites. Early eighteenth-century country lanes, like Brick Lane in Spitalfields, had become paved city streets. The New Road, constructed in mid-century to by-pass the built-up area to the north of London, was 'skirted on both sides with houses' within fifty years.[4] London was expanding over a larger area and at a faster rate than at any time in its previous history. Although new building advanced unevenly in different directions from the City, and inevitably booms alternated with troughs in the construction industry, there was a steadily increasing demand for new houses from both the huge increase in population and rising commercial prosperity from the middle of the

eighteenth century onwards. Private landowners led the way in pro-
moting building developments, together with City livery companies,
the Church, the Crown and charitable institutions.

It was the landowners of a comparatively few great estates who
led the way for the development of Mayfair and the West End as
areas of fine squares and streets for the residence of the fashionable
and wealthy. Mayfair had already been laid out by the 1730s but the
golden age of Georgian architecture was from the early 1760s to
the outbreak of war with France 30 years later. In that period came
the Adelphi, Piccadilly, Berkeley Square, Cavendish Square, Portland
Place and Fitzroy Square. At the same time, as the rich moved west,
the poor crowded into districts forming a belt around the City,
especially to the north and east, and by the 1780s a foreign visitor
could remark that 'the East End, especially along the shores of the
Thames, consists of old houses; the streets there are narrow and ill-
paved ... The contrast between this and the West End is astonishing'.[5]
Into this area more and more people crammed in the subsequent 50
years. Between 1801 and 1831, the population of just six of the most
crowded districts – St Giles, Clerkenwell, Spitalfields, Bethnal Green,
Whitechapel and Wapping – increased by 140,000.

After the Napoleonic wars there was another construction boom.
To the west this included the development of Tavistock and Gordon
Squares and Belgravia. London's industrial areas were also expanding
rapidly. The development of London's docks transformed the districts
on both sides of the Thames. A huge new labour force required
streets of small cheap dwellings to house them. Between 1799 and
1813, 1500 houses were built around the new Commercial Road
alone. At the same time new housing developments sprang up to the
north in Camden Town, Islington and Hackney, and to the west in
Kensington and Chelsea, although numbers of new houses never
kept up with the growth in population resulting in ever greater
overcrowding.

This period also saw major public building in London. During the
war years government offices in Whitehall, Newgate prison, naval
dockyards and army barracks were all built or extended. Somerset
House dates from this period and work began on the British Museum
and the National Gallery. Also built were the first dedicated shopping
streets and covered shopping arcades such as Woburn Walk and the
Burlington Arcade. In 1820–21 came the Theatre Royal, Haymarket.

Hyperbole though it was, it is no coincidence that it was in the year 1827 that James Elmes published his somewhat premature *Metropolitan Improvements; or, London in the Nineteenth Century* and wrote:

> Augustus made it one of his proudest boasts, that he found Rome of brick, and left it of marble. The reign and regency of George the Fourth have scarcely done less for the vast and increasing Metropolis of the British Empire; by increasing its magnificence and its comforts; by forming healthy streets and elegant buildings, instead of pestilential alleys and squalid hovels; by substituting rich and varied architecture and park-like scenery, for paltry cabins and monotonous cow-lairs.[6]

In this period came the first real improvements to public health and public facilities. From the 1760s there were innumerable schemes for the improvement of paving, starting with the Westminster Paving Act of 1762, for lighting and drainage, and for the demolition of dangerous or obstructive buildings. By the 1780s London's pavements, street-lamps, water supply and sewers were regarded with awe by foreign and provincial visitors alike. Lighting went through two rounds of improvement. First came oil lamps in the last quarter of the eighteenth century and then, from 1812, gas. In that year the Westminster Gas Light and Coke Company was incorporated and by 1815 there had been laid 15 miles of gas mains.

The Commercial Topography of London Population growth and the infrastructure to serve it was both the cause and effect of industrial and commercial growth. In this respect, the expansion of London's docks was one of the most significant developments of the period. Throughout the eighteenth century, London's maritime trade had increased steadily. Not least in importance was the enormous amount of coastal traffic entering the Thames. Even so, the only new enclosed dock to be constructed in the second half of the eighteenth century was the Brunswick Dock opened in 1790. By 1800 there were only 18 acres of enclosed dock and this led to severe overcrowding in the Pool of London between the Tower and London Bridge; yet by 1813 the area of enclosed dock had increased ten-fold to almost 180 acres. In 1802 the West India Docks were opened and linked to the City by the new Commercial Road. Three years later came the London Docks, downstream from the Tower at Wapping. By 1807 there had also been built the East India Docks at Blackwall, linked to the City by the new East India Dock Road, the Surrey Commercial Docks, connected to the river by the Grand Surrey Canal, and the Wapping basin. All were accompanied by massive new warehousing complexes and all quickly became focal points for industrial and commercial development in the first quarter of the nineteenth century.

Of particular significance in this period was the rapid industrial expansion of the East End. In 1770 the Hackney Cut had by-passed the River Lea to provide access to the Thames at Blackwall for water-borne traffic from Hertfordshire and Essex, and the Limehouse Cut did the same to the west of the Isle of Dogs. Later, in 1812, the Regent's Canal gave the area a direct link to north and west London and on to the Midlands and Lancashire. By the 1820s over 20 per cent of London's manufacturing firms were located in the East End.

London's spectacular population growth would not have been possible without a road network to carry the food, fodder and fuel it required, to carry raw materials and finished goods to and from the provinces and to carry people to and from their places of work and to the other towns and cities of the kingdom. By 1750 the turnpike trusts had already brought about substantial improvements in the road network radiating outwards from London. This continued right through to the onset of the railway age 80 years later. Within the built-up area of the metropolis traffic congestion was already a major problem. There were some road widening and improved surfacing schemes, but the major improvement, and the world's first planned by-pass, was the New Road built in 1756–61 to by-pass the City to the north. South of the river, the major improvements were St George's Circus, Westminster Road and Blackfriars Road. All of these were associated with new bridges across the Thames. Westminster Bridge was opened in 1750 and Blackfriars Bridge in 1769. After the Napoleonic wars came a further bridge-building programme with Vauxhall Bridge being completed in 1816, Waterloo in 1817 and Southwark in 1819. All required new approach roads and connecting roads, such as Union Street linking Blackfriars Road with the Borough, which in their turn became focal points for trade and industry.

To feed London, both human beings and livestock, required the produce from an area of surrounding countryside about ten miles in diameter. There were some three dozen markets dealing in different commodities, such as Smithfield (meat), Covent Garden and Borough (fruit and vegetables), Spitalfields (vegetables), Billingsgate (fish),

Leadenhall (meat, fish, poultry, herbs, plants and provisions) and Bermondsey (hides and leather). All of these, too, were centres of industry and commerce.

Traditional studies most often imply that London was characterised by individual districts overwhelmingly devoted to single trades or industries and particular streets devoted to shops and shopping. Of course this was true to a certain degree. However, the overwhelming characteristic of London as a whole during the late eighteenth and early nineteenth centuries was the bewildering industrial and commercial diversity to be found in every district and in many of its maze of largely unplanned streets. Equally remarkable was the density and concentration of this commercial activity. The traditional view can be readily exemplified by two nineteenth-century descriptions. In mid-century it was claimed that 'as London has gradually swelled itself into its present huge dimensions, circumstances of adaptation have enabled the leading branches of trade to localise themselves in various districts. The geographical distribution of trades and professions are therefore as well defined in London as the natural produce of the earth in its different climes';[7] 50 years earlier, in 1803, *The Picture of London* described a 'shopping centre' in which,

> There are two sets of streets, running nearly parallel, almost from the eastern extremity of the Town to the Western, forming (with the exception of a very few houses), a line of shops. One lying to the South, nearer the river, extends from Mile End to Parliament St, including Whitechapel, Leadenhall St, Cornhill, Cheapside, St Paul's Churchyard, Ludgate St, Fleet St, the Strand, and Charing Cross. The other to the North reaches from Shoreditch Church almost to the end of Oxford St, including Shoreditch, Bishopsgate St, Threadneedle St, Newgate St, Snowhill, Holborn, Broad St, St Giles and Oxford St.
>
> The Southern line, which is the most splendid, is more than three miles in length; the other is about four miles. There are several large streets also occupied by retail trade, that run parallel to parts of the two grand lines, or intersect them, among the most remarkable of which are Fenchurch St and Gracechurch St in the City of London; and Cockspur St, Pall Mall, St James St, Piccadilly, King St, Covent Garden, and New Bond St, at the West end of the town.[8]

Both of these descriptions are gross over-simplifications of the distribution of trade and industry in London. Thus, for example, in the 1820s nearly two-thirds of London's immensely important clock-

and watchmaking firms were to be found in and around Clerkenwell. However, these firms accounted for only 12 per cent of all businesses in Clerkenwell; the other 88 per cent was made up of businesses involved in no fewer than 67 other trades.[9] Even in two of the most intensive clock- and watchmaking areas around Clerkenwell Green, of 67 firms trading in 1817 in St James's Street, Walk and Place, to the north, and St John's Square and Lane, to the south, only 20 were in various watchmaking trades, including watch movement makers, watch case makers, escape wheel cutters, escapement makers and secret springers, as well as clock- and watchmakers. Among the diversity of other trades to be found in these five small streets were a tailor and breeches maker, a snuff and tobacco manufacturer, a tea dealer, a pastry cook and confectioner, a bedstead and mattress manufacturer, a musical instrument maker, a patent sash line maker, a hearth rug manufacturer, an iron plate manufacturer and three printers. The mix of trades is exemplified by one of these streets. In 1817 the 182½ yards of St John's Lane contained 37 houses. In these were to be found no fewer than 15 businesses. At number 2 was T. Davies, a pastry cook and confectioner; next door was W. Collins, a snuff and tobacco manufacturer; at number 3 was John Kerby, a springer and liner; and next door to him J. Brookes, a watch spring maker; at number 8 was William Leaver, a tea dealer; and, at number 9, R. Corrall, a book- and music seller. Then at numbers 11, 12 and 16 came three clock- and watchmakers, John Storer, Robert Storer and R. Lawrence respectively. At number 18 was D. Evans, a bedstead and mattress manufacturer; at number 21, W. Webb, bricklayer and plasterer; and at number 22, the firm of Madgwick and Cooper, Japan manufacturers. At the far end of the lane were A. Austin, a watch motion manufacturer at number 30; and T. Giles, a brass, copper and wire drawer at number 31. Finally, at number 23 was a solicitor, Benjamin David.

Two other geographically concentrated industries were silk and leather. Nevertheless, although nearly 60 per cent of London's silk manufacturing firms were to be found in Spitalfields and Bethnal Green in the 1820s, these accounted for only 17 per cent of all businesses in these two districts. Again, 36 per cent of leather working firms were to be found in and around Bermondsey, but they accounted for only 20 per cent of all businesses there. In other words, no district of London was characterised by an overwhelming concentration of firms in any one trade. To a very large extent, almost every London trade was to be found everywhere. Thus, with clock- and watch-making, even if nearly two-thirds of firms were to be found in Clerkenwell, small numbers were to be found all over London in such diverse areas as the City, Chelsea, Poplar, Bloomsbury, Soho, Kennington, Walworth, Paddington, Hackney, Holborn, Whitechapel, Islington and Southwark.

It is equally misleading to imagine that there were the exclusive shopping streets implied by the contemporary account quoted above. Some were, of course, more so than others. In Cheapside in 1817 were to be found no fewer than 165 businesses located in only 157 houses. Of these, 112, which was just over two-thirds, were either wholesalers or retailers or both. Nevertheless, even in Cheapside there were still 26 firms engaged in manufacturing. Many buildings housed more than one business; number 108 as many as five and number 66 four. Further west, High Holborn's 325 houses contained 251 businesses. Of these, 159 or 63 per cent were retailers. However, 77 or nearly a third were manufacturers. These included manufacture of such diverse products as tobacco and snuff, mattresses, fire escapes, worsted trimmings, combs, soap, guns, umbrellas, optical instruments, trunks, coaches, blacking, toys, fancy moulds, mangles and presses, wooden clocks, brushes, metal fanlights and musical instruments. The longest and most quintessential shopping street in London was Oxford Street. As early as 1775 Sophie von la Roche had marvelled in a letter home to Germany: 'Just imagine, dear children, a street taking half an hour to cover from end to end.'[10] By 1817 its mile and a quarter length contained 397 businesses and although retailing accounted for just over two-thirds of them (271), there were still 112 engaged in a variety of manufacturing trades as diverse as spruce beer brewing, water closet manufacturing, coachmaking and the manufacture of venetian blinds.

At the other end of the social scale, there were 125 businesses in Rotherhithe Street. Nearly half were either directly involved in shipbuilding or served the maritime trades, as for example ship chandlers or slopsellers. However, the greater number of firms were engaged in a bewildering variety of retail and other trades which included millers, linen drapers, hat manufacturing, watchmaking, cheesemongers, grocers, tallow chandlers, confectioners, a brass founder, chemists and undertakers.

It is also interesting to note the existence of business on a substantial scale very close to some of the most socially exclusive areas of London. This was still a time when even the greatest households required the full range of goods and services necessary to their comfort to be available literally just around the corner. Such arrangements had usually grown up without the necessity for any planning. However, Nash left nothing to chance when creating Regent Street between 1813 and 1820. The old St James's Market had been demolished to make way for the new thoroughfare but Nash made sure that a new market was constructed between Regent Street and Haymarket and that around it were to be found the small retailers and workshops necessary to serve an entire and socially diverse neighbourhood. An example of this bewildering pattern of businesses close to the houses of the wealthiest and most eminent of London's inhabitants is Mount Street. Located between Park Lane to the west and South Audley Street to the east, just a few yards from where the latter joined Grosvenor Square, it possessed 30 businesses in 1817. These included three wax chandlers, three wine merchants, three statuaries, two oilmen and grocers, a chemist and druggist, a haberdasher, a dealer in foreign china, a furnishing ironmonger, a bookseller, an undertaker, a coffee and spice dealer, a house painter, two household furnishers, and a ladies' shoe warehouse. There were also four professional men, an apothecary, two surgeons and a surveyor, but most interesting of all there were eight manufacturing businesses; a hat manufacturer, a saddle maker, a brushmaker, a brazier, a cabinet maker, a breeches maker, an artificial florist and a coachbuilder. Pall Mall contained 75 businesses, 10 of which were manufacturers. Among these was the very down-to-earth business at number 97 of Messrs Statham and Company, blacking manufacturers.

Finally, it is interesting to note the sheer density of London's commercial activity. John Lockie's *Topography of London*, published in 1813 for the Phoenix Fire Office, gives 10,000 street names, down to the obscurest alley and courtyard. Comparing this with Faden's 1813 edition of Horwood's map suggests that about 4000 of Lockie's entries were tiny alleys and courtyards with about 6000 streets and thoroughfares of rather more substance. On this basis, there were on average over eight businesses located on each and every thoroughfare of any substance in London in the first quarter of the nineteenth century. This is more than double the average number to be found in

London in the last decade of the twentieth century. Some examples from 1817 illustrate the density of commercial activity in individual thoroughfares. Frith Street in Soho had 35 businesses in its 308-yard length; Green Street, off Leicester Square, had 14 in 82 yards; and Hatton Garden no fewer than 61 in only 242 yards. Examples of longer streets are Tottenham Court Road, which had 155 businesses in its length of 1177 yards, and the Borough with 275 businesses in 781 yards. The 253 yards of Red Lion Street in Clerkenwell not only had 52 businesses in a length of only 253 yards, but 29 of these were in manufacturing trades. No fewer than 17 businesses were to be found in even such a short thoroughfare as Middle Row in Holborn, which was only 66 yards in length. Three were quite substantial manufacturing firms, two hat manufacturers and a tinplate worker.

CHAPTER 3

Industrial London

Classifying London's Trades

No doubt one of the principal reasons why there has been no previous attempt by historians to look in depth and detail at the economy of London during the Industrial Revolution has been the absence of any means of classifying its innumerable industries and trades in such a way as to allow meaningful comparative analysis, whether by trade, size of firm, geographical location or over time. Indeed, a tool to enable such analysis for Britain in the present century has existed only since 1948. This is the Standard Industrial Classification (SIC), first introduced in 1948 and modified many times since. In the words of the Central Statistical Office:

> The United Kingdom economy is made up of a wide range of economic activities through which goods are produced or services rendered by firms and other organisations. For analytical purposes, economic activities of a similar nature may be grouped together into 'industries', for example into agriculture ... retail distribution (or) catering ... A system used to group activities in this way is described as an industrial classification, [it] usually starts with a small number of broad groups of activities which are then subdivided into progressively narrower groups so that the classification can be used with varying amounts of detail for different purposes. Thus a broad group 'Transport and communications' may be subdivided into the different modes of transport (road, rail, water, air) and communications (postal services, telecommunications) and these in turn into smaller subdivisions such as road haulage, bus and coach services, etc.[1]

Such a tool is as necessary for analysis of the economy of London during the Industrial Revolution as it is for the British economy as a whole in the second half of the twentieth century. Only Campbell in *The London Tradesman* of 1747 attempted any rudimentary industrial classification, and this only linked certain peripheral trades to the

TABLE 3.1 Example of Standard Industrial Classification modified for period 1775–1825

SIC and Class	SIC and Group	SIC and Activity
46 Furniture & timber	461 Sawmilling & planing	
	463 Builders' carpentry	
	464 Wooden containers	
	465 General carpentry	
	466 Cork, baskets & brushes	4661 Cork
		4662 Basketware
		4663 Brushes & brooms
	467 Furniture	

main trade on which they were dependent.[2] All other eighteenth- and nineteenth-century directories, career guides and commercial treatises simply listed trades alphabetically. However, for the purposes of this book it has been found possible to classify the industries and trades of London in the period 1775–1825 in accordance with a modified version of the 1980 SIC. Of course, it contains numerous technologies which neither existed nor had any equivalent in the later eighteenth and early nineteenth centuries. Nevertheless, it is also true that every trade and industry found in that period still exists today and can be identified in the 1980 SIC.

The 1980 SIC is divided into 10 Divisions, 60 Classes and 222 Groups. Firms are to be found in London in the period 1775–1825 in 31 of those Classes and 117 of the Groups, probably a higher proportion than in the 1990s. Below the level of 'Group' is 'Activity'. At this level the detail is too late twentieth-century orientated to be viable in the context of the earlier centuries. However, for the purposes of the modified SIC used in this book, 'Groups' are reclassified into 'Activities' similar to the modern, but more directly relevant to the period 1775–1825. The modified SIC used in this book is set out in full in the Appendix. Table 3.1 shows the example of furniture and timber.

There are, of course, difficulties in assigning tens of thousands of individual businesses to the various categories within such a classification, no less for the period 1775–1825 than for the present day. The application of the classification can be illustrated by some of the more typical examples of how the major difficulties have been overcome in practice. One of the principal problems with any industrial classification is distinguishing between wholesalers and retailers. In some cases it is not a meaningful distinction at all. However, for the purposes of this book, businesses are assumed to be predominantly retail unless either described as wholesale in the fire insurance registers or there is compelling evidence in the policy itself to regard it as wholesale. Examples of the latter are John Kittermaster and Samuel Bostock. The first is described as a fishmonger in a Sun Fire Office policy of 1775, but it may be inferred that he was a wholesaler because the address is Billingsgate and he insured a warehouse for £200 as well as stock and utensils for £800. These values are far in excess of anything which would be expected from a retail fishmonger.[3] Samuel Bostock was a cheesemonger of 105 Borough who in 1777 insured stock, utensils and goods for £3000. Both the considerable sum and the fact that they are described as held in his warehouse suggest that he was a wholesaler.[4]

Another of the major problems is distinguishing between manufacturing and bespoke production. In many cases there was no distinction between production of an article and its sale by a shopkeeper/craftsman. However, the convention adopted for this book is that where no contemporary distinction is drawn and no specific indication is given in the policy register of a production process, the business is classified as retail. Again, where there is an indication of bespoke production, this too is treated as retailing, which is in line with modern SIC practice. Where there is some production process, but also distribution, this too is classified as distribution. Only where there is a clear indication that the production process is paramount is it treated as falling within the appropriate manufacturing sector.

Patterns of Industry in London

To most people the word 'industry', especially used in the context of the Industrial Revolution, inevitably conjures up pictures of coal and iron, steam engines and belching chimneys, cotton and woollen mills, heavy engineering and the beginnings of mass production. However, for the purposes of this book it is argued that it is impossible to make sense of the economy of London in the period 1775–1825 without acknowledging the more modern use of the term 'industry' to denote any area of business enterprise, whether agricultural, extractive, manufacturing, construction, distribution, transport or other services. All too often it has been assumed, not least in our own day, that only the first three really count; that the rest are somehow mere froth on the surface of the economy. The truth is that all may be equally important, depending entirely on the circumstances of time and place. In practice, all except the first two were enormously important in and to London and taken together explain the pre-dominance the metropolis exerted in the economy of Britain as a whole. Roy Porter puts it rather well in describing a slightly later period: 'Historians have sometimes written about London's reliance upon "service" employment as if that meant the capital were some-how less "productive" than other regions' – parasitic in fact. But this is a false assumption. The truth is that in the Victorian era jobs in services accounted for over half the *national* increase in employment, and the service sector contributed no less to economic activity than manufacturing.'[5] The Central Statistical Office puts it more prosaically in the context of the modern Standard Industrial Classification: 'Industry ... is not restricted to extractive or production activities but extends to the provision of goods and services of all kinds.'[6]

This book concentrates heavily on the individual business. Again, some definition is necessary. A business may be taken as any in-dependently owned unit of production or service, whether or not employing persons other than the proprietor or proprietors. In other words, an independently self-employed carpenter with no other employee is regarded as a 'business' in exactly the same way as, say, a manufacturing firm with a thousand employees. This is both the modern definition for government economic statistical purposes and the basis on which late eighteenth- and early nineteenth-century fire office records and trade directories were compiled. In this context it is interesting to note that no contemporary source of industrial data from the late eighteenth and early nineteenth centuries ever dis-tinguished between occupation or craft on the one hand, and industry or trade on the other. Thus, hundreds of terms such as 'carpenter', 'cabinet maker', 'baker', 'musical instrument maker', 'plumber' or 'linen draper' are used interchangeably to mean both. However, where fire office records show capital valued at hundreds or thousands of pounds or trade directories have an entry designed for the information of the general public, it may safely be assumed that a 'business' is being described rather than an individual employed by someone else.

To take one example, Peter Mestaer of New Hermitage Street, Wapping, was described in a Sun policy issued in 1769 as a 'shipwright'. However, he was in fact the proprietor of a very substantial business which insured wharves and industrial buildings for £1500 and stock, utensils and goods for £950.[7]

An example of how an individual trade designation could cover a multitude of differently organised businesses is 'cabinet maker'. It could be used for an employed craftsman, a self-employed person, a sole proprietor, a partnership or a company. For the purposes of this book, all except the first are regarded as 'businesses'. Examples of the other four are in the above order: John Benjamin Osborne of 6 West Street, Soho, who in 1820 insured tools valued at £10;[8] Charles Judson of 37 Little Alie Street, who in 1819 insured stock and utensils valued at £2140;[9] Deacon and Davis of 35 Piccadilly, who in the same year insured stock and utensils valued at £2000;[10] and Henry Russell and Co of 67 St Martin's Lane, who took out policies in every year but one between 1819 and 1825 for stock and utensils valued at up to £4000 and for a manufactory insured for £500.[11]

Data derived from fire office registers and trade directories demonstrate just how diversified was the economy of London by the 1770s, and how much more so again it was half a century later. By far the most comprehensive surviving trade directory for the entire period from 1775 to 1825 was Pigot and Co's *London and Provincial New Commercial Directory for 1826–27*. This lists alphabetically over 900 separate trades and every individual business within each of those trades, some 49,000 in total but with about 3000 firms double-counted in more than one trade. It should be noted that, for the purpose of this book, the professions are excluded, whether medical, legal, educational, financial or artistic. Thus, neither banks nor insurance companies are included, nor are schools. The figure of 49,000 excludes all such businesses. Of these, 14,500 were manufacturing firms, 23,500 were engaged in wholesale or retail distribution, over 2600 were merchants or commission agents, brokers or factors, over 2000 were in the construction trades, nearly 3900 were inns, hotels, eating or coffee houses, 1400 were involved in transport and over 700 in the provision of other services.

Nothing remotely as comprehensive as Pigot was published in the last quarter of the eighteenth century when trade directories were intended far more as guides for the wealthy and fashionable to just those businesses they might be inclined to patronise. Rarely do they include the more mundane and numerous trades, such as butchers, bakers, carpenters, dressmakers, launderers or victuallers. Typically, directories of the 1770s contain about six or seven thousand entries at most.[12] However, it is possible to estimate from detailed studies of a number of individual trades that London in the mid-1770s had about 30,000 businesses in total. This suggests that over the period 1775–1825 the number of businesses in London rose by a little over 60 per cent, compared with an increase in population of nearer 80 per cent. Of the total of 30,000, a little under half (14,000) were engaged in wholesale or retail distribution, nearly 10,000 in manufacturing or construction trades, just over 1700 were merchants, factors, agents or brokers and about 3500 innkeepers or victuallers.

The sample of firms derived from the fire office registers for this book is statistically very high for any study of this sort. For the 1770s it is 16,700 out of an estimated 30,000, which is nearly 56 per cent, and for the 1820s just over 14,000 out of 46,000, or over 30 per cent. The reason for the lower sample size in the 1820s is that the Sun had by that time lost a substantial amount of business to newer fire offices, the records of which have not survived.

Diversity and specialisation, the latter Adam Smith's key to economic growth, increased as rapidly as did the numbers of businesses overall. By 1776, when The Wealth of Nations was first published, the fire office registers record 754 separate trades in London; by the mid-1820s the number had increased to 1042. A little over 250 trades to be found in London in the mid-1770s can no longer be separately identified 50 years later. However, there are over 550 trades separately identified in the mid-1820s which did not yet exist in a separately identifiable form in the 1770s. Taking the period 1775–1825 as a whole, over 1300 separate trades can be identified in London from the registers of the various fire offices.

The significance of the incidence of business in the community in the 1770s and 1820s can be compared to the 1990s. London in the mid-1770s had about one business for every 26 inhabitants; by the mid-1820s the ratio was about one business for every 28. In the early-1990s, the ratio of VAT-registered business to the total population of the United Kingdom was about one to 38. An interesting comparison can also be made of the ratios of retail businesses to the total population. In London in the mid-1770s it was probably about one to 40 and in the mid-1820s about one to 45; in 1989, for the United Kingdom as a whole, it was about one to 240.

The fire office registers also reveal something of how capital was structured in London. The large majority of policies were taken out in the name of a single individual. However, the proportion taken out in the name of more than one individual increased significantly between the 1770s and the 1820s, from under 9 per cent to 13.5 per cent. Very few firms used the designation 'and company' in the 1770s, under 0.1 per cent; by the 1820s this had risen to over 3 per cent. Such firms insured for an average of £11,741 in the 1820s, almost eight times the overall average of £1510. It is clear that the greater the capital requirements of the trade, the greater the proportion of firms with more than a single proprietor. Thus, in the 1820s the proportion of merchants, factors and wholesalers taking out policies in more than one name was over 41 per cent and the average value of capital insured was £6982. At the other end of the spectrum the proportion of such businesses was under 10 per cent in both the retail and services sectors and the average value of capital insured was only £804 and £909 respectively. Manufacturing stood between the extremes; 18 per cent of policies were taken out in more than one name and the average value of capital insured was £1412. A similar pattern is to be found in the 1770s. Nearly 31 per cent of policies taken out by merchants, factors and wholesalers were in more than one name and the average value of capital insured was £2910; at the other end of the scale, the proportion was under 9 per cent for the retail and services sectors and the average value of capital insured only £462 and £323. The proportion of 'family' businesses actually increased considerably between the 1770s and 1820s, from 25 per cent of those with more than one proprietor to nearly 40 per cent. This suggests that even in the most modestly capitalised of London's trades the large increase in capital required to maintain a business successfully over the period 1775–1825 necessitated the involvement of more than one family member in a growing number of cases.

In the remaining chapters of this book, data on the numbers of businesses in different trades and industries, the capital employed by them, their numbers of employees and the changes in these factors over the period 1775–1825, will be used to suggest answers to some of the most controversial questions surrounding the role of London during that period. Taken together, these answers amount to a factually based revision of many of the assumptions which have prevailed for most of the twentieth century. The five sets of questions to be answered are as follows:

1. What was the significance of manufacturing in and to London? Was it a manufacturing backwater or the most important manufacturing centre in the kingdom? Was it growing or declining between 1775 and 1825? Was it reliant on particular industries, or types of industry, such as the finishing or luxury trades, or on a wide and growing range of manufactures? Was it characterised by large firms or small, or did both play significant roles? How far were individual trades concentrated in particular districts, and what is the significance of whether they were or were not in particular instances? How were they affected by technological change? Was London's industry bypassed by steam, or at the leading edge?

2. To what extent did London experience a construction boom in this period? What was the contribution of the construction trades to the economy of London as a whole? How did they impact on other industries?

3. Was there a consumer revolution and, if so, to what extent was London the dynamic behind it? Was there a distinct distributive sector in this period? What was the growth in wholesale and retail distribution, and how did it impact on other trades? Was the growth in the wholesale and retail sectors consistent across all such trades, all social classes and all districts of London, or were there differences between them?

4. Did London in this period evolve a prototype service economy? What were the developments in, for example, transport, catering and personal services, and how important were they to the economy as a whole? Was their importance growing or declining? How did they impact on other parts of the economy? What was their inter-relationship with other sectors, for example transport and coach-building? To what extent were they too a response to the changes in consumer habits?

5. How important was commercial London, and was that importance growing or declining? What were the roles of, and relationships with other trades, of merchants, factors, brokers and agents of all kinds?

. . . .

CHAPTER 4

The London Manufacturing Trades

Manufacturing as a Whole

Perhaps the most radical of the recent revisions of London's role in the Industrial Revolution is the proposition that it was the largest and most important manufacturing centre in Britain, certainly until well into the nineteenth century. Pigot and Co's *London and Provincial New Commercial Directory for 1826–27* listed just under 49,000 businesses. Of these, just over 14,500 may be classified as engaged in manufacturing, excluding bespoke production. This was almost 30 per cent of all businesses in London. They also accounted for nearly a quarter of all the capital insured by London businesses with the fire offices. In fact, if the capital insured by London's huge mercantile sector of merchants, agents, factors and brokers is excluded, manufacturing accounts for 35 per cent of the remainder.

Throughout the half century from 1775 to 1825, the manufacturing sector was increasing in size and importance in the metropolis. Although there is no reliable count of manufacturing firms as a whole in the 1770s, it is likely that there were between 7000 and 8000 and that this accounted for about a quarter of all firms. This would imply that the total number of firms engaged in manufacturing trades about doubled between the 1770s and the 1820s. A more precise statistical comparison can be made for two industries, the furniture and book trades. These showed increases in the number of firms of 165 and 180 per cent respectively.[1]

The size of individual businesses in the manufacturing trades, as measured in terms of the fixed and working capital insured by them for fire insurance purposes, also increased considerably. In the 1770s, the average value of capital insured was £712; by the 1820s this had

TABLE 4.1 Size of manufacturing firms in London by value of capital insured

Capital insured (£)	No. of firms 1770s	Percentage of total	No. of firms 1820s	Percentage of total
100 and under	1560	35.2	843	23.6
101–500	1751	39.5	1282	35.8
501–1000	507	11.4	491	13.7
1001–2999	373	8.4	520	14.5
3000 and over	241	5.4	443	12.4
Total	4432	100.0	3579	100.0

Source: Sun and other London fire office registers

exactly doubled to £1415. The median value also increased by a similar proportion, from £200 to £380. These figures also demonstrate that most of the increase in size was to be found among larger firms. Nevertheless, both large and small businesses played their role in the contribution made by manufacturing to the economy of the metropolis in the period 1775–1825. Changes over the period are highly instructive. Data from the fire office registers show the size of manufacturing firms in London in the 1770s and 1820s in terms of capital insured (see Table 4.1).

Clearly, the proportion of smaller firms reduced over the period. Nevertheless, even though the proportion insuring £500 or less reduced from nearly three-quarters in the 1770s to just under 60 per cent in the 1820s, it was still well in excess of half in the later period. Conversely, the proportion of firms insuring fixed and/or working capital valued at over £1000 nearly doubled between the 1770s and the 1820s, from just under 14 per cent to nearly 27 per cent. Within the highest size band, the proportion rose from just over 5 per cent to over 12 per cent. It is particularly instructive to consider how much of the total capital insured was accounted for by firms of differing sizes (see Table 4.2).

In the 1770s, over 30 per cent of capital insured by London manufacturers came from firms with capital valued at £1000 or less, 18 per cent by those insuring £500 or less. By the 1820s, firms with capital valued at £1000 or less for insurance purposes accounted for nearly 16 per cent of the total; those insuring for £500 or less accounted for

TABLE 4.2 Capital insured by manufacturing firms in London of different size

Capital insured (£)	Sum of capital insured (£) 1770s	Percentage of total	Sum of capital insured (£) 1820s	Percentage of total
100 and under	97,992	3.1	51,100	1.0
101–500	470,473	14.9	364,017	7.2
501–1000	384,695	12.2	382,105	7.6
1001–2999	648,462	20.6	912,965	18.1
3000 and over	1,553,618	49.2	3,344,010	66.2
Total	3,155,240	100.0	5,054,197	100.0

Source: Sun and other London fire office registers

just over 8 per cent. Although these are small proportions, they are not insignificant. The trend is clear: whereas at the beginning of the last quarter of the eighteenth century nearly a third of all manufacturing capital was accounted for by small and medium-sized firms, half a century later this proportion had fallen to about one-sixth. Interestingly, the proportion of manufacturing capital accounted for by medium to large firms actually fell slightly between the 1770s and the 1820s, from 21 per cent to 18 per cent. However, the proportion insured by large firms increased very significantly, from under a half to exactly two-thirds.* At the very least, it would seem that the

---

* An estimate of the total value of capital insured in London in the 1820s has been made for every major London trade or industry by grossing up the actual risk insured by those firms taking out policies with the Sun, Royal Exchange, Hand in Hand, Globe and London fire offices to the total number of firms in those trades or industries as listed in Pigot and Co's *London and Provincial New Commercial Directory for 1826–27*. It has to be noted that this underestimates the overall value of capital insured to the extent that we do not always know whether the very largest firms insured with another fire office for which records have not survived. On the other hand, it overestimates total values to the extent that larger firms are over-represented in the fire office registers and the sums insured by them are, therefore, given too high a weighting factor in the grossing-up process. On balance it is reasonable to believe that the total values of capital insured in any trade or industry are broadly of the right order of magnitude and represent the relative position of any one trade or industry compared with another.

conclusion reached by one recent historian is a gross oversimplification. It is far too sweeping to assert: 'Manufacturing industry in London was characterised by the predominance of small scale production in which the unit of production was the workshop or home.'[2] Self-evidently, if nearly half of all capital utilised in manufacturing was insured by large firms as early as the 1770s, and if this had increased to two-thirds by the 1820s, and if medium-sized firms made up a large proportion of the remainder, small firms can scarcely have been 'predominant'.

It can, therefore, be seen that while all sizes of firm continued to play a significant role within the manufacturing trades as a whole, clearly the most significant increase is in the number in the highest size band. Measuring changes in the size of individual firms in particular industries over time or between different London trades is necessarily relative: absolute criteria do not exist. Nevertheless, there is a measure which can reasonably be applied to businesses in any London trade which is external to both their geographical location and the particular trade or industry and which, if not an *absolute* criterion, is at least an *objective* and *consistent* one. In Tables 4.1 and 4.2, £3000 has been deliberately set as the bench-mark for capitalisation above which *any* business may be regarded as 'large'. This was the figure for which the many standard design Arkwright cotton mills of the 1780s were usually insured, £1000 for the standard three- or four-storey building of about 90 feet by 30 feet, £1000 for the 10-horse-power water mill, thousand spindles and other machinery, and £1000 for stock. Such a mill employed 200 to 300 people. Cotton was in many ways the archetypal industry and these mills the archetypal industrial undertakings of the Industrial Revolution. The point is that they were insured by the same London fire offices as every other industrial undertaking in Britain at the time, whether in London or the provinces. Such mills were large by any objective standard and it is reasonable, therefore, to regard any business with capital insured for £3000 as *large* in this period, and any insuring for over £3000 as *very large indeed*.[3]

On a much more subjective basis, it should be noted that Dodd identified 22 different London industries in 1843 in which factories were to be found on a massive scale: brewing, distilling, sugar refining, shipbuilding, coachbuilding, gasmaking, bell founding, bookbinding, printing and marble working, and the manufacture of tobacco and snuff, vinegar and British wine, hats, leather, soap and candles, blacking, flint glass, floorcloths, pianofortes, rope and sailcloth, church clocks and copper and lead.[4]

Another measure of the relative size of London manufacturing firms can be gathered from the statements of profits contained in over three-quarters of Bankruptcy Commission files. A sample of the balance sheets of 403 bankrupt London firms in the period 1820–31 gives an annualised profit of £583. Obviously, the incidence of bankruptcy was by no means identical to the structure of industry in London as a whole. Even had it been so, it would still not be possible to draw conclusions from such a small sample. Nevertheless, it is interesting to note that the average annual profit for 92 manufacturing firms was £781, slightly higher than for all firms.

Steam Power Another measure of the extent to which London was a major industrial and manufacturing centre is the use of steam power. Many historians have implied, or even openly stated, that steam power was virtually unknown in London at this time. One writes of London's disadvantage relative to the new industrial districts because it could not utilise the new technology based on coal and steam owing to its distance from the coalfields.[5] Another that 'London was not revolutionized ... its industries remained small-scale in organization and traditional in technology'.[6] Neither is true. As early as 1733 London had seven steam engines at work, though these would have been used for pumping rather than for the transmission of power. Nevertheless, another 20 had been installed by 1780. The first Boulton and Watt engine was installed in Cooke and Co's distillery at Stratford in 1776.[7] By 1780, 4.5 per cent of all steam engines installed in Britain were in London. Between 1781 and 1800 there was a huge increase in numbers. In Britain as a whole, 1566 engines were installed, of which 109 or 7 per cent were in London. To put this into perspective, the 109 installed in London was far more than in Durham (38) or Northumberland (37), much the same number as in Shropshire and Staffordshire (111 each) and nearly half the number in the whole of Lancashire (240), the West Riding (228) or in all other parts of the country put together, including both Scotland and Wales (226).[8]

In 1804 and 1805 a very extensive survey was carried out by John Farey. He claimed to have visited every establishment in London utilising steam power and to have found 112 engines. Breweries topped the list with 17, followed by ten foundries and machine makers and eight dye houses and distilleries. There were also tanneries, vinegar makers, calico printers, sailcloth weavers, colour and starch makers, drug and mustard mills, cutlers, ropemakers, glass and diamond cutters, silversmiths and a number of others. In all, Farey noted the use of steam power in 21 different London industries. By the 1820s this had increased to 29 trades in which fire insurance policies covered a steam engine. When he actually published his *A Treatise on the Steam Engine* in 1827, Farey noted that there were 290 steam engines in use in London, an increase of 159 per cent since 1804–5. He compared this with 240 in Manchester, 130 in Leeds and 80 to 90 in Glasgow.[9] At the very least, this is a measure of the extent to which London not only shared the technological advances being made in the more traditionally recognised centres of manufacturing growth, but remained in the forefront throughout the period 1775–1825.

The Geography of Manufacturing in London

A recent geography of London attempts a very precise description in which the different districts of the metropolis are classified within very distinct zones,

> In the first half of the nineteenth century London's economic geography crystallised around three complementary but distinctive zones. At the centre the City of London was a clearly defined commercial and financial core containing a mix of offices, commercial premises and warehouses. The outer suburban zone consisted of homes of the professional and commercial middle classes ... sandwiched between core and suburb was the inner industrial perimeter stretching in a belt around the City of London, from Holborn in the west to Poplar in the east and southwards to Lambeth. This contained the bulk of manufacturing employment. Many of London's traditional trades were concentrated in this inner perimeter. Other trades, such as printing, watchmaking, silk weaving and engineering were also concentrated in particular localities within the inner zone.[10]

Hobsbawm also described three distinct labour markets: the West End, which was dominated by bespoke production carried out by skilled artisans; the East End, in which manufacturing was for the wholesale trades and dominated by unskilled labour; and the south, which stood between the two.[11] Although there is some truth in both

TABLE 4.3 Distribution of manufacturing firms in London by postal district

London postal districts	Manufacturing firms 1770s	Percentage of all firms in district	Manufacturing firms 1820s	Percentage of all firms in district
E	818	29.4	732	27.0
EC	1426	27.8	1184	26.7
W	565	23.4	503	25.8
WC	892	25.2	547	25.5
N	31	26.1	59	21.2
NW	2	16.7	37	17.9
SE	519	29.2	424	25.2
SW	179	19.7	93	15.4
Total	4432	100.0	3579	100.0

Source: Sun and other London fire office registers

of these classifications, they are again an oversimplification. The distribution of manufacturing firms into precise areas was far from clear-cut. Tables 4.3 and 4.4 show manufacturing firms in London for which fire insurance records survive for each of the main geographical groupings of London postal districts used for the last hundred years or more.

From Table 4.3 it can be seen that manufacturing accounted for a very little different proportion of businesses in the City, either in the 1770s or the 1820s, than it did in the East End or the districts south of the river. Nor were the west central or west end districts significantly different. The newer and more residential suburbs to the north, north-west and south-west had smaller proportions, but never below 15 per cent. Nor was there much difference between the 1770s and 1820s within any of the broad postal district areas. Only south of the river was there a small reduction in the proportion of all firms engaged in manufacturing, from 29.2 per cent to 25.2 per cent.

There was very little difference in the distribution of London's manufacturing businesses between the 1770s and 1820s. In both periods about a third were located in the City, about a fifth in the East End and 12 per cent in the districts south of the river. The only significant decrease was in the proportion to be found in the west central area, which declined from over 20 per cent to only just over

TABLE 4.4 Manufacturing firms by postal district

London postal district	No. of firms 1770s	Percentage of total	No. of firms 1820s	Percentage of total
E	818	18.5	732	20.5
EC	1426	32.2	1184	33.1
W	565	12.7	503	14.1
WC	892	20.1	547	15.3
N	31	0.7	59	2.6
NW	2	0.1	37	1.0
SW	179	4.0	93	2.6
SE	519	11.7	424	11.8
Total	4432	100.0	3579	100.0

Source: Sun and other London fire office registers

15 per cent. The universality of manufacturing in London was still a feature in the 1840s when George Dodd recorded his impressions of both the City and Southwark. Of the former, he noted that in Shoe Lane there were 'many factories for articles of copper, and also of brass, lead, tin, and other metals';[12] of the latter, he observed:

> Those dwellers in and visitors to the 'Great Metropolis' who cross South-wark Bridge from the City to the Borough can scarcely fail to have observed the array of tall chimneys which meets the eye on either side of its southern extremity; each one serving as a kind of beacon or guide-post to some large manufacturing establishment beneath – here a brewery, there a saw-mill, further on a hat factory, a distillery, a vinegar factory, and numerous others. Indeed Southwark is as distinguishable at a distance for its numerous tall chimneys and the shrouds of smoke emitted by them, as London is for its thickly-congregated church-spires.[13]

Everywhere, 'the way to wealth [was] generally through some narrow, dirty, dark, and crowded street, bounded on either side by ranges of factories, warehouses, or wharves; with waggons and porters and cranes and bales of goods meeting the eye at every few steps'.[14] Impressionistic though Dodd's descriptions are, they fit the statistical framework outlined above better than arbitrary modern attempts to divide Industrial Revolution London into neatly differentiated 'zones'.

TABLE 4.5 Numbers of London manufacturing firms and value of capital insured by manufacturing sector

Manufacturing sector	No. of firms	Percentage of total	Capital insured (£)	Percentage of total
Metals	58	0.4	33,000	0.2
Non-metallic products	356	2.5	526,000	3.0
Chemicals	388	2.7	767,000	4.4
Metal goods	1241	8.5	1,182,000	6.7
Engineering	386	2.7	408,000	2.3
Shipbuilding	217	1.5	290,000	1.6
Coachbuilding	567	3.9	819,000	4.6
Watchmaking	627	4.3	235,000	1.3
Precision instruments	261	1.8	106,000	0.6
Food, drink and tobacco	626	4.3	3,019,000	17.1
Textiles	1224	8.4	2,341,000	13.3
Leather	983	6.8	1,396,000	7.9
Clothing	1139	7.8	1,327,000	7.5
Timber	2318	16.0	960,000	5.4
Furniture	1718	11.8	1,217,000	6.9
Paper and printing	1291	8.9	2,280,000	12.9
Other manufacturing	1124	7.7	722,000	4.1
Total	14,524	100.0	17,628,000	100.0

Sources: Pigot and Co's *London and Provincial New Commercial Directory for 1826–27*; and Sun and other London fire office registers

Classification of Manufacturing Trades

The numbers of businesses in each manufacturing sector and the value of capital insured with the London fire offices in the 1820s are tabulated in Table 4.5.

Of course, these are not absolutely self-contained industrial sectors. Indeed, it is the inter-relationship between them which makes up one of the most fascinating areas of analysis of London's industrial profile in the last quarter of the eighteenth century and the first quarter of the nineteenth. These are dealt with more fully below, but to take just a few of the more obvious examples: shipbuilding cannot be discussed without reference to either anchorsmiths (metal goods manufacturing), rope- or sailmaking (textiles) on the one hand, and chronometer and mathematical and optical instrument making (precision instruments) on the other; and coachmaking clearly depends on the transport services sector and heavily influences the leather trades of saddle, harness and trunk making. In addition, every manufacturing trade influences and is influenced by the wholesaler and retailers who distribute its products.

Table 4.5 shows that some industrial sectors accounted for much larger proportions of London's manufacturing businesses than they did of the capital insured, and vice versa, marking the distinction between the more and less highly capital intensive of them. Eleven industrial sectors each accounted for over 4 per cent of either London's manufacturing firms or of capital insured by them, or both: food, drink and tobacco, paper, printing and publishing, textiles, furniture, leather and leather goods, clothing, metal goods, the timber trades, coachbuilding, chemicals and watch- and clockmaking.

This is not to say that these were the only important industries. Indeed, many of the individual trades within the above broad sectors were of enormous importance in themselves, for example sugar refining, brewing, distilling, printing and silk, soap and hat manufacture. Others such as shipbuilding or musical instrument making were important though not part of any larger grouping. Nevertheless, the above list forms the starting point for an analysis in depth of the role played by manufacturing in London in the period 1775–1825. What is most immediately evident from this list is that it does not fit any simplistic notion of London's manufacturing industries as dominated by luxury or finishing or any other one type of trade. If there is one factor which does link them all, it is that they are precisely the trades one would expect to find in a city which both formed an enormous immediate market for its own products and was the focal point and set the fashion for other parts of the country which looked to it for a lead.

Food, Drink and Tobacco

The colossal task of feeding the largest and wealthiest city the world had ever seen explains the huge scale of food manufacturing in London in the last quarter of the eighteenth and the first quarter of the nineteenth centuries. It was still true, of course, that much, if not most, food production was carried out routinely by the retailer – butcher, baker, confectioner, cheesemonger, grocer or provision merchant of one sort or another – and many types of foodstuff – fish, fruit, vegetables, meat and poultry – required no real processing at all. George Dodd pointed out the 'difference exhibited between those [manufactures] relating to solid food and those relating to liquids; the former being mostly carried on in comparatively small establishments, while the latter involve arrangements of great magnitude'. He did allow that there were exceptions such as sugar and mustard, and that tobacco and snuff involved large-scale production processes.[15] In practice, there were rather more exceptions than this and it is certainly true overall that production of food, drink and tobacco involved some of the largest and most highly capitalised manufacturing trades in London, and had done so since at least 1700.

Pigot listed 626 firms engaged in food manufacture in 1826–27, 4.3 per cent of all London's manufacturing firms. Even more to the point, over 17 per cent of all manufacturing capital insured by the London fire offices was accounted for by these firms. There was little place for the smaller firm in any of these industries. Only 29 per cent insured capital valued at £500 or less in the 1820s, compared with 63 per cent for all London trades, and they accounted for only 1.3 per cent of all capital insured.

Undoubtedly, brewing was on the largest scale of all. Alone it accounted for nearly 7 per cent of all capital insured by London's manufacturing trades, indeed nearly 2 per cent of capital insured by all London businesses. Pigot listed 177 brewers in 1826–27 and there are fire office records for 120 in the 1770s and 57 in the 1820s. Even in the earlier period the average value of capital insured by brewers was £2621 and by the 1820s this had increased by over 150 per cent to £6607. In the early eighteenth century there had been innumerable small brewers in London. However, by the last quarter of the century their number was declining drastically and this accelerated over the period 1775–1825. In the 1770s, over a third insured their businesses for £500 or less; by the 1820s this had decreased to only 19 per cent. Using the £3000 criterion, 20 per cent of London's brewers can be described as large in the 1770s, and 50 years later this had increased to 28 per cent. A small proportion of firms were very large indeed. As early as the 1770s over 14 per cent insured capital valued at £5000 or more, and 5 per cent insured over £10,000. By the 1820s these proportions had leapt to over 26 per cent and nearly 16 per cent. Table 4.6 shows the full breakdown by value of capital insured.

TABLE 4.6 Brewers

Capital insured (£)	No. of firms 1770s	Percentage of total	No. of firms 1820s	Percentage of total
100 and under	5	4.2	3	5.3
101–500	38	31.6	8	14.0
501–1000	22	18.3	14	24.6
1001–2999	31	25.8	16	28.1
3000 and over	24	20.0	16	28.1
Total	120	100.0	57	100.0

Source: Sun and other London fire office registers

Demand for beer escalated enormously throughout the period 1775–1825. Between 1818 and 1825 alone, output nationally of strong beer rose by nearly 17 per cent, from 5.573 million gallons to 6.5 million. Over the more limited period from 1820 to 1825, annual per capita expenditure on alcohol increased by 22 per cent from £2.43 to £2.97.[16] The market in London was a perfect size, its outermost districts within the daily reach of a dray, and it required no new technological breakthrough before large-scale production was feasible, although 14 steam engines were in operation by 1801. The larger brewers were not slow to seize such a marketing opportunity from an early date. By 1748 the 12 largest firms accounted for 42 per cent of London's production. This rose to 55 per cent by 1776, to 78 per cent by 1815 and to 85 per cent by 1830. In that latter year the 12 had a total financial resource of £6 million. The top three alone – Whitbread's, Barclay's and Truman's – accounted for nearly 36 per cent of London's total output[17] and in 1843 Dodd described such firms as 'the "lions" of the metropolis, so vast are their dimensions'.[18]

The increase in capitalisation between the 1770s and 1820s is exemplified by Calvert and Co of Campion Lane, Upper Thames Street. They had insured capital valued at £31,400 in 1771; by 1820 the sum insured by them had risen to £84,100. In the latter year this included their counting house valued at £3000, two storehouses, a brew house and its plant insured for £8800, a steam engine house for £500, the steam engine for £800, a vat house for £700, a warehouse for £700, and an assortment of other industrial buildings for £6700. This was in addition to stock and utensils valued at £62,900.[19] On the other hand, there was very little change in the capital insured by Goodwyn and Co. They moved from Butcher Row, Ratcliffe Cross, in 1771 to Lower East Smithfield in 1820, increasing the capital they insured only from £30,790 to £33,000.[20] Interestingly, there was a similar ratio of fixed to working capital insured by Goodwyn and Co in the 1770s to that insured by Calvert and Co in the 1820s. The industrial buildings insured by Goodwyn in 1771 included a brew house and two storehouses for £3000, two still houses for £160, two engine houses for £40, a mill house, coal house and malt house for £500, three warehouses for £1350, and three store cellars for £650. They also insured stock and utensils for £24,900. Barclay Perkins insured capital valued at £37,000 in 1820;[21] 43 years earlier, in 1777, the original brewery on the Park Street site had been insured by Henry Thrale, friend of Dr Johnson and originally employer of John Perkins, for £8000.[22] Both firms exemplify the family continuity which was a feature of the brewing industry.[23] An example of a still substantial, but considerably smaller, risk was the policy taken out by George Ball and Co in 1825. They insured the Bowl Yard brew house in Broad Street, St Giles, for £3000, a steam engine for £800, their counting house, cooperage, stables and other industrial buildings for £1040, and stock and utensils for £9710.[24]

As early as the 1770s, firms insuring capital valued at £500 or less accounted for only 4 per cent of all capital insured and even this fell dramatically by the 1820s to only just over half of one per cent. However, even though this was the most highly capitalised of all London's manufacturing industries it was still just possible for small brewers to survive: in 1824, Edward Little insured the Canal Brewery in the Kent Road for £150, and stock and utensils for the same sum.[25] Throughout the period 1775–1825 most brewers were located in the City, or just to the east or south. This both gave access to the river and provided the central location from which their drays could supply the whole of the metropolis.

The second of London's three major food and drink manufacturing industries was distilling. The great age of gin had been the first quarter of the eighteenth century but the social evils associated with its consumption had led to a series of Acts between 1729 and 1751 restricting its sale. Even as late as 1745 consumption nationally had approached 8 million gallons. However, by the early 1780s this had declined to little more than one million, although consumption edged up again from the 1780s. Distilling was primarily a London trade and in 1783 the London corn distillers claimed to produce 'upwards of eleven-twelfths of the whole distillery of England'.[26] In 1747 Campbell remarked that 'The London Distillery is now arrived at a very great Perfection'[27] and a century later Dodd described the typical London distillery as exhibiting a 'remarkable largeness of feature'.[28] There were two branches of the trade, malt distilling and compound distilling or rectifying, the former usually being much the more highly capitalised. As well as gin, houses such as Seager and Evans and Burrough's produced liqueurs and cordials, with such almost forgotten names as shrub, lovage, caraway and aniseed, as well as cordials for medicinal purposes.[29]

The period 1775–1825 saw a decline in the number of London distillers. *Kent's Directory for the Year 1774*, which is a very incomplete count of London's tradesmen, listed 74 distillers. In 1826–27 Pigot's far wider count listed only 60. Similarly, the fire office registers contain the policies of 69 in the 1770s and only 24 in the 1820s. However, if their numbers decreased, their size undoubtedly increased. In the 1770s the average value of capital insured was £2719, a very large figure by comparison with other trades. By the 1820s it had increased almost four-fold to £10,328. Even the median values were extremely high, £1550 in the 1770s and £5900 in the 1820s. In the earlier period nearly a quarter of all firms insured capital valued at £500 or less; 50 years later there was none, and less than 30 per cent could even be described as medium-sized. The proportion of 'large' firms insuring for £3000 or more rose from over 30 per cent in the 1770s to a massive 71 per cent in the 1820s. In the earlier period, 16 per cent insured for £5000 or more; in the later it was over half, and a third insured for over £10,000. This was one London manufacturing trade incontestably dominated by large firms. Table 4.7 shows a full breakdown by value of capital insured.

As with brewers, London's distillers displayed a considerable degree of continuity over the entire period 1775–1825. John Bockett and Joseph Houghland insured their counting house, still house and warehouse at 273 Borough for £1700 in 1777, and the contents for £16,000. As Joseph Bockett and Son, and relocated across the river in New Bridge Street, they insured for £21,000 in 1819 and 1821.[30] Typically, fixed capital was not large in relation to the valuations put on stock and utensils in the 1770s. Thus, when William Van Strate and Peter

TABLE 4.7 Distillers

Capital insured (£)	No. of firms 1770s	Percentage of total	No. of firms 1820s	Percentage of total
100 and under	0	0	0	0
101–500	16	23.2	0	0
501–1000	12	17.4	3	12.5
1001–2999	20	29.0	4	16.7
3000 and over	21	30.4	17	70.8
Total	69	100.0	24	100.0

Source: Sun and other London fire office registers

Edel insured their still house, rectifying house and warehouse in Lower Street, Islington for £200 each in 1771, they insured their stock and utensils for nearly eleven times that sum (£6650).[31] The largest sum insured in the 1820s was £50,000 by Currie and Co of Vine Street, Bloomsbury. Their distillery was located on the east bank of the River Lea at Bromley-by-Bow. By the 1820s fixed capital was being insured for very much larger sums than half a century earlier.[32] Seager and Evans, founded in 1805, moved from Brewer Street, Pimlico to Millbank in 1822 and two years later insured their distillery for £3000, as well as stock and utensils for £5000.[33] As an illustration of the process of concentration of production in fewer and fewer firms, Seager and Evans were to take over three other substantial distilleries in the next few years, Pigeon's in the Borough, Jackson's in Dockhead and Hore and Griffiths in Whitechapel.[34] Another famous name, Charles Gordon and Co, insured their still house and warehouse at 67 Goswell Street for £500 and their steam engine, stock and utensils for £4500 in 1823 and 1824.[35] In both the 1770s and 1820s distilleries were to be found all over the metropolis, but far fewer south of the river by the later period.

The third of London's great food and drink manufacturing industries was sugar refining, characterised like brewing and distilling by the necessity for very high levels of capitalisation. However, unlike the two major drink manufacturing industries, capitalisation of sugar refining did not greatly increase over the period 1775–1825. In the 1770s, the average value of capital insured was £4914 and this increased by only 14 per cent to £5620 by the 1820s. On the other

TABLE 4.8 Sugar refiners

Capital insured (£)	No. of firms 1770s	Percentage of total	No. of firms 1820s	Percentage of total
100 and under	0	0	3	4.6
101–500	2	2.0	4	6.2
501–1000	9	9.2	3	4.6
1001–2999	63	64.3	13	20.0
3000 and over	24	24.5	42	64.6
Total	98	100.0	65	100.0

Source: Sun and other London fire office registers

hand, as in brewing and distilling, there was very little place for the small firm. The industry underwent a steep decline in the 1780s. There were an estimated 140 sugar houses in 1776, and this is said to have reduced by a third in the 1780s.[36] Thereafter the industry would appear to have stabilised because there were 88 in 1826–27. Table 4.8 shows a full breakdown by value of capital insured.

There were many contemporary published estimates of capital required to set up in most of London's innumerable trades. Most estimated that at least £500 was required for any of the three major food and drink manufacturing industries. However, sugar refining was at the top with virtually every contemporary source setting a minimum figure of £1000; indeed, *Kearsley's Table of Trades*, published in 1786, stated that up to £10,000 might be required as start-up capital. Only just over 11 per cent of all firms in the 1770s, and 15 per cent in the 1820s, insured capital valued at £1000 or less. Conversely, nearly a quarter insured capital valued at £3000 or more in the 1770s and nearly two-thirds in the 1820s. A number of firms were very large indeed. Over 10 per cent insured for over £10,000 in the 1770s and more than 15 per cent 50 years later. In 1777 Spalding, Slack and Hawes of Gravel Lane, Whitechapel, insured for £22,000.[37] Similar valuations were made in the 1820s when Holthouse and Co in New Road insured for £20,000 in 1822.[38] Fixed capital could be substantial. Typically, Martin Wackerbath, one of the many people of German extraction in London's sugar refining industry, insured his sugar house in Hoxton Square for £700, and a shed and lofts for £150 in 1777. He also insured stock and utensils for £4400.[39] By 1820, James Nasmyth was insuring his sugar house and steam engine house in Old Gravel Lane for the immense sum of £6000, a steam engine and other machinery for £2000, a storehouse for £1000 and an 'experimental house' for £150.[40] Nasmyth is a good example of the early application in London of steam power to food production on a very large scale.

In terms of location, sugar refining required access to the river. However, over the period 1775–1825 the industry moved steadily east. In 1782 there had been two distinct clusters. The larger was along Upper Thames Street, where there were 25 with 6 others close by. The smaller was in Whitechapel and Goodman's Fields, where there were 20 between the Whitechapel Road and Wellclose Square. By the 1820s, less than 10 per cent were still located in the City, with 89 per cent in Whitechapel and around Wellclose Square.

Throughout the period 1775–1825 most of London's food was either processed by retailers or imported already processed from other parts of the country or abroad. Nevertheless, there were a number of examples of food production in London on a substantial scale. Pigot listed 189 firms in 24 different trades in 1826–27. The fire office registers record an even greater number of trades, 31 in total. These provide a vivid impression of the range of food processing trades in the capital. They included fat and oil, mustard, vinegar, British wine, confectionery, soda and mineral water and ginger and spruce beer manufacturers, bacon curers, sausage and savaloy; jelly, lemon juice, chocolate and cider makers, millers, slaughtermen and sea biscuit bakers. Together they accounted for capital insured in the 1820s for over £734,000, greater than that for either distilling or sugar refining and over 4 per cent of capital insured by all manufacturing firms in London.

Within these trades were to be found some very large businesses indeed. Vinegar manufacture involved some particularly large firms. In 1777 John Potts and Son insured their mill house, warehouse and brew house at 17 Mansell Street for £4000, a storehouse and lofts for £2100, and stock, utensils and goods for £15,000. Nearly half a century later, on 29 November 1821, Charles, Arthur and William Potts, insured their fixed and working capital for a total of £53,600. By then they were located at New Bridge Street, Southwark, where their liquor backs, cooperage, warehouses and sheds were valued at £5000, four stove or cockle houses at £4500, two brew houses at £4600, their counting house at £1600, various coach houses and stables at £800, a steam engine at £400, a coal house at £100, and fences, railings and gates at £200. They also insured stock and utensils valued at £36,400.[41] Very large too were Beaufoy and Co of South Lambeth. Their brew house was valued at £7000, their warehouse at £1500, a cooperage at £400, a steam engine at £600, a mill and the machinery therein at £3000 and assorted other industrial buildings at £3200. Their stock and utensils were insured for £13,300.[42] Again it is worth noting the use by both firms of steam power in food production.

At least seven other food manufacturing or processing industries required large or moderately large levels of capitalisation; mustard, soda water, starch and sweet manufacture and milling, sea biscuit baking and bacon curing. Lingard and Sadler were mustard makers who insured their mill house at 24 Winchester Street, Borough, for £150 in 1774, their warehouses for £200, and stock and utensils for £1250.[43] Soda water had been invented in 1767 and the name first used in an advertisement by Schweppes in 1798.[44] By 1820 one soda and mineral water manufacturer, Philip de Gruchy of 17 Silver Street, Cheapside, was insuring stock and utensils valued at £1500.[45] Starch manufacture could require very large amounts of capital and in 1824 William Randall insured his mill at Princes Street, Lambeth, for £1975, his counting house for £300, his warehouse for £2800, several granaries for £4200 and a forge house for £25.[46] Very large too was the business of William Phone and Son. They were confectioners who insured their manufactory and warehouse at 38 Watling Street for £3000 in 1820, as well as stock utensils and goods for £1700.[47] An example of a substantially capitalised miller was Thomas Rutter and Co of Lambeth who insured for £3400 in 1820.[48] Sea biscuits were also manufactured on a considerable scale. Morrison Coverdale had insured his bake house alone for £1000 in 1777,[49] and Hill, Boulcott and Hill of 80 Wapping Wall took out a policy for £12,000 in the 1820s.[50] Finally, it should be noted that Thomas Hemmings, a bacon curer in Peters Lane, Clerkenwell, valued his stock and utensils at no less than £8000 in 1819.[51]

Overall, just over 21 per cent of these food and drink manufacturers insured capital valued at £3000 or more in the 1820s and can be regarded as large. However, smaller businesses made an important contribution too; 6 per cent of all capital employed was accounted for by firms insuring £500 or less and these made up 55 per cent of all businesses in the 1820s and 63 per cent in the 1770s. There were many firms like G. R. Mitchell, a French bread, gingerbread and biscuit baker at 32 Gibson Street, Lambeth, whose trade card assured potential trade customers that 'Muffins, Crumpets, Prussian Cakes' were supplied to 'Taverns, Coffee Houses and Shops'.[52] Another example is John Hinxman, a tripe dresser, who insured his boiling house at 10 Clare Street for £250 in 1820, his slaughterhouse for £200, and stock, utensils and livestock for £220.[53] Far smaller still was Moses Hooper, a lemon-juice maker in Botolph Alley, who insured his total stock for £100 in 1769.[54]

Finally, it must be noted that tobacco and snuff manufacture was a major London trade throughout the period although it is difficult to distinguish between manufacture and retail sale because many firms were engaged in both. An invoice sent out by Fribourg and Treyer on 21 August 1787 stated that they 'Make and Sell all Sorts of French Rappees, Spanish, Portuguese, Scotch, and High Dry'd Irish Snuffs'.[55] As late as 1820, snuff was still 90 per cent of their business. Three years later they carried stock weighing 6 tons 14 cwt.[56] However, of 112 manufacturers in 1826–27, Pigot listed 98 who were tobacco and snuff manufacturers, 10 snuff makers and 4 cigar makers. Dodd noted that they 'involve manufacturing arrangements of much ingenuity'.[57] In 1820 the snuff manufactory of Samuel Stock near the Minories was valued at £2875, his steam engine at £300, other machinery at £700, and stock and utensils at £4000.[58] Interestingly, horse mills were still being used by tobacco manufacturers in that year; John Barker insured his at 157 Shadwell for £300, as well as a manufactory valued at £400, and stock and utensils at £650.[59]

Paper, Printing and Publishing

Printing and publishing was one of the most substantial of all London trades throughout the period 1775–1825. There can be little doubt of the truth of the contemporary observation that, 'In no other British town or city are there printing offices on so large a scale, or so many printing machines congregated in one spot, or so many workmen'.[60] Certainly, the statistics are impressive. There were 1162 London printers and publishers in 1826–27, over 8 per cent of all manufacturing firms; they accounted for 10 per cent of all capital insured by manufacturers. Fire office registers contain policies for firms engaged in 19 specialised printing, 5 specialised bookbinding and 4 specialised publishing trades. Apart from general printers, book-binders and publishers, there were, for example, separately identified copperplate, letterpress and lithographic printers, music printers and engravers, book folders and sewers, book edge gilders and vellum binders, and chart, law and music publishers.

Numerically, the largest trades identified separately by Pigot in 1826–27 were printers (of which there were 393), engravers (358), bookbinders (255) and publishers (48). *The Earliest Directory of the Book Trade* listed 124 London master printers in 1785 and various other contemporary sources list 200 to 300 in the period 1818–26.[61] Cowie's *Bookbinder's Manual* of 1828 listed 295 bookbinders.[62] In practice, of course, it is very difficult to distinguish between these trades since they substantially overlapped, not only one with another, but also with wholesale and retail booksellers and with the stationery trade. Writing in 1837, Nathaniel Whittock described a five-tier pyramid with wholesale booksellers and publishers, who buy copyrights from authors and publish at their own expense to sell to retail booksellers, at the top, followed by specialist publishers of, for example, religious or children's books, publishers of works in parts, publishers of period-icals and, lastly, retail booksellers.[63]

The major turning point for the publishing industry came in the 1770s with the ending of 'perpetual' copyrights. This threw into the public domain the profitable works on which the London trade had depended for nearly a century, leading to greater competition and lower prices.[64] Retail booksellers began to combine to act as pub-lishers. Forty got together to publish Johnson's *Lives of the Poets* in 1777 and 35 for publication of Charnock's *Marine Architecture* in 1800.[65] Strahan and Cadell had made a profit of over 60 per cent in 1777 on the third edition of the first volume of Gibbon's *Decline and Fall of the Roman Empire*, two-thirds of which went to the author. They were also the original publishers of *Wealth of Nations* the previous year.[66]

There were 685 booksellers in London in 1826–27, an enormous increase from just over 300 at the turn of the century. In fact, book sales had rocketed. As early as 1792, James Lackington claimed in his *Memoirs*: 'I suppose that more than four times the number of books are sold now than were sold twenty years ago'.[67] In fact, the number of books published annually rose from 600 in the 1770s to over 990 in the first half of the 1820s, an increase of 65 per cent. More spectacularly, the average number of pamphlets published annually

TABLE 4.9 Printing and publishing

Capital insured (£)	No. of firms 1770s	Percentage of total	No. of firms 1820s	Percentage of total
100 and under	70	34.7	60	22.3
101–500	86	42.6	84	31.2
501–1000	21	10.4	38	14.1
1001–2999	19	9.4	43	16.0
3000 and over	6	3.0	44	16.4
Total	202	100.0	269	100.0

Source: Sun and other London fire office registers

more than doubled between 1769–77 and 1819–25, from 2542 to 5087. Over the shorter period from 1769 to 1800, the number of periodicals published annually rose from 34 to 83.[68]

Printing is also distinguished as a trade in which there was a substantial place for the smaller firm. In the 1770s nearly 35 per cent insured capital valued at £100 or less and another 43 per cent insured between £100 and £500. Even 50 years later the proportions were still 22 per cent and 31 per cent. Firms insuring £500 or less accounted for nearly a quarter of all capital insured in the 1770s. It was much less, but still 7 per cent, in the 1820s. There was always room for the smaller-scale general printer or engraver. Contemporary trade cards suggest a trade very little different to the present day. Thus, Redford and Robins in 1830 described their printing business at 36 London Road, Southwark, as 'Pamphlets, Auctioneer's Work, Cards, &c ... Posting and Hand Bills ... Engraving and Bookbinding, Stamps, Account Books, and Stationery of every description'.[69] Typical of the many small engravers in London was G. Berry of 70 Long Acre. His trade card circulated in 1800 said: 'Arms found & printed ... Visiting Cards, Compliments Cards, Bills etc.'[70] Table 4.9 shows a full breakdown by value of capital insured.

In terms of capital insured, firms increased substantially in size between the 1770s and the 1820s, the average value trebling from £533 to £1541. Publishers cannot be identified separately until 1820, but thereafter the average value of capital insured by them was £2838. For printers, the average value increased from £908 to £2118. The lesser capitalised trades were bookbinding and engraving, for which the average value of capital insured rose from £219 to £790 and from £196 to £400 respectively. In the 1770s just under 3 per cent of all firms can be considered 'large' using the £3000 criterion. However, by the 1820s this had risen to over 16 per cent and well over 7 per cent insured £5000 or more. 'His Majesty's Printers', Eyre and Strahan, illustrate the trend. In 1773, located in New Street, Shoe Lane, they insured for £9000; by 1820, and moved to East Harding Street, they had doubled their insurance cover to £18,000.[71] The first William Strahan (1715–85) had been a London printer since 1737. He had been a close friend of Dr Johnson and was printer of the great *Dictionary* in 1755. By 1820 the Strahan involved in the firm was Andrew, third son of the original founder. By 1832, Andrew Strahan having died the previous year, the company had become Eyre and Spottiswoode. Andrew and Robert Spottiswoode were grandsons of the first William Strahan and it is interesting to note that before the merger, when they were located like Eyre and Strachan half a century earlier in New Street, they had insured capital valued at £8200 in 1820. The previous year they had separately insured two printing offices, specified as measuring 864 and 486 square feet respectively, for £300.[72] By the 1820s the use of steam power was widespread. In 1820 John Walter of *The Times* insured a printing office, counting house and steam engine house at the original Printing House Square in Blackfriars for £3250, a steam engine for £400 and printing machinery for £3500.[73] Another famous name, Hansard, insured his printing office at 6 Great Turnstile for £1000 in 1821, as well as stock, utensils and goods for £8000.[74]

The Bankruptcy Commission files contain examples of very substantial profits made by City printers. Over a period of seven years and nine months prior to his bankruptcy in 1829, Thomas White of Johnson's Court averaged annual profits of £2019. Two years earlier, Littlewood and Green in Old Bailey were also declared bankrupt, having shown average annual profits of £865 over the previous five years.[75]

The term 'publisher' was not used prior to about 1820. Two very substantial firms in the 1820s were Simkin and Marshall of 3–5 Stationers Court, Ludgate Hill, and John and Walter Thomas Clarke of 22 Portugal Street, Lincoln's Inn Fields. The former insured for £14,000 in 1823;[76] the latter, who were law publishers, insured for £11,000 in 1821.[77] However, Longman and Co, who throughout the period 1775–1825 described themselves as 'booksellers', insured for £71,000 in 1822. In 1775, they had insured for just £5000.[78] Also describing themselves as 'booksellers' were John Murray, who insured for £25,350 in 1820,[79] and George Whitaker and Co, who insured for £22,000 the following year.[80]

Capital insured by smaller firms is exemplified by a copperplate printer, William East of 31 Warwick Lane, who insured for £200 in 1771.[81] Engravers tended to be even smaller; Elizabeth and James Lake of 15 Tokenhouse Yard insured for £100 in 1822.[82]

London's huge printing and publishing trade made it the major national market for paper but, although production needed to be located near at hand, it was not a major London manufacturing trade in this period. However, it is worth noting that Pigot listed 86 London rag merchants in 1826–27. Rags were a major raw material for paper-making and in 1819 one rag merchant, Joseph Bonsor, appropriately carrying on his business from Salisbury Square off Fleet Street, insured a stock of rags valued at no less than £2000.[83] By this time papermaking was predominantly located in Kent and Hertfordshire where there was the necessary supply of clean water, though many of the great Home Counties papermakers were also major London stationers. On the other hand, there were a number of London makers of paper products. Pigot listed 129 in 1826–27. These included manufacturers of card, pasteboard and pasteboard goods, account books, paperhangings, paper toys and ornaments and papier mâché. The perfection reached by papier mâché is shown by the firm of Mechi of 4 Leadenhall Street who advertised manufacture of 'papier mâché articles consisting of tea trays, tea caddies, ladies' work, cake and note baskets, card cases, card pools, fruit plates, fruit baskets, netting boxes, hand screens, card racks, chess boards'.[84]

London was the centre of the wallpaper trade. Plastered walls replaced panelled walls in the 1760s and by 1834 production was over 1.2 million pieces. As early as the 1770s John Sigrist of Piccadilly was advertising that he manufactured 'the New Invented Paper Hangings from off Copper Plates' and that he 'Imitates India Landscapes, Figures, Flowers, Birds &c. Matches Silks, Chintzs, Cottons, Linnens &c'. Including retailers and paperhangers as well as manufacturers, there were 241 businesses involved in the trade in the first quarter of the nineteenth century. Although no fire insurance policy survives, Harwood and Co employed 600 people in about 1813.[85] Cooke,

Hinchcliffe and Matthews insured a complex of industrial buildings in Chelsea with the Sun and British fire offices for £4100 in 1825, as well as stock, utensils and goods for £4750.[86]

One substantial paper manufacturer with premises at the outermost edge of the metropolis in Kingsland Road and Bethnal Green was Bening Arnold and Son. They insured their manufactory for £2300, an engine house for £500, and a steam engine and other machinery for £1700 in 1822.[87] They also insured working capital valued at £2800. In 1774, Benjamin Johnson, a card maker in the Strand, insured two workshops for £1200, and stock and utensils for £2500.[88] Fifty years later in 1825, Heath, Vaughan and Coveney, pasteboard manufacturers in Queen Street, Cheapside, insured for £2500.[89] Manufacture of account books was another specialised trade. About 1820 Ann Biddulph of 9 Blackman Street, Borough, advertised that she made 'Account Books, School Books (and) Memorandum Books'.[90] The capital required was very modest; Joseph Evans of 2 Dean Street, Soho, insured for just £250 in 1824.[91] At the very lowest end of the paper products trade were businesses like those of Sarah Walker, a mask, paper toy and cap maker of 2 Castle Street, Long Row, who insured stock and utensils for just £30 in 1825.[92]

Textiles

Alongside the necessity to feed London's huge and growing population was the need to clothe it. Although they are not usually regarded as London-based industries, taken together the textile and clothing manufacturing trades accounted for 2363 of London's manufacturing firms in 1826–27, almost one in six. Indeed, they comprised nearly 5 per cent of all businesses and accounted for over one-fifth of all capital insured by London manufacturers in the 1820s. The textile trades alone involved 1224 firms, 8.4 per cent of all businesses engaged in manufacturing. These firms insured fixed and working capital valued at £2,341,000 in the 1820s, over 13 per cent of the total sum insured by all manufacturing trades. A measure of London's contribution to these trades may be gathered from the fact that during the eighteenth century as a whole, it has been calculated that London and the south-east were far and away the largest centres of both patented and non-patented textile inventions, accounting for 44.6 per cent of the former and 36.5 per cent of the latter. Lancashire and the north-west accounted for 14.9 per cent and 14.3 per cent respectively, and Yorkshire 12.2 per cent and 1.6 per cent.[93]

One of the major controversies surrounding the role of manufacturing in London in the period 1775–1825 is the extent to which it was dominated by 'finishing' trades. This is of particular significance in respect of the textile trades although in one sense the whole debate is rather sterile. The implication is that 'finishing' trades, like the service sector, are somehow less real, and certainly much less important, than those manufacturing trades involved with processes earlier along the production chain. In reality all stages of production are of equal economic importance. The important point with regard to the textile trades is that both initial production and finishing are to be found in London in this period. Much the most important of the former was silk. The industry had been of prime importance to London since the early seventeenth century, certainly since long before the arrival of the Huguenots in 1685. The London Weavers Company had 6000 members between 1681 and 1733–34. The trade continued to expand until the mid-1820s, though it was moving away from its traditional location in Spitalfields from the latter part of the previous century. Despite the complete ban on imports of foreign silk fabrics throughout the period 1775–1825, the industry suffered enormous variations in trade. In addition to the impact of trade cycles in general, silk was subject to both seasonal factors and the vagaries of fashion. It was also characterised by an over-supply of labour. The Spitalfields Act of 1773 had banned combinations and fixed prices and wages. However, this had comparatively little impact on levels of trade, contrary to the belief at the time.[94]

As late as 1826–27 Pigot listed 237 firms engaged in six silk trades, together with another 86 in the cotton, calico and crêpe manufacturing trades which are classified with silk for standard industrial classification purposes. This excludes the finishing trades which are dealt with below. The fire office registers identify even more specialised firms. Apart from silk manufacturers, usually termed simply 'silk weavers' in the 1770s, there were silk sorters, throwsters, turners, weavers and winders. There were also manufacturers of oil silk, crêpe, cotton, muslin, velvet, damask, gauze, moss, mop yard and lamp cotton.

Dorothy George gave pride of place to silk in her account of London industry in her classic study of *London Life in the Eighteenth Century*. Table 4.10 shows that she was right in her assessment that

TABLE 4.10 Silk and cotton

Capital insured (£)	No. of firms 1770s	Percentage of total	No. of firms 1820s	Percentage of total
100 and under	60	36.1	51	29.0
101–500	38	22.9	33	18.8
501–1000	27	16.3	11	6.3
1001–2999	23	13.9	31	17.6
3000 and over	18	10.8	50	28.4
Total	166	100.0	176	100.0

Source: Sun and other London fire office registers

'The small master and the large master existed side by side, though there was a progressive tendency to greater capitalization' and both were supplemented by 'the working weaver who owned or hired his own loom'.[95]

Undoubtedly, capitalisation increased substantially over the period 1775–1825. The average value of capital insured with the London fire offices more than doubled, from £1103 in the 1770s to £2449 in the 1820s. The median value of policies actually trebled, from £300 to £925. The many contemporary authors of trade guides noted this. Thus, in 1747 both Campbell's *The London Tradesman* and the anonymous *A General Description of All Trades* estimated a required start-up capital for a silk weaver of £50 to £500. By 1819 Mortimer's *General Commercial Dictionary* was estimating £250 to £2000. The proportion of firms insuring capital valued at £3000 or more rose from under 11 per cent in the 1770s to over 28 per cent in the 1820s. By the latter period 9 per cent were insuring for £5000 or more and nearly 3 per cent for over £10,000. On the other hand, there were also numerous smaller businesses. Silk was not an industry of large-scale manufacturing operations. In the 1770s, 59 per cent insured for £500 or less, of which over 36 per cent insured for £100 or less. Although these proportions had fallen by the 1820s, they were still 48 per cent and 29 per cent respectively. Nevertheless, the proportion of total capital accounted for by firms insuring for £500 or less was only 8 per cent in the 1770s and by the 1820s this had fallen to little more than 3 per cent.

Although a contemporary observed that 'with respect to silk ...

although a large quantity is manufactured at Spitalfields, yet it is here totally distinct from factory operations',[96] the industry was dominated by the larger firms. As early as 1777, Vansommer and Paul of Pall Mall insured for £21,000 with four different fire offices: for £6000 each with the Sun and Royal Exchange; for £5000 with the Union; and, for £4000 with the London.[97] Two Spitalfields weavers, James Walker of 7 Duke Street and Lewis Jouenne of 1 Chapel Street, from his name of Huguenot descent, insured £10,500 in 1777 and £9000 in 1773 respectively.[98] By 1820 much larger sums were being insured; Doxatt and Co valued stock, utensils and goods at their Bishopsgate Street premises at £50,000.[99] In a few cases, fixed capital was very considerable. In 1774 Wells and Rickards of 23 Ludgate Street insured their silk mill and its machinery for £3000.[100] More typical was Henry Robinson who insured his silk manufactory at 36 Gun Street, Spitalfields for £500 in 1822. The following year he insured stock, utensils and goods for £6000.[101] An interesting insight into the growth of one Spitalfields firm is provided by John and Francis Giles of 18–19 Church Street. They insured stock, utensils and machinery for £1550 in 1819, for £2550 in 1821, and for £4500 in 1822, before increasing the risk to £6500 in 1823.[102]

Throughout the period 1775–1825 most firms were located to the east of the City, 64 per cent in the 1770s and 59 per cent in the 1820s. The most significant change was the growth of Bethnal Green and, to a lesser extent, Mile End as centres of the trade by the 1820s, though Spitalfields still predominated.

There were also very large numbers of London firms involved in a wide variety of individually smaller textile manufacturing trades which none the less amounted to a substantial part of the textiles sector when taken together. Altogether, Pigot listed 661 firms in 1826–27 and the fire office registers for the 1820s show that they accounted for an insured capital valued at over £1.1 million. A very large number of separate trades were involved. Pigot listed 32 and the fire office registers contain policies entered under 45 self-described trade specialisms. These included manufacture of sailcloth, hemp floor coverings, carpets and rugs, hair and hair cloth, ribbon, braid, lace and trimmings, net, and rope, line and twine. There were also flax and hemp working, a few framework knitters and stocking dressers and a handful of firms in the wool and worsted trades. In the latter trade, Perrott and Beale had established themselves as clothworkers as early as 1710 and were still in business in the second half of the twentieth century. They were able to take advantage of the fashion for fine wool cloth started by Beau Brummell.[103]

Most firms were small. Within these trades as a whole, 61 per cent insured capital valued at £500 or less in the 1770s and 45 per cent in the 1820s. The two major trades were ribbon, lace and trimmings, and rope and twine, of which Pigot listed 270 and 105 respectively in 1826–27. Both trades were characterised by small businesses. Typical was Matthew Winter, a lace and fringe maker in Long Acre. An invoice of 1777 stated that he 'Makes & Sells all Sorts of Livery and Army Lace & Fringe for Beds, Coaches & Saddles, Shoulder Knots in Gold, Silk, Silver, Mohair or Worsted, Sashes for Officers, Tassels and Lines for hanging large Lanterns or Chandeliers &c'. Winter was connected with the very important coachbuilding industry centred in Long Acre. So also were Block and Hopwood, lace and fringe manufacturers at number 65. Their 1785 trade card mentions 'Coach Laces' as a product line.[104] In the 1770s the average value of capital insured was £871. However, by the 1820s this had more than doubled to £1823. A few firms were of a substantial size. In 1775 William Poole, a ribbon weaver of 53 Cheapside, insured stock and utensils for £5600.[105] A rare female-owned firm was that of Ann Spiers, a trimming manufacturer who insured her manufactory at 122 Church Street, Bethnal Green, for just £10 in 1819, but stock, utensils, fittings and machinery for £800.[106]

Rope, line and twine manufacturers tended to be of an even smaller size. The average value of capital insured by them rose only from £819 in the 1770s to £1043 in the 1820s. Often they were linked closely to shipbuilding and a few were quite large, such as William Sims and Son who in 1822 insured stock, utensils and machinery for £2500, as well as a wide range of industrial plant in Sun Tavern Fields for £1900. The latter is worth quoting in detail. It included:

	(£)
Hemp warehouses	200
Rope warehouse	75
Two counting houses	38
Tar capstan and yarn house	125
Tallow and oil houses and tar shed	20
Store houses	75
Carpenter's shop, coach houses etc.	100
Ropewalk and sheds	600

Steam engine, boiler, spinning and tar houses	375
Workshop	37
Rigging house	50
Leanto shed	62
Cart shed	13
Machine spinning house	50
Cold register houses	20
Engine and other sheds	60[107]

By no means all ropemakers were involved in shipbuilding. Located well to the north of the river, the range of products offered in 1776 by R. Tidswell of Windmill Hill was 'all sorts of Ropes, as Packers Ropes, Crane Ropes, Barr Ropes, Cart Ropes, Waggon Lines, Bricklayers and Swayers Lines, Corded Traces and Halters, Jack and Sash Lines, Cloaths, Chalk and Fishing Lines, both for Sea and Rivers, with other Lines, Packthread and Twine'.[108]

What *was* closely linked to shipbuilding was the weaving of sailcloth. Again, a few businesses were very large. In 1819 Turner and Co insured their warehouse and counting house in Narrow Street, Limehouse, for £1500, their spinning sheds for £250, a tar house for £75 and a number of other buildings for £200, as well as stock, utensils and goods valued at £5525.[109] There were other substantial trades, too, for example a number of floorcloth manufacturers in the Knightsbridge area, such as Nathan Smith who insured his floorcloth manufactory there for £900 and a workshop and counting house for £100 each in 1775, as well as a warehouse for £900 two years later. In 1775 he had also insured stock and utensils for £700.[110] By the 1820s capitalisation had grown considerably so that in 1822 Harvey and Knight insured their manufactory in George Street, Lambeth, for £5000. Their showroom was at 57 Broad Street, Bloomsbury, where they held stock, utensils and goods valued at £5000 in 1821.[111] Carpet manufacture was not a major London trade although there were a few firms, such as Robert Morrell who insured a workshop at 43 Chiswell Street for £300 in 1770 and utensils and goods valued at £1500 in 1775.[112] An interesting firm was Welch, Collins and Wells. They were horsehair manufacturers who insured their business for £2500 in 1777, when it was located at 1 Round Court, St Martins le Grand, but for £9500 in the 1820s, by which time they had moved to Chancery Lane.[113]

Overall, the textile finishing trades were of lesser importance than manufacturing. Pigot listed 240 firms in 1826–27, which was only 19 per cent of all firms involved in London's various textile trades, and the fire office registers show that they accounted for just over 18 per cent of all capital insured. There were four major groupings of textile finishing trades, dyeing and bleaching, callendering and hot pressing, textile dressing and other finishing trades, including printing. Many individual firms were involved in a number of the 25 trades to be found in the fire office registers. These included bleachers, dyers and scourers, callenderers and hot pressers, silk, satin, flax, hemp and gauze dressers, packers and calico and woollen printers.

Very often these were trades which had had a greater significance for London in the early part of the eighteenth century but which had begun to move out by the period 1775–1825. It has been amply demonstrated, for example, that calico printing played a fundamental role in the growth of industrialisation and commerce in both Britain and Europe in the eighteenth century. London had been the original centre of the English trade in the late seventeenth century, but by the middle of the eighteenth century it was moving to Lancashire. As with a number of trades, it was London's river which had ceased to be suitable. It was too congested for the industry's requirements for water power so that what textile printing remained in the area of the metropolis moved along the Lea from Bow to Waltham Abbey, along the Wandle from Wandsworth to Croydon and along the Cray to Crayford and Dartford.[114] Even so, a significant number of textile finishing firms were left in London itself. Most were small and, although capitalisation did rise over the period 1775–1825, the number did not increase by very much. In the 1770s the average value of capital insured with the London fire offices was £1264. Fifty years later it had risen by only 39 per cent to £1763. Median values rose only from £500 to £575. The proportion of 'large' firms insuring for £3000 or more increased from just under 10 per cent in the 1770s to only 19 per cent by the 1820s. This compares with 11 per cent and 28 per cent respectively for silk manufacture. Conversely, well over half of all firms insured for £500 or less in the 1770s, and it was still nearly half in the 1820s. These businesses accounted for just over 8 per cent of all capital insured in the textile finishing trades in the 1770s. By the 1820s this had fallen to under 5 per cent. Table 4.11 shows the full breakdown by value of capital insured.

Despite the predominance of smaller firms, a few companies were very large indeed. In 1777 Robert Allan, a calico printer, insured for £18,900[115] and Crutchley, Farmer and Goodwin, dyers, for £13,400.[116]

TABLE 4.11 Textile finishing

Capital insured (£)	No. of firms 1770s	Percentage of total	No. of firms 1820s	Percentage of total
100 and under	39	22.8	20	16.7
101–500	51	29.8	37	30.8
501–1000	29	17.0	17	14.2
1001–2999	35	20.5	23	19.2
3000 and over	17	9.9	23	19.2
Total	171	100.0	120	100.0

Source: Sun and other London fire office registers

The latter insured their dye house in Clark Street, Southwark, for £1400, warehouses for £600, a mill house for £150, horses for £100, and stock, utensils and goods valued at £11,150. The former is an excellent example of the move outwards in search of an unpolluted water supply. Although the firm was based in the Old South Sea House in Broad Street, it insured a wide range of industrial buildings on the River Lea at Stratford for £2800, and stock, utensils and goods for £16,100. The buildings insured included a counting house and warehouse (valued at £800), a madder house, mill house and callender shop (£300), a blue shop (£100), a white shop and lead backs (£150), a printing house, stove house and warehouses (£500), a printing house and two brick sheds (£500) and a copper house (£350). By the 1820s steam power was in use on a considerable scale. One of the largest female-owned businesses in London was Elizabeth Whitehead and Son, dyers of Bankside. In 1822 she insured a steam engine and other machinery for £1300, her dye house, warehouse, steam engine house, and coal hole for £2000, a mill house for £100 and other industrial buildings for £1650, and stock, utensils and goods for £1950.[117] On an even larger scale were Wilkinson, Fisher and Co. They were callenderers and hot pressers who in 1819 insured their steam engine house at Hill Street, Windmill Street, for £2900, and stock, utensils and goods valued at £10,900.[118]

Smaller, and more typical firms, are exemplified by John Baynes, a dyer at 118 Blackman Street who insured his dye house for £250 in 1821, and stock, utensils and goods for £250,[119] and Charles Powell, a presser and packer, who insured his workshop at 12 Wilson Street for

£200, and stock and utensils for £100 four years later.[120] Fifty years earlier there was the similar example of Benjamin Tickner, a callenderer who insured two workshops in Archer Street for £200, a shed for £10, and stock, utensils and goods for £160 in 1771.[121] The ups and downs of the trade are illustrated by the case of George Yeathead, a dyer in Deal Street, Coverley's Fields. In 1819 he insured capital valued at £4000. This rose to £5000 in 1820 and to £7300 in 1821. Over the next two years it fell to £2300 and £2000, and to only £800 in 1824. No policy is recorded in the registers for 1825.[122]

Geographically, the textile finishing trades were located mainly in the City and East End, 74 per cent in the 1770s and 70 per cent in the 1820s. Most of the rest were to be found south of the river. Overall, the conclusion must be that finishing did not dominate London's textile trades and that in all of them smaller firms played a significant role, though not a large one.

Thirteen bankruptcy files for the textile trades as a whole give an average annual profit of £559. The same sample of firms had an average start-up capital of £3455, suggesting profit as a percentage of capital of 18.9 per cent. However, there were very large variations. Le Mare and Bestage in Wood Street, bankrupted in 1828, showed an average annual profit of £1277 over a two-and-a-half-year period; at the other end of the scale, James Brownell of Steward Street, Spitalfields, had a profit of only £163 in the year prior to his bankruptcy in 1826. Frederick Martin of Cheapside, described as a silk ribbon manufacturer, showed average profits of £675 over a two-and-a-half-year period prior to his bankruptcy in 1831. Of the same order of magnitude were the profits of Sodo and Collingwood, dyers in Cleveland Street, Mile End Road. They were bankrupted in 1825, having shown average profits of £674 over the previous three years and four months.[123]

Furniture

When he wrote *A Tour through the whole Island of Great Britain* in the mid-1720s, Daniel Defoe took it for granted that his example of a 'middling tradesman', a grocer from Horsham, would possess cane chairs, tables, chests of drawers, looking-glasses and other furniture which was made in London.[124] Certainly, a fast-growing population in London itself, used to rising standards of living, ensured that there was a huge market for furniture quite apart from any demand from the provinces for what was most highly fashionable. As in the first quarter of the eighteenth century, furniture making was one of London's primary manufacturing trades throughout the last quarter, and the first quarter of the next century. Pigot listed 1718 businesses engaged in 23 specialised trades within the furniture making sector in 1826–27, almost 10 per cent of all London's manufacturing firms and nearly 4 per cent of all businesses in the metropolis. Sir Ambrose Heal's classic work *London Furniture Makers 1660–1840* lists 416 firms in the period 1765–80 and there are fire policies recorded for 510 in the period 1769–77. This suggests that there may have been as many as 750 in total in the 1770s. On that basis the number would seem to have more than doubled over the period 1775–1825.

Furniture making is a classic example of a trade where it is difficult to distinguish between manufacturing, bespoke production and retailing. This section deals with those firms which made furniture as distinct from the dealers in new and second-hand furniture, most often known as 'brokers of household goods' in the 1820s or simply 'brokers' in the 1770s, dealt with in the retail sector below. There were, in fact, some 478 such dealers listed by Pigot in 1826–27. Another problem in the terminology of the period is the 'upholder'. To Campbell in 1747, the upholder was the key to the whole furniture trade:

> I have just finished my House, and now must think of furnishing it with Fashionable Furniture. The Upholder is chief Agent in this Case. He is the Man upon whose Judgement I rely in the Choice of goods … he has not only Judgement in the Materials, but Taste in the Fashions, and Skill in the Workmanship. This Tradesman's Genius must be universal in every Branch of Furniture … The Cabinet Maker is his right-hand Man.[125]

However, by 1824 the term had become synonymous with 'upholsterer' and was regarded as simply another branch of the manufacturing trade so that 'The business of the cabinet maker, and that of an upholsterer, are now so generally linked together, that any observation on either [may] be comprehended under one general head'.[126]

Among the 32 separate specialised trades to be found in the fire office registers are bed, bedstead and mattress makers, with a sub-division of child bed makers, bedpost carvers, general carvers and gilders, chair makers, carvers, stuffers, painters and japanners, clock-case and barometer case makers, couch and sofa makers, desk and desk base makers, with specialist makers of portable desks, frame makers, inlayers, screen makers and, of course, general cabinet makers and upholsterers. In 1826–27 Pigot listed 667 general cabinet makers, 264 carvers and gilders, 221 upholsterers, 142 bed and mattress makers and 136 chair and sofa makers. Eleven firms had been described as 'master carvers' in 1813 when it was noted that 'gilding on wood both in oil and burnish is at present at its highest perfection and is executed in London better than in any part of the world'.[127]

Hundreds of trade cards and shopbills issued by furniture makers survive in the Guildhall and British Library collections, many of them superbly illustrated with contemporary pieces. A trade card circulated by Turnley and Sons of Garden Row, London Road, Southwark, in 1800 exemplifies the range of products made by the manufacturer supplying the retail trade. They described themselves as a 'Wholesale Manufactory for Every Description of Sofas, Settees, Fancy Drawing Room, Solid Rosewood, Mahogany, and other Chairs, Bedsteads, Bed Pillars, Mattresses, Writing Desks, Tea Caddies, Looking Glasses, &c, &c'. A typical range of products from thirty years earlier was that of Thomas Chapman of Old Bedlam. He was in business from about 1760 to 1769 and his oddly spelled trade card states that he 'Maketh and Selleth all sorts of Mahogany Tea & Dining Tables, Chamber-Tables, Tea Boards, Waiters, and Tea Chests, likewise all sorts of Bed Carving and Joyner's Work, as Bed Cornishes, Teasters and Head Boards, Settees, Beauroes, and Field Beds'.[128]

The large majority of businesses were very small. Dodd noted in 1843: 'The tables, chairs, the bedsteads, the beds, the mattresses, the glass-frames, the picture-frames, the window cornices, – all are made to a vast extent in London, but not generally in large factories. They are the production of tradesmen, each of whom can carry on a tolerably extensive business without great extent of room, or a large number of workmen'.[129] The average value of capital insured was £479 in the 1770s. This had increased by only 48 per cent to £708 by the 1820s. Median values were even less, £200 and £300 respectively. In the 1770s well over three-quarters of all businesses insured for £500 or less, and this fell only marginally to two-thirds by the 1820s. In the earlier period such small firms accounted for over 20 per cent of all capital insured; by the 1820s this had fallen to only just over 5 per cent.

TABLE 4.12 Furniture

Capital insured (£)	No. of firms 1770s	Percentage of total	No. of firms 1820s	Percentage of total
100 and under	164	32.2	135	26.4
101–500	232	45.5	202	39.5
501–1000	71	13.9	77	15.1
1001–2999	31	6.1	75	14.7
3000 and over	12	2.4	22	4.3
Total	510	100.0	511	100.0

Source: Sun and other London fire office registers

Large firms, insuring £3000 or more, accounted for only 2 per cent of all firms in the 1770s, and for little more than 4 per cent 50 years later. Table 4.12 shows the full breakdown by value of capital insured.

Nevertheless, throughout the period 1775–1825 there were a few very large firms. In 1774 Richard and William Gomm, a name to remain famous in the trade for another two centuries, insured their workshop and warehouse in Clerkenwell Close for £1000, as well as stock valued at £6000.[130] John Mayhew and William Ince of Marshall Street had insured for the even larger sum of £10,000 two years earlier.[131] By 1824, Whiteside and Redmaine of 176 Oxford Street were insuring for £14,900.[132] Thomas Dowbigging insured his workshop alone for £3000 in 1821, in addition to stock, utensils and goods valued at £8400.[133] In the case of Seddon's of Aldersgate Street, very little change in size occurred between 1771 and 1822; they insured for £5250 on the first occasion and for £5000 on the second.[134] That this was a labour-intensive trade is shown by the fact that they employed 400 people in 1786 making an enormous range of furniture across a wide market range. In that year they were visited by the ubiquitous Sophie von la Roche who observed that they employed,

> on any work connected with the making of household furniture, joiners, carvers, gilders, mirror-workers, upholsterers, girdlers – who mould the bronze into graceful patterns – and locksmiths. All these are housed in a building with six wings. In the basement mirrors are cast and cut. Some other departments contain nothing but chairs, sofas and stools of every description, some quite simple, others exquisitely carved and made of all varieties of wood, and one large room is full up with all the finished

articles in this line, while others are occupied by writing tables, cupboards, chests of drawers, charmingly fashioned desks, chests, both large and small, work and toilet tables in all manner of wood and patterns, from the simplest and cheapest to the most elegant and expensive.[135]

Four generations of Seddons maintained the business from 1750 to 1868. All of these firms described themselves as cabinet makers. An interesting picture emerges of another substantial firm from the bankruptcy file. Sharpe and Clarke of Berners Street were described as upholsterers and cabinet makers who started their business in 1816 with an initial capital of £1500. Their balance sheet showed substantial but fluctuating profits over the ten years 1816–25, varying from £788 in 1818 to £1406 in 1823. However, profits plummeted to £120 in 1826 and they were declared bankrupt in 1828 with their stock valued at £1932.[136]

There were no large firms in the more specialist trades. Thus, for example, Abraham Dunton, a chair maker of Compton Street, insured his workshop for £180, and stock and utensils for £240 in 1771,[137] and Martha Gee, a feather bed and mattress maker, insured her workshop in Newington Causeway for £50, and stock, utensils and goods for £250 in 1822.[138] The vast majority of cabinet making firms were also small, such as Joseph Sugden who insured his workshop for £200 at 7 Harcourt Street, Lisson Green, in 1823, as well as stock and utensils for £100.[139]

Throughout the period 1775–1825, a little over a quarter of all firms were located in the City, and about the same proportion in the West End. The historian of Heal's describes Tottenham Court Road as still the centre of the trade when the first Heal moved there in 1818. However, the proportion of London firms located in the area fell from 27 per cent in the 1770s to under 16 per cent by the 1820s. These areas were characterised by higher quality and more expensive products. Although the great expansion of the cheaper end of the market, largely catered for by firms in the East End, did not happen until the 1830s, the proportion of businesses located there had already risen from only 8 per cent in the 1770s to 13 per cent in the 1820s.[140]

Leather and Leather Goods

Leather and leather-working was yet another very large scale London trade. It divided into three distinct sectors – leather prepara-

TABLE 4.13 Leather tanning and dressing

Capital insured (£)	No. of firms 1770s	Percentage of total	No. of firms 1820s	Percentage of total
100 and under	20	17.9	10	6.1
101–500	48	42.9	47	28.7
501–1000	23	20.5	25	15.2
1001–2999	16	14.3	50	30.5
3000 and over	5	4.5	32	19.5
Total	112	100.0	164	100.0

Source: Sun and other London fire office registers

tion and dressing, saddle and harness making and the manufacture of luggage and other goods – which between them accounted for nearly a thousand firms in 1826–27, 7 per cent of all manufacturing businesses. They insured capital valued at almost £1.4 million, 8 per cent of the total in the 1820s. Table 4.13 shows the full breakdown by value of capital insured. Pigot listed 443 firms engaged in leather tanning and dressing, covering such trades as tanners, curriers, fellmongers, grinders, leather cutters, dyers, dressers, japanners and stainers, patent leather manufacturers and vellum makers.

Very unusually, the largest risk insured in the 1770s was by a woman. Ann Varnham, a fellmonger in Five Foot Lane, Southwark, insured several warehouses, a storeroom and a number of lofts and other industrial buildings for the very precise sum of £1838 in 1769, as well as stock and utensils valued at £5550.[141] Another large Southwark business in the 1770s was a firm of fellmongers and leather dressers, the proprietors of which are shown in the Sun Fire Office register as a husband and wife, John and Mary Simpson. They insured a leather mill in White's Grounds, Barnaby Street, for £1000, a shed for £200, and stock and utensils for £4820 in 1771.[142] The huge increase in capitalisation between the 1770s and 1820s is exemplified by a tanner and Spanish leather dresser, George Choumert. In 1777, when the business was located at 84 Bermondsey Street, he insured sheds and warehouses for £400, and stock and utensils for £900; by 1821, the firm had moved to Russell Street, also in Bermondsey, where he insured his counting house, a warehouse, tan, press, salt and mill houses, a bark barn, several shaving shops and various other sheds, lofts and buildings for £5800, and stock and utensils valued at £20,100.[143] By that time it was by no means unusual to find firms insuring for risks in excess of £20,000. Francis and Ellis Brewin were tanners in Willow Walk, Bermondsey, and in 1819 they insured their steam engine for £1000, the steam engine house for £500, other machinery for £1000, drying sheds and a communicating bark barn for £4400, a counting house and another bark barn for £800, drying lofts for £300 and several sheds for £300. They also insured stock and utensils valued at £14,500.[144] The 1827 bankruptcy file of James Fry, a currier in Artillery Street, Bermondsey, showed average profits of £1716 over the previous four years.[145]

Typical of the numerous much smaller firms in the trade were James Engleheart and William Crook. The former was a currier who insured his workshop at 4 Bond Street for £30, and stock, utensils and goods for £70 in 1775;[146] the latter a leather dresser in Crown Mead, Bermondsey New Road, who insured his workshop for £230, and stock and utensils for £150 in 1822.[147]

It was remarked in 1824 that the tanner 'Requires considerable capital, and room and water'.[148] With regard to the last of these, a slightly later observer commented that 'Bermondsey has been for many years the principal seat of the leather manufacture in England [because] a series of tide-streams ... twice in every 24 hours supply a large quantity of water from the Thames for the use of the tanners and leather dressers'.[149] In fact, the fire office registers show that only 36 per cent were actually located there throughout the period 1775–1825. However, most of the rest were located near the north bank of the Thames, either in the City or the East End. One firm of Bermondsey tanners was Crookendon and Spilsbury who achieved profits of £1000 over the two years prior to their bankruptcy in 1828.[150]

Neither of the other two main branches of the leather trade was either as numerically significant or as highly capitalised as tanning and leather dressing. In the 1826–27 edition, Pigot listed 304 makers of saddles and harnessing. A significant minor trade within this sector was whipmaking for which Pigot listed 34 firms. Campbell provided an overview of the diversity of trades related to the saddler which, although written in 1747, changed very little over the next 80 years:

The Sadler ... furnishes us with Saddles of all Sorts, Housings, Caps,

Bridles, Caparisons, Girths, Surfingles, Brushes, Spunges, and Curry-Combs with every Thing else related to Horse Furniture ... He finishes his Work by the Help of Several distinct Tradesmen: such as the Tree-Maker, who makes the wooden Part of the Saddle; the Rivetter, who makes the Iron Work of the Tree; the Founder, who casts Buckles, Bars, Studs, Brasses, etc for his Bridles ... the Bridle-Cutter, who cuts out Leather in Patterns for Saddles, Bridles etc; the Embroiderer, who works Devices, Crests, and Coats of Arms, etc in Gold, Silver, or Worsteds upon his Housings.[151]

Small firms predominated. In the 1770s, over 90 per cent insured fixed and/or working capital valued at £500 or less. Fifty years later it was still well over three-quarters. No firm insured for £3000 or more in the 1770s and only two in the 1820s. On the other hand, over two-thirds of all capital insured in the earlier period was for firms taking out policies for £500 or less and it was still over 37 per cent in the 1820s. The most highly capitalised firms were whipmakers such as Charles Griffiths who insured a workshop and warehouse at 322 High Holborn for £2200 in 1822, as well as stock, utensils and goods for £2500.[152] Two years earlier, John Townes, a fashionable saddler with branches at 68 Barbican and 141 Cheapside, insured stock, utensils, goods and fittings for £4200.[153] Also in 1820, William Cairns, a collar and harness maker, insured several workshops at 43 Whitechapel Road for £450, and the stock, utensils and fittings in them for £600.[154]

Pigot listed 236 manufacturers of luggage and other leather goods in 1826–27 and the fire office registers record policies for no less than 20 separate and specialised trades, including trunk makers, letter and dressing-case makers, bellows makers, army accoutrement makers, pocket book manufacturers, razor strap and case makers, shagreen case makers and telescope and instrument case makers. The largest category was trunk makers, of which Pigot listed 91. A good example of the range of products made by the trunk maker is provided by the trade card of Samuel Forsaith of Long Acre. Circulated in the last quarter of the eighteenth century, it states that he

Makes and Sells all sorts of campaign, and strong iron bound trunks for travelling in foreign Roads, Sumpters and Portmanteau Trunks, Budgets and Trunks for Post Chaises, Cover'd Hampers, Canvas and Leather Valeses for Bedding, Leather Portmanteaus, Saddle Bags, Fire Buckets, Jacks, Powder Flasks, Harvest Bottles, Peruke Boxes, travelling Writing

Desks, Cases for Plate, China, Glasses and Musical Instruments ... Gentlemen, Merchants and Shopkeepers in Town and Country may be well supplied with all Sorts of Packing Trunks, and Hair & Gilt Nests of Trunks for Exportation, &c.[155]

Both Forsaith's place of business in Long Acre and his product line suggest a close connection with the coachbuilding industry.

Again, most firms were very small, although a few were more substantial in size. Nearly 90 per cent insured capital valued at £500 or less in the 1770s and the proportion was still almost three-quarters fifty years later. These small firms accounted for well over half of all the capital insured in the 1770s and 17 per cent in the 1820s. Nevertheless, there were few large trunk makers: Mary Townsend of Leadenhall Street insured for £1850 in 1769.[156] An 1819 Hand in Hand policy illustrates the size of a typical trunk maker's premises: Stephen Ponder insured three separate buildings at 28 Great Eastcheap – a 112-square-foot counting house for £60, a 169-square-foot shed for £40 and his actual shop, measuring 1180 square feet, for £500.[157] Bellows makers were invariably quite small. Typical was Sarah Frazier. She insured her workshop at 14 Little Alie Street for £100 in 1820, as well as stock and utensils for £400.[158] Capitalisation was rather larger in one or two other leather goods manufacturing trades. Jackson and Learmouth, who were army accoutrement makers, insured their counting house and workshop at 4 Great Poultney Street for £650 in 1822, as well as stock and utensils valued at £6500.[159]

Clothing

It is notoriously difficult to distinguish between bespoke production of clothing and manufacture for the retail market. However, it has become much clearer in recent years that the preoccupation with material betterment that characterised the eighteenth century included an increasing demand for clothing that was both cheap and fashionable. This led to both manufacture of ready-made clothing on an extensive scale, and to a network of retail dealers for its distribution. Campbell referred to the trade as early as 1747[160] and in 1771 a typical advertisement in the *Public Advertiser*, placed by Bromley's Linen and Shirt Warehouse in Charing Cross, stated: 'Any Gentleman having an immediate Call for ready made Shirts may be supplied with any Quantity, from 5s 6d to 21s finished in the neatest manner.'[161] At about the same date, the trade card sent out by Mary Dennis from her establishment in Houndsditch stated that she sold 'all Sorts of ready-made Linnen, Shirts and Shifts of all Sizes ... Women's Gowns, Women's and Children's Stays ... Coats, Frocks and Petticoats. Wholesale and Retail'.[162] London was the centre of this trade. Another substantial London trade was glove making. It was noted in 1834 that 50,000 dozen gloves were being manufactured in the metropolis, exclusively from imported French kid leather and employing 1500 to 1700 people.[163] In fact, manufacture of clothing in London, including household and other made-up textiles, involved 1139 firms in 1826–27. They insured capital valued at £1,327,000. In both cases this was almost 8 per cent of the total for all London manufacturing trades.

The one area of clothing manufacture in London which was profoundly different to all the others was hatmaking. From the early eighteenth century, hatmaking, unlike other pre-industrial clothing trades such as shoemaking or tailoring, had been characterised by a clear separation between manufacturing and retailing. This was because there was no need for measuring and fitting; hats could be easily ready-made for retail sale on different-sized blocks.[164] Fire insurance policies frequently contain the term 'manufacturer' and often describe a production process or list specific manufacturing facilities. London early dominated the trade in felt hats and, although it has been said that it was in decline from about 1750, by 1805 it was being claimed that Southwark hatmakers alone had produced five million hats over the previous seven years using the new method of detaching the silky wool from the coarse hairs of seal skins developed by Thomas Chapman in 1795.[165] However, evidence from the fire office registers suggests that the London hatmaking trade in general grew very substantially in the period 1775–1825. The number of fire insurance policies trebled between the 1770s and the 1820s, from 36 to 109. Conversely, the number of milliners and retail hatters insuring in the 1770s was over twice the number of those insuring in the 1820s: 493 compared with 190. The earlier fire office registers do not record the specialised manufacturing trades found fifty years later, such as waterproof or straw hat making, or the finishing trades such as dyers and binders. The *Book of English Trades* for 1824 remarked: 'Hats of the finest Quality, are made in large quantities in London ... The master Hat-maker employs frequently a large capital and numerous hands.'[166]

Twenty years later, Dodd distinguished hatmaking from virtually every other form of clothing: 'The whole article is made from the raw material, and to a greater extent in London than anywhere else, by a connected series of processes in one establishment.'[167] He had Christy's in mind, but they were far from unique in early nineteenth-century London.

Pigot listed 662 hat manufacturers in 1826–27, 58 per cent of all clothing manufacturing firms. The largest specialised trade was straw and chip hat manufacturing which involved 375 firms. Another 212 were listed as general hat manufacturers. The other major specialism was manufacture of waterproof hats, in which trade 25 firms were engaged. The fire office registers also record such specialist trades as manufacture of hat linings, crêpe hatbands, bonnets, army caps, cauls, beaver hats, japanned leather hats and hat tips and bindings.

The average value of capital insured almost doubled between the 1770s and the 1820s, from £759 to £1368. However, in both periods the trade was very much a mixture of large and small firms. Over 58 per cent insured capital valued at £500 or less in the 1770s and this actually rose to over 64 per cent by the 1820s. However, whereas the fire office registers record only one firm insuring for over £3000 in the 1770s, by the 1820s nearly 15 per cent did so. In the 1770s firms insuring for £500 or less accounted for nearly 15 per cent of all capital insured. With the increase in large-scale manufacturing, the proportion fell to under 8 per cent by the 1820s. By the mid-1820s, hatmaking involved insurance of capital valued at over £900,000, 5 per cent of all capital insured in manufacturing. Table 4.14 shows the full breakdown by value of capital insured.

Two of the major hat manufacturers of the nineteenth century were Christy's and Lock's.[168] Neither was of any great size in the eighteenth century. Lock's, for example, insured for only £610 in 1775.[169] By 1820, Christy and Co of 35 Gracechurch Street were insuring their damping and finishing shop in Bermondsey Street for £100, a dye house for £150, a stiffening shop for £50, one workshop for £50, another interconnecting with one of their warehouses for £750, a finishing shop for £300, various other warehouses, sheds and storehouses for £1070, and stock and utensils valued at £18,765, a total of £21,235.[170] Twenty years later it was noted that they were employing 1500 people.[171] In 1822 the firm which was to give its name to the 'bowler', John Bowler and Co, insured their manufactory,

TABLE 4.14 Hatmaking

Capital insured (£)	No. of firms 1770s	Percentage of total	No. of firms 1820s	Percentage of total
100 and under	8	22.2	36	33.0
101–500	13	36.1	34	31.2
501–1000	9	25.0	10	9.2
1001–2999	5	13.9	13	11.9
3000 and over	1	2.8	16	14.7
Total	36	100.0	109	100.0

Source: Sun and other London fire office registers

warehouses and other industrial buildings at 52 Castle Street, Southwark, for £2220, as well as stock and utensils valued at £7850.[172] Just how substantial hat manufacturing could be in the 1820s is illustrated by the firm of John Townend in the Minories. In the five and a quarter years prior to his bankruptcy in 1829 he had achieved average *annual* profits of no less than £9332, the highest figure shown in any Bankruptcy Commission file.[173]

By the 1820s there were also a number of substantial firms engaged in more specialised hat manufacturing trades; a japan leather hat manufacturer, Henry Fricker at 182 Fleet Street, insured his manufactory for £400 in 1824 in addition to stock, utensils and goods valued at £550;[174] and a firm of beaver cutters, Mary Phillips and Son, insured their warehouse at 5 Middlesex Street for £100 in 1819, and stock, utensils and fittings for £3100 four years later.[175] A typical smaller hatmaking firm was James Shallis, a chip hat manufacturer. In 1820 he insured two workshops at 27 Exmouth Street for £150, as well as stock and utensils for £200.[176] Most of the largest hat manufacturers were located in Southwark, where about a quarter of all firms were to be found. Smaller firms were to be found all over London, with the largest numbers in the City and East End.

Pigot listed 305 firms involved in the manufacture of other clothing and footwear, with breeches and shawl makers the most numerous. Most were very small. In the 1770s the average value of capital insured was £143; 50 years later it was still only £663. The proportion of businesses insuring for £500 or less was over 98 per cent and they represented 65 per cent of all capital insured in these trades. By the

1820s these proportions were still two-thirds and 21 per cent respectively.

The armed forces were an important market. The eighteenth century saw the emergence of distinct uniforms and by 1763 there were 18 major London contractors to 115 regiments, all benefiting from their continuity of demand compared with the uncertainties of the fashion trades.[177] One very large army clothier, Thomas Harley at 152 Aldersgate Street, insured for £8000 in 1777.[178] Buckram stiffening was another highly capitalised trade. In 1775 Robert Ledger insured a dye house, callender house, warehouse and counting house at 3 Maze Pond for £300, in addition to stock and utensils for £1800.[179] In the 1820s, two of his descendants were in the same trade on a larger scale still. Edward Ledger and Son insured a steam mill and steam engine house at Back Street, Horsleydown, for £800, a warehouse for £200, and stock, utensils and machinery for £1400,[180] and George Ledger insured a steam engine and other machinery for £500 at Maze Pond, a warehouse, counting house, dye house and workshop for £1600, and stock, utensils, goods and livestock for £1600 also.[181] There were also a number of substantial boot and shoe manufacturers in the 1820s, such as Thomas Cotton and Co of 1 London Road who insured for £1500 in 1824.[182]

Worthy of note as a major London trade in the 1770s was peruke making. In that period of fashionable demand for wigs, the fire office registers record 253 peruke makers. Very little capital was required; the average risk insured was £78. A rare example of a more substantial sum was the £530 insured by John Ollivier of Belton Street, Piccadilly, in 1769.[183] Other small-scale trades were brace and stock, fan, breeches, shawl, artificial flower and umbrella and parasol manufacture. Pigot listed 132 umbrella and parasol makers in 1826–27.

Two other much smaller sectors were manufacture of household and other made-up textiles and fur goods. Pigot listed 114 firms in the former and 58 in the latter in 1826–27. Within the former there were two distinct trades: manufacture of household textiles such as blankets and bed linen; and sails, sacks and tarpaulins. Household textiles rarely involved firms of any great size. Typical was Mary Sophia Mannering, a child bed linen maker of 8 Swinton Street, Grays Inn Road. She insured stock, utensils and goods valued at £50 in 1825.[184] Sailmaking, on the other hand, involved some very substantial firms and these are dealt with under shipbuilding. However, there were also a few larger businesses in the sack and tarpaulin trades. Thomas Gamson, a sack and sacking manufacturer, insured his warehouse, manufactory and starching shop in Kingsland for £1500 in 1821, in addition to stock and utensils for £800,[185] and Ann Petty, a tent maker of Love Lane, Rotherhithe, insured her working capital for £1000 in 1777.[186]

Within the fur trade, most furriers were retailers. However, there were a small number of firms predominantly involved in manufacturing, such as Charles Edwards in Gough Square whose bankruptcy file described him in 1821 as 'buying Skins and Furs wholesale and Manufacturing the same into Muffs Tippetts Hats Bonnetts Trimmings and other Articles and selling the same when so manufactured by wholesale and retail'.[187] A few firms were very large indeed: Lee and Sons, manufacturing furriers of Loman Street, Southwark, insured machinery for £2000, and stock, utensils and goods for £18,000 in 1822.[188]

Metal Goods

Throughout the period 1775–1825, London, although never on the scale of the west Midlands and the north of England, was none the less a major centre for the manufacture of metal goods of all kinds, in particular to satisfy its own domestic market. In total, Pigot listed 1241 London firms involved in the metal trades, 8.5 per cent of all London's manufacturing firms. In the 1820s they insured for £1,182,000, nearly 7 per cent of all manufacturing capital insured in London.

In terms of finished metal goods, there were three major trades; implements and tools, household goods and other finished metal goods. Pigot listed 812 firms. Of these, 110 were shown within 14 separate tool and implement manufacturing trades, 239 within 17 household goods manufacturing trades and 463 in 23 other finished metal goods trades. The fire office registers contain policies for 306 firms in the 1770s and 202 in the 1820s and there are 77 separately identified trades. Within the implements and tools category, the most common were sawmakers, planemakers, general toolmakers and makers of agricultural implements. Most common among manufacturers of household goods were makers of kitchen ware and wireworkers. The remaining sector was very diverse, but most frequently found were general brassworkers, tinplate workers and smiths of every kind (blacksmiths, whitesmiths, coppersmiths, anchor-smiths and so on). The two principal firms of tinplate workers in London in 1813 were Jones and Taylor in Tottenham Court Road and Howard and Co in Old Street Road. Both were described as 'wholesale traders' and it was noted that they 'have travellers in various parts of the kingdom'.[189]

A flavour of the rich variety of specialist London trades is provided by Pigot's 1826–27 directory. Among many others he listed the names of 16 planemakers, 34 sawmakers, 43 lamp makers, 25 needle and pin makers, 16 roasting jack manufacturers, 16 toymakers, 7 sieve makers, 12 file cutters, 11 sword cutlers, 9 table knife and fork makers, 9 lathe makers, 3 thimble makers, 3 hinge makers and 7 tea tray and urn makers. In practice, however, all overlapped one with another, and with foundries and manufacture of nails and screws and metal finish-ing. The diversity noted in the Birmingham brass and copper trades at this time was undoubtedly equally true of the London metal manufacturing trades:

> there is an infinite variety of trades. At one stage we have the brass founder, who required a small amount of capital and employed several workpeople ... and going through all the operations in the production of such articles as locks, door handles, hinges, brass fittings for furniture and for carriages and harness etc: at another stage we have the specialised worker producing buttons or buckles, and using different materials of which brass was usually one, or we have the brass candlestick maker, the cock founder, the locksmith, the thimble maker, the brass nail maker, etc: all concerned solely with the making of particular commodities and all using brass. At one point the brass and copper trades fade off into the toy trade, at another into the iron trade, or into the jewellery trade, or ... into the engineering trade.[190]

The difference between London and the Midlands and north was summed up by Dodd in 1843:

> The manufactures in metal are ... carried on in London generally on a smaller and more divided scale than in the north, especially those which relate to iron and steel ... Copper is worked very largely in London, and so is Lead ... the sheet-lead for roofs and terraces, lead tubes for water pipes, copper vessels for brewing, distilling, sugar refining, steam boilers, etc, are all manufactured to a considerable extent in the metropolis. The mixed metals such as brass, gun-metal, bell-metal, and fusible metal are

all worked up into useful forms here, but generally in establishments of no great extent.[191]

Of equal importance, this shows how London metal manufacturing firms, although predominantly small in scale, were able to supply directly the requirements of some of the capital's most important industries such as brewing, distilling, sugar refining and construction.

The vast number of trade cards, handbills, invoices, advertisements and the like which survive for these trades show how wide was the range of goods manufactured and how difficult it is to distinguish between the different branches. Thus, although James Sharp of 15 Leadenhall Street described himself as an 'agricultural implement maker', the trade card he circulated in 1770 lists among the product lines made at his manufactory at 133 Tooley Street anchors and shipwork as well as ploughs and harrows.[192] Similarly, in 1825 Holtzaptfel and Co described themselves in a handbill as 'manufacturers of mechanical and edge tools'. Their showroom was at 64 Charing Cross and their manufactory a mile or so away at 3 Chapel Court, Long Acre. Their handbill illustrated a variety of lathes, drills, workbenches, flatting mills, grinding machines and other tools, but they also manufactured 'cutlery in all its branches'. Eleven years earlier a German visitor had marvelled at their stock of lathes and at the fact that the cheapest was priced at 30 guineas. Holtzaptfel was by no means the only surviving London manufacturing cutler.[193] In 1824 the trade card of Henry Verinder of 79 St Paul's Churchyard advertised his 'London made Cutlery of the Best Quality'.[194]

At the top end of the market, Richard Baker, who described himself as 'Patent Mangle and Press Maker to His Majesty and the Royal Family', and who traded from three establishments in Fore Street, Oxford Street and Fenchurch Street, advertised no fewer than 139 product lines in 1827.[195] Fifty years earlier in 1776, James Powell, an iron manufacturer, brazier and hardwareman, circulated a handbill which listed the goods he made in brass, copper, iron and steel as stoves, fire irons, chandeliers, locks, door furniture, hooks, kitchen furniture, pots and pans, tools, candlesticks, salvers, cisterns, watch chains, knives, dog collars, bells and general smith's work.[196] Yet another range of products is described in the 1820s catalogue of John Porter of 81–2 Upper Thames Street. At his manufactory at Dowgate Dock in the City were made 'Iron Park & Field Fences, Hurdles,

TABLE 4.15 Finished metal goods

Capital insured (£)	No. of firms 1770s	Percentage of total	No. of firms 1820s	Percentage of total
100 and under	124	40.5	55	27.2
101–500	139	45.4	83	41.1
501–1000	27	8.8	31	15.3
1001–2999	12	3.9	22	10.9
3000 and over	4	1.3	11	5.4
Total	306	100.0	202	100.0

Source: Sun and other London fire office registers

Gates, etc, Wire Fences, Flower Stands, Trainers & every description of wire work. Iron Bedsteads of all kinds'.[197]

All these trades were dominated by small firms. In the 1770s nearly 86 per cent insured for £500 or less, over 40 per cent for £100 or less. Fifty years later the proportions were still 68 per cent and 27 per cent. Firms insuring for £500 or less accounted for 40 per cent of all capital insured in the 1770s, although by the 1820s it had fallen to 16 per cent. Although the average value of capital insured doubled, this was only from £372 to £769. More significantly, median values rose only from £150 to £250. All this is in line with evidence given to a House of Commons committee about the Black Country 'that the greater part of the manufacturers of Birmingham did not require large capitals, and many worked with less than £100'.[198] Even by the 1820s, only just over 5 per cent of firms insured for £3000 or more. In the 1770s it had been only just over 1 per cent. Table 4.15 shows the full breakdown by value of capital insured.

Among the very small number of larger firms in the finished metal goods manufacturing trades was Robert Wallis and Co. They described themselves in 1827 as furnishing ironmongers and manufacturers. Their advertisement shows their manufactory at Brooke House, Brooke Street, Holborn, to have been a three-storey building measuring perhaps one hundred feet by thirty feet judging from the number of windows.[199] Unfortunately, no fire insurance policy survives for the company. However, William King, a tinplate worker, insured his manufactory and workshop at 66 Snow Hill for £530 and £320 respectively in 1824, in addition to stock valued at £6350.[200] Even larger were

Henry and Joseph Tylor, coppersmiths and braziers at 4 Cripplegate Buildings. They insured their manufactory for £3500 in 1825, as well as stock, utensils and goods valued at £8000.[201] On a smaller scale, William Hurst, a filemaker at 8 Greenhill Rents, West Smithfield, insured his workshop for £200 and stock and utensils for £800 in 1819.[202] An interesting glimpse into the businesses of one of the trade's larger firms is provided by the bankruptcy file of John Pontin, a wireworker and sieve maker in Turnmill Street. He was declared bankrupt in 1831, but over a prior eight-and-a-half-year period achieved a profit of £3574 on a turnover of £12,766, which was 28 per cent. On much the same scale were the profits of William Hassan, a brass-founder and lamp maker at 4 Charles Street, who made an average annual profit of £438 over a ten-year period prior to his bankruptcy in 1823.[203] An unusually large firm in the 1770s was Alexander French, a manufacturing ironmonger in East Lane, Rotherhithe. In 1775 he insured his workshop for £900, a warehouse for £1300, and stock and utensils for £7790.[204]

A few examples must suffice to give a flavour of the innumerable small firms in the trade. In 1772 William Nesbitt, a smith and brazier, insured his workshop in Orange Street for £30, and stock and utensils for £120,[205] and Rebecca Champion of Brick Lane was a scissors maker who insured for £100.[206] Nearly fifty years later in 1821, John Bartlett, a whitesmith, insured his workshop at 8 Clare Street for £200, and stock and utensils for £300.[207]

There was also a large number of foundries in London; Pigot listed 353. Although the centre of the English brass and copper industry was in the Black Country, it is interesting to compare Birmingham's 71 brassfounders in 1797 with the 77 in Kent's 1818 London directory and 129 listed for London in 1826–27 by Pigot. Most London foundries were small, three-quarters insuring for £500 or less in the 1770s and nearly 40 per cent in the 1820s. However, the average value of capital nearly doubled from £790 to £1417. A few ironfounders insured a wide range of heavy fixed capital. As early as 1769 Raby and Rogers insured their furnaces, water wheels, forges and bellows in Dockhead, Southwark, for £1800, as well as stock, utensils and goods valued at £8000.[208] Nearly sixty years later in 1825, Crundall and Hallen insured a counting house for £150, a smith's shop for £50, a foundry for £350, a smithy for £100, stables for £200, and stock, utensils and goods for £1150, all at the Roebuck Iron

Foundry in Great Dover Road, Southwark.[209] Two other much smaller trades, both involving very small firms, are worth a mention, nail and screw making and metal treatment. In 1822 Thomas Bayman, a hand screw smith at 35 Old Gravel Lane, insured for £100.[210] Japanning and enamelling employed rather more capital, but again not very large sums. Thus, Joseph Le Jeune insured his workshop at 12 Denmark Street for £200 in 1777, as well as stock and utensils for £500.[211]

All London's metal manufacturing industries were to be found throughout the metropolis; about half in the City and East End and about a third in the west central districts and the West End. Most of the remainder were to be found south of the river.

Timber Trades

Taken as a whole, its timber trades were almost as important to London as its metal trades, and as varied and numerous. Pigot listed 2318 businesses, 16 per cent of all manufacturing firms. However, they were overwhelmingly small in scale and accounted for only just over 5 per cent of all capital insured in the 1820s, £960,000 in total. By far the most numerous were general carpenters and turners, of which Pigot listed 1565, one in thirty of all London businesses. Throughout the eighteenth century and the first half of the nineteenth, the term 'carpenter' could either mean a small-scale general craftsman in wood, trading with very little capital, or could be synonymous with the term 'builder' in the construction trade, and involve huge capital investment. The latter are dealt with as part of the construction industry. The former were invariably very small, although none the less important for the economy of London by virtue of their enormous numbers. The average value of capital insured was only £185 in the 1770s and this had risen very little to £202 by the 1820s. Throughout the period 1775–1825, half insured capital valued at £500 or less, and around 95 per cent for £500 or less. The few larger firms were turners such as Edward Beesley of Fleet Street who stated in his 1784 trade card that he 'Turns and Sells all sorts of Cane and Stick Heads, with Canes, Oak, Hickery & other Sticks'.[212] Other specialised trades working in wood were makers of gun stocks, saddle trees, fan sticks, pattens, hat blocks, artificial limbs and ladders.

Coopers and makers of other wooden containers were a very

considerable and rather more highly capitalised London timber manufacturing trade. Pigot listed 302 in 1826–27, the majority being coopers (252), but also small numbers of backmakers, hoop benders and packing case and tea chest makers. The fire office registers also contain policies for specialist box, plate case and medicinal chest makers. One such specialised firm was that of Thomas Peake of 3 Windsor Court, Monkwell Street. He described himself in his trade card of around 1800 as a plate case, knife case and cabinet maker and his business as making 'Canteens, Portable Desks, Tea Chests, & Gun Cases'.[213]

Coopers were a rare example of a trade within which the numbers of large firms declined over the period 1775–1825. The median value of capital insured was the same in the 1770s as the 1820s, £350, but the average value fell from £1100 to £770. The proportion of 'large' firms insuring for £3000 or more decreased from 11 per cent to 6 per cent, although the proportion insuring for £500 or less remained constant at 60 per cent. The proportion of total capital insured accounted for by small businesses rose from 11 per cent in the 1770s to 18 per cent in the 1820s. The reason lay in the trend towards large-scale users of the cooper's product making their own barrels and casks as the size of firms in such industries increased, as for example in vinegar making. Dodd remarked of Beaufoy's Lambeth vinegar factory in 1843: 'The cooperage is more extensive [than any other workshop] for all the casks employed in the vinegar and wine departments are both made and repaired on the premises'.[214] The fire office registers show that 87 per cent of firms insuring cooperages in the 1770s were coopers; by the 1820s it was only 40 per cent and among the other 60 per cent were such large users as brewers, sugar refiners, spirit colour manufacturers and vinegar manufacturers. A little later, and in Burton, Bass's cooperage handled half a million casks a year.[215] The biography of William Hart, who worked as a London cooper from the 1790s through to the 1840s, shows that he was employed by Wigram's, the shipbuilders, to make casks to be used to hold ships' stores.[216] Table 4.16 shows the full breakdown by value of capital insured.

An example of the large cooper to be found in the 1770s is Edward Layton of 163 Borough who, between 1769 and 1775, took out various policies for a workshop and sawpits valued at £1900, two workshops and several sheds valued at £600, and stock and utensils valued at £3100.[217] A rare cooper trading on a larger scale in the

TABLE 4.16 Coopers

Capital insured (£)	No. of firms 1770s	Percentage of total	No. of firms 1820s	Percentage of total
100 and under	35	24.6	16	20.5
101–500	53	37.3	33	42.3
501–1000	13	9.2	14	17.9
1001–2999	25	17.6	10	12.8
3000 and over	16	11.3	5	6.4
Total	142	100.0	78	100.0

Source: Sun and other London fire office registers

1820s was Charles Dowding in Wapping, who had employed William Hart mentioned above from 1796 to 1799. He managed average annual profits of £1081 over a five-and-a-half-year period between 1819 and 1825 but was declared bankrupt in 1826.[218] More typical was Michael Davis who insured a cooperage at 4 Allington Place for £100 in 1824, in addition to stock and utensils for £140.[219] An interesting Hand in Hand policy specified that the cooperage insured by John French in Cowcross Street in 1819 measured just 14 feet by 24 feet and was valued at £50.[220] In the 1770s about a third of coopers were to be found in both the City and the East End, with a quarter south of the river. By the 1820s, the proportion located in the East End had risen to half.

The other major 'timber' trade was manufacture of brushes, baskets and cork articles. Pigot listed 314 firms in 1826–27 and they insured capital valued at £365,000. Again, most businesses were small, though there were a few exceptions. In many ways these were the archetypal manufacturing trades serving the everyday domestic needs of a rapidly expanding city in a period of rising living standards, and mainly through small-scale production. Pigot listed 150 brushmakers, 72 basket makers and 71 cork cutters. In practice, many businesses dealt in the manufacture and sale of all, or at least several, of these. A handbill circulated in 1830 by James Brand of 43 Blackman Street, Borough, listed not only a wide range of mops, brushes and baskets, but also mats, rugs, lanterns, pails, tubs, clothes horses, blinds, kitchen chairs, trays, stools, rules, wooden kitchen implements, mousetraps, cradles, coat and umbrella stands, gaming boards, cricket bats and

TABLE 4.17 Brushes, baskets and cork articles

Capital insured (£)	No. of firms 1770s	Percentage of total	No. of firms 1820s	Percentage of total
100 and under	11	12.8	9	14.5
101–500	19	48.7	32	51.6
501–1000	5	12.8	8	12.9
1001–2999	3	7.7	8	12.9
3000 and over	1	2.6	5	8.1
Total	39	100.0	62	100.0

Source: Sun and other London fire office registers

balls, chess sets, children's toys, wooden shoes and billiard equipment.[221]

The average size of capital insured rose from £509 in the 1770s to £1163 in the 1820s. Most businesses were small: 77 per cent insuring for £500 or less in the 1770s and 66 per cent in the 1820s. However, by the 1820s, 8 per cent insured for £3000 or more. Table 4.17 shows the full breakdown by value of capital insured.

Brushmaking could take place on a very large scale. Wright and Cartwright insured their manufactory in Christopher Street, Hatton Garden, for £1000 in 1821, several warehouses for £3000, and stock and utensils for £12,000.[222] However, more typical was William Brailey. He insured his workshop at 21 Skinners Street for £70 and stock and utensils for £80 in 1819.[223] Basket making and cork working were invariably small-scale trades. Although firms were to be found all over London, there was a particular concentration of small specialised brushmakers in Kent Street, Southwark. They were described as men 'who had a little capital and a small stock of materials' and often to be found three to a house. A nostalgic description had it that:

> Here the proverb, 'As poor as a brushmaker', seemed true to the last degree. The street was composed of big dingy houses with different persons living on every floor. Many a room was a workshop and a kitchen as well. We could say that the tenant lived from hand to mouth. Each in business on his own account, he was not a journeyman, neither could he be called a master, as he employed nobody but his family.[224]

Coachbuilding

London was both literally and metaphorically at the centre of the revolution in personal mobility which occurred in Britain long before the railway age. This transport revolution was in many ways part of the consumer revolution. Both are discussed at length later in this book, but they provide the context within which London's coachbuilding industry evolved to a peak of development in the period 1775–1825. The story had started long before; by the mid-seventeenth century, London was already the centre of a national stagecoach system. The trade card circulated in 1791 by one Long Acre coachmaker, I. Brooks, reads very much like the routine claims of the twentieth-century motor trader: 'Carriages built on true Mechanical principles which are not liable to overturn, and follow the Horses with less draught. Axletree & Boxes on an entire new & simple construction, in which the Friction is so reduced, & the Oil preserved, that they will go three thousand miles without a fresh supply.'[225]

Most carriages were built for private use. The total number of carriages paying duty rose from 60,000 in 1814 to 99,000 in 1834, an increase of 65 per cent in 20 years. Statistics of duty on carriages produced for sale compiled in the 1870s give a figure of 3600 vehicles built for private use in 1814 and 15,000 in 1824. The number in private use was 55,000 in 1814 and 75,000 in 1824 at the height of the post-war boom. A direct comparison of numbers of private to public service vehicles can be made only for 1814 when the former was 55,000 out of 60,000 or nearly 92 per cent. If it is assumed that the proportion of vehicles in private use was about 90 per cent of the total, this means that it rose from 55,000 in 1814 to 75,000 in 1824 and to 90,000 in 1834. The duty figures show that almost exactly half were two-wheeled and half four-wheeled. The number of mail coaches also increased sharply, from 180 in 1799 to 700 in 1835, most built and maintained under contract in London. It is also worth noting that in 1823 David Davies built the first 12 cabs in London, stationing them in Great Portland Street.[226]

Campbell had already drawn attention to the size and complexity of the trade in London in 1747[227] and nearly a century later it was still remarked that 'Coach-making is carried on in the metropolis to a greater extent, and probably in a higher state of excellence, than anywhere else. From the light gig to the state-coach, from the cab to the heavy wagon, all are manufactured here'.[228] Indeed, contemporaries were still describing London as the centre of the trade in the 1880s.[229]

That this was a luxury trade *par excellence* is beyond doubt. A number of surviving examples of invoices, catalogues and quotations show that the average price of a London-built carriage in the late eighteenth and early nineteenth centuries was £170. It was possible to purchase a basic perch phaeton for £37, but a crane-neck coach with a full set of optional extras ran to £337. Optional extras alone could run to well over £200. A 'fashionable barouche driving seat [and] cloth cushions' were priced at £26 10s alone.[230] A typical estimate prepared for a potential customer in 1824 promised:

> able shifting bodies and a large locker underneath, made of best material, seasoned timber and workmanship, neatly carved and run, painted and picked out to order and the panels highly varnished and polished, a four hoped circular head with japanned joints and a japanned dashing leather to one of the bodies, two neat leather knee-boots and floor cloths to the bottom ... a perch carriage with hoop tyre wheels, turned and hardened axles and boxes. Long under springs to the fore part of the body and circular whip springs with braces and jacks to their backs to the hindpart of the carriage and painted and picked out and clear varnished and a pair of japanned lamps fixed with socket ironwork, the whole complete, duty included, £225.[231]

It is little wonder that a major West End coachbuilding firm for nearly 75 years, William Leader at 73 Wells Street, had a stock of carriages valued at £28,000 when declared bankrupt in 1826.[232]

Pigot listed 567 firms directly engaged in coachbuilding in 1826–27. This was 4 per cent of all manufacturers and they accounted for nearly 5 per cent of capital insured by such businesses. In related trades Pigot listed 91 trunk makers, 20 herald painters, 65 general lamp manufacturers and over 300 involved in the saddle and harness making trades. In all, probably about one in 14 of all London's manufacturing firms were engaged directly or indirectly in the coachbuilding industry. Coachbuilders insured capital valued at £820,000 in the 1820s. If the other related trades are included, the total would have been well in excess of a million pounds.

It was remarked in 1837 that 'few carriage builders carry on every branch of work on their own premises; none carry on all the branches, for it would not be worth their while on a small scale, and on a large scale it would be too enormous an undertaking'.[233] Certainly, the fire office registers record 22 specialised London coachbuilding trades, a specialisation greater than for any London manufacturing trade other than clock- and watchmaking. In addition to general coach, carriage, light cart and chaise makers, and wheelwrights, there were specialised coach axletree, blind, lamp, lining, spring and sedan chair makers, coach carvers, engravers, founders, joiners, lace mercers, painters, platers, tyresmiths, smiths, and coachmakers finishers and machinists. Pigot listed 234 coachbuilders and 152 wheelwrights. The other numerically most common trades were coachsmiths and tyre makers (47), coachfounders and platers (40), coach painters (21), coach spring makers (19), coach machinists (18), coach lamp makers (8) and axletree makers (7). There was also a repair and maintenance side to many of these trades. Thus, for example, virtually all Britain's mail coaches, the numbers of which rose from 180 in 1799 to 700 in 1835, were both built and maintained in London.

A high proportion of firms in the industry were quite small. In the 1770s, 68 per cent insured capital valued at £500 or less, and 50 years later it was still over 43 per cent. However, the average value of capital insured increased nearly three-fold, from £540 to £1444. These figures conceal a considerable difference between the general coach-builder and the specialised supporting trades within the industry. In the 1770s the average value of capital insured by coachbuilders was £786 compared with £319 for the firms in the related specialised trades; by the 1820s the difference was even more marked: £2060 compared with £596. There was a very large increase in the number of 'large' firms insuring for £3000 or more. In the 1770s it was less than 3 per cent, but by the 1820s the proportion had risen to over 15 per cent. Small firms accounted for 28 per cent of all capital insured in the industry in the 1770s; by the 1820s this had fallen to the much smaller but still significant proportion of 8 per cent. Table 4.18 shows the full breakdown by value of capital insured.

A number of unusually detailed fire insurance policies have survived for coachbuilders. Hachett and Boyes insured a shed and coach platform in Long Acre for £350 in 1772, their counting house, warehouse and the lofts above for £150, another warehouse with lofts above for £700, two workshops, one for coach painting, for £300, and stock, utensils and goods for £3800.[234] Fifty years later, in 1823, Stubbs and Hancock of 243–7 Whitechapel Road took out a policy for £9500. Workshops in George Street, Montague Street, were valued

TABLE 4.18 Coachbuilding

Capital insured (£)	No. of firms 1770s	Percentage of total	No. of firms 1820s	Percentage of total
100 and under	33	22.0	17	12.3
101–500	69	46.0	43	31.2
501–1000	32	21.3	28	20.3
1001–2999	12	8.0	29	21.0
3000 and over	4	2.7	21	15.2
Total	150	100.0	138	100.0

Source: Sun and other London fire office registers

at £500 and their contents at £1500; stands for carriages and a smith's shop were valued at £1500, and the stock and utensils therein at £2000; a smith and wheelwright's shop was valued at £100 and its contents at £150; and a warehouse with lofts above was insured for £100, and the oil and varnish stored in it for £100 also. Another set of carriage stands with lofts above was insured for £800 and the stock and utensils therein for £1950. Finally, sheds and lofts in Great Garden Street 'for making coach bodies' were valued at £450 and their contents at £350.[235] In both these cases, the stock at risk in the policies would have been actual carriages, complete or incomplete, because little machinery and few large tools were required. William Felton, author of the standard technical work on coachmaking throughout the nineteenth century, *A Treatise on Carriages* (published between 1794 and 1796), was in business from at least 1790 to 1825. In the latter year he insured his workshop at 6 Long Acre for £2000, and stock, utensils and goods for £1000.[236]

An example of a much smaller and more specialised firm was Giles Widger, a tyresmith who insured his workshop at 13 Coal Yard, Drury Lane, for £200 in 1819, specifying its size as 3240 square feet.[237] Isaac Harper, a wheelwright, insured a workshop in Market Street, Horseferry Road, for £60 in 1821, a smith's shop for £20, and stock, utensils and goods valued at £170.[238]

Long Acre was the major centre of the trade throughout the period 1775–1825, certainly for the finest vehicles. Nearly 40 per cent of all firms were located there with another large concentration in the West End, especially around Berkeley Square and Oxford Street, where about a quarter were to be found. In the 1770s, about 20 per cent were to be found in the City. Very few were located there in the 1820s, though 14 per cent were to be found in and around Whitechapel. With regard to Long Acre, it was perfectly natural for Macartney, on his famous embassy to China in 1792–94, to write of his journey to the Emperor's summer palace that his was 'the first piece of Long Acre machinery that ever rattled up the road to Jehol'.[239]

Chemicals

Taken as a whole, manufacture of chemical products in the broadest sense was an important London industry throughout the period 1775–1825, though no individual trade was in itself particularly large. With regard to industrial chemicals, the growth of manufacturing industries, particularly textiles, created the technical and economic conditions suitable for the development of applied chemistry. Although London was never to rival Glasgow, Tyneside or south-west Lancashire as a centre of the heavy chemicals industry, there were dyestuffs manufacturers, and a number of manufacturing chemists established themselves to supply such industries as brewing, distilling, vinegar making, food processing, printing, the leather trades and soap and candle making with the chemicals they needed. Indeed, the last two were themselves part of the chemicals industry in the broadest sense. Taken together there were 388 firms involved in the chemical trades and these insured capital valued at £770,000 in the 1820s, 4.4 per cent of all capital insured in manufacturing.

Pigot listed 125 manufacturers of industrial and other specialised chemicals. These included manufacturers of vitriol, saltpetre, pitch and tar, whitelead, acetous acid, alum, aquafortis (sulphuric and nitric acid) and size. The largest single industry was dye-stuffs with 35 firms manufacturing blue, black, annato, verdigris, orchell and spirit colour. London remained a moderately important centre until the 1850s; that is, until the first major technological breakthroughs occurred.[240] There were also such specialised firms as makers of anti-corrosion and anti-mildew preparations. Five London firms made coach and cart grease. A trade card circulated around 1800 by Joseph Perceval of 10 Green Street, Blackfriars Road, offered 'Merchants, Farmers, Dealers and Others' a 'Superior Fine Grease Preparation for Carage [sic] Wheels & Mills of every description'.[241]

Most firms were of a moderately large size, with few either very small or very large. Thus, 60 per cent insured capital valued at over £500 in the 1770s, and 78 per cent in the 1820s. Even in the 1770s, there were a number of quite substantial firms. In 1774 Walker and Singleton of 42 Cheapside, who described themselves as oil of vitriol and aquafortis manufacturers and brimstone refiners, insured their laboratory and warehouse for the immense sum of £3000, as well as stock and utensils valued at £6100.[242] Five years earlier, William Palmer, a saltpetre refiner, insured his refining house in Gravel Lane, Houndsditch, for £300 and stock and utensils for £1200.[243] A blue maker, Thomas Marshall of Hog Lane, Shoreditch, insured a horse mill for £100 in 1774 and stock and utensils for £750.[244] Half a century later there were a number of still larger firms. In 1820 Grace and Freeman, whitelead and turpentine manufacturers in Chelsea insured a horse mill, a workshop and a scouring house for £50 each, a drying house for £300, their counting house, warehouses and furnaces for £400, and stock, utensils and fittings for £4550.[245] Four years later Francis and Co, saltpetre manufacturers in Nags Head Court, insured their manufactory for £700, a warehouse for £500, and the stock and utensils stored therein for £2700.[246] Pigot listed 11 glue manufacturers, some of whom were very large, like John and Joseph Barton who insured their manufactory and boiling house in Grange Road, Bermondsey, for £700 in 1821, two drying sheds for £500, two glue rooms, a warehouse and stable for £600, two adjoining sheds for £200, a counting house for £250 and several other sheds, lean-tos and industrial buildings for £800, as well as stock and utensils valued at £5720.[247]

Another major sector was paints, varnishes and printing inks. Pigot listed 114 such firms of which the most common were colour manufacturers (42), varnish makers (25) and printing ink makers (16). Campbell's description of the relationship between the colourman, that is the retailer of paints and varnishes, and colour manufacture in the late 1740s held true for the next hundred years:

> The Colour-Man buys all manner of Colours uncompounded: He is, in some shape, the Apothecary to the Painter; as he buys the simple colours and compounds some of them; He grinds such as require grinding … There are some others employed in preparing Colours, such as, in making Powder-Blue, commonly called Prussian Blue … The work is chiefly carried on in the Borough of Southwark … There are some who prepare

that beautiful Colour called Carmine ... There are Works at Whitechapel, and some others of the suburbs, for making of White and Red Lead, with the rest of the Preparations of that the work is performed by Engines, Horses and Labourers.[248]

Most firms were of a substantial size, such as Giles and Pilcher who in 1824 insured their manufactory in Morgans Lane, Tooley Street, for £750, a steam engine for £200 and the steam engine house for £50, their counting house for £200, a warehouse for £1390, a shed for £20, and stock and utensils for £6800.[249] Bowman and Thompson, described as colour and paint manufacturers in their bankruptcy file in 1831 had achieved average annual profits of £2320 over the previous six and a half years.[250] Manufacture of printing ink was carried out on a more modest scale. In 1819 Robert Colvin insured his manufactory at 14 King Street, Clerkenwell, for £100, and stock and utensils for £400.[251]

Manufacture of pharmaceutical products and perfumery were also significant London trades. It is not at all easy to distinguish these from the far more numerous retail druggists, apothecaries and perfumers. The 1824 edition of *The Book of English Trades* attempted a distinction: 'The Chemist of trade, might be defined the maker of medicines; the Druggist the seller of them. In London ... a Chemist and Druggist are frequently combined in the same person ... The Chemist and Druggist usually makes some of his articles, even if he is only a retailer; he also sells numerous quack medicines ... The Chemist and Druggist generally, also, dispenses Physicians' prescriptions.'[252] Prior to the Apothecaries Act 1815, medical practice, drug dispensing and drug manufacturing were all likely to be carried out within the same business. Only after the requirement for apothecaries to be licentiates of the Society of Apothecaries did some become medical practitioners and others dispensers or manufacturers of drugs. Despite this, the distinction was far from clear even 30 years later. The first 200 years of Allen and Hanbury exemplify the overlap. The founder, Sylvanus Bevan, described himself as an apothecary in 1715. However, by 1765 his brother Timothy was calling himself a chemist and druggist. Ten years later the firm was definitely engaged in manufacturing drugs and selling them both wholesale and retail. The dispensing side of the business was still expanding in the 1830s and, even after the first technological breakthroughs in pharmaceutical manufacture in the 1850s, dispensing was still a major activity. It was not until the move from the City to Bethnal Green in 1874 that manufacturing really took off. Indeed, it was not to become solely a manufacturing entity until 1893.[253]

The manufacture of perfumery and cosmetics had reached a high level of sophistication by the first quarter of the nineteenth century. *Lillie's British Perfumer*, published in 1822, described 16 types of perfume, 40 natural aromatic products, 27 perfumed spirits and oils, 17 perfumed waters, 5 pomatums and cold creams, 22 perfumed hair products, 7 powders and pastes, 7 tooth powders and 17 types of cosmetics.

Again, there were some very considerable firms. In 1821 James and Henry Vallance, who described themselves as chemists, druggists and manufacturers of castor oil, insured their warehouse and manufactory in Bakers Row, Clerkenwell, for £800, and stock, utensils and goods for £4500. They also insured stock, utensils and goods to the same value at 19 Garlick Hill.[254] Typical perfume manufacturers were Bentley and Wood who insured a steam engine and other machinery at 7 Little Queen Street for £250 in 1821, as well as stock, utensils and goods valued at £1650.[255] By 1817 William Yardley was already in business as a lavender and cosmetics manufacturer in Thorney Street, Bloomsbury, having previously been a sword cutler.[256]

There was also a considerable section of the industry producing chemical products for household use. Pigot listed 139 such firms in 1826–27. Not least under this heading came soap manufacturers of which Pigot listed 44, and many of which were very substantial firms indeed. The fire office registers show that nearly a quarter could be classified as large in the 1770s and 60 per cent in the 1820s. The average value of capital insured was £2018 in the earlier period and then more than doubled to £4760 in the later. This was around three times the average value of capital insured in London manufacturing trades as a whole. Certainly, all the contemporary sources estimated that at least £1000–£5000 was required as starting capital. The large investment of capital required reflected the size of plant needed to satisfy steeply rising demand as the population grew and living standards improved; as the historian of one Lancashire firm put it, there was 'an increased need for soap in the growing, smoke-begrimed towns'.[257] Not least was this true of London. Indeed, few industries illustrate better the rise in living standards over the period covered by this book. *Lillie's British Perfumer* described 46 varieties of soap in

1822. Annual consumption of soap per head in Britain rose from 3.6 lb to 7.1 lb between 1801 and 1851. Production had risen from 17,000 tons in 1785 to 35,000 tons in 1814 although excise returns show that the number of soap makers fell from 971 to 468 over the same period. Average output per firm increased from 19 tons to 527 tons over the first half of the nineteenth century.[258] London experienced the same trend; the fire office registers show that the number of soap makers fell by nearly half between the 1770s and 1820s.

A large soap boiling house contained numerous soap pans and in addition there would normally be a frame room, warehouses, laboratory, carpenter's and blacksmith's shops for making boxes, crates and equipment, sheds, stables and yard, and a counting house.[259] The capital required by a London soap maker is exemplified by George and Jesse Russell, later simply Jesse Russell, of Goodman's Yard, Minories. They had insured for £11,010 in 1771; by 1819 this had risen 53 per cent to £16,800.[260] The following year Peter Kendall and Co insured their counting house, soap house and warehouse in Goodman's Yard for £2000, and stock and utensils for £10,000.[261] In comparison, Joseph Crosfield and Sons of Warrington, who survived into the second half of the twentieth century, insured for £2860 in 1828, of which £1130 was for fixed capital.[262]

On a much more modest scale, the making of candles overlapped with that of soap. It also overlapped with the retail trades of wax and tallow chandlers, although the fire office registers show that a minority were predominantly manufacturers. Another related trade was the manufacture of sealing wax and wafers. Before 1800 candle making was a craft requiring little capital; by the 1820s it was beginning to evolve into an industry using both new machinery and better controlled materials.[263] The fire office policy registers suggest that the number of such firms nearly trebled between the 1770s and 1820s and that the average value of capital insured more than doubled from £687 to £1414. By 1821 George, William and Mary Pratt were insuring a manufactory and melting house in Salmon Lane, Limehouse, for £600, a mill house for £100, and stock and utensils for £1750.[264] Four years later the term 'candle manufactory' is to be found when William Huxtable insured his at 13 King Street, Holborn, for £200. He also insured his warehouse for £300, and stock and utensils for £3600.[265]

Another minor trade reflecting increasing living standards is the manufacture of household cleaning products. Pigot listed 65 London firms, including 42 blacking and 12 whiting manufacturers. There were also such specialised trades as soda, plate powder, lamp and ivory black, and brass and copper cleaning composition makers. Few were very large, but Joseph and William Cooper insured their whiting manufactory and counting house at 16 Millbank for £1200 in 1825. This was another trade in which horse mills survived into the 1820s; the Coopers insured theirs together with stock and utensils for £1500, and livestock, presumably in part for the horse mill, for £400.[266] All these, together with pharmaceuticals and soap, were trades in which science was being applied to industry at an early date and the fire office registers record the insurance of a number of laboratories in both the 1770s and the 1820s.

Watch- and Clockmaking

Another of London's highly important and long-established luxury trades was watch- and clockmaking. Like many other London trades, it was distinguished both by a high degree of specialisation and by the difficulty of distinguishing between manufacturing proper and bespoke production for the individual customer. Over seventy years ago Dorothy George described how, in the eighteenth century: 'The maker ... might be either a shopkeeper or a chamber-master working for the shops, in which case the name of the shop would be put on the dial – sometimes the name of a jeweller, a toyman or even a pawnbroker, who knew nothing of watchmaking.' However, by 1824 specialisation had been acknowledged: 'When watches were first made, the whole business was performed by one man, who was then properly called a watch-maker; but the name is now given to him who puts the various movements together, adjusts their several parts, and finishes the whole machine.'

From about 1750, British watchmakers in general, and London firms in particular, enjoyed a century of both technological superiority and commercial dominance over all other major European manufacturers. Jewelled bearings had become a necessary feature of any good watch and watch jewelling had become the monopoly of British watchmakers. By the latter part of the eighteenth century Clerkenwell alone was estimated to be producing 120,000 watches a year, with 70,000 of these for export. Output from London's watchmakers was estimated to comprise about half the total for the whole of Europe.

The export trade extended well beyond the boundaries of Europe, frequently being found, for example, throughout the Ottoman Empire. One watchmaker alone, Bayley in Red Lion Street, was reputed to be producing 3000 to 4000 a year in the mid-1790s. Even in the 1820s it was still being claimed that the 'Best watches in the world are made in London'.

Watchmaking has been described as 'probably the most highly developed division of labour of any branch of British industry'. This is readily illustrated by both the contemporary London trade directories and the fire office registers. Pigot listed 627 businesses in 1826–27 under 25 separate trade headings. There were also 25 separate trades represented in the fire office policy registers, including clock chain makers, engravers, smiths, movement and dial makers, watch cap, case, hand and spring makers, watch jewellers, chasers, finishers and gilders, chronometer makers and makers of wooden clocks. Subdivision was almost endless; Dorothy George quoted an estimate of 102 distinct trades in 1817.

Although watchmakers accounted for 4.3 per cent of all London manufacturing firms, they insured only 1.3 per cent of all manufacturing capital. Partly because of the intense division of labour, watchmaking was far more labour than capital intensive. In 1798 it was estimated that 7000 people were employed in Clerkenwell alone, with another 1000 in St Luke's Without Cripplegate. Over a quarter of a century later it was still being said that the trade 'employs a great number of hands'.[267] The 1831 Census showed 2642 men aged 20 or over and the 1841 Census counted 4344 employees. However, most firms employed comparatively little capital. The average was £214 in the 1770s and this rose only to £375 in the 1820s. Median values were only £110 and £123. In the 1770s over 92 per cent of firms insured capital valued at £500 or less; nearly 48 per cent of them £100 or less. Even by the 1820s these proportions were still 82 per cent and 36 per cent. Firms insuring for £500 or less accounted for exactly two-thirds of all capital insured in the 1770s. By the 1820s this had fallen to the still relatively high proportion of 37 per cent. Even in the 1820s there were still virtually no large firms although a significant number of middle-sized businesses, insuring between £1000 and £3000, had emerged. Table 4.19 shows the full breakdown by value of capital insured.

Among the larger firms to be found in the 1770s was that of

TABLE 4.19 Watch- and clockmaking

Capital insured (£)	No. of firms 1770s	Percentage of total	No. of firms 1820s	Percentage of total
100 and under	122	47.8	57	36.1
101–500	113	44.3	72	45.6
501–1000	12	4.7	15	9.5
1001–2999	8	3.1	13	8.2
3000 and over	0	0	1	0.6
Total	255	100.0	158	100.0

Source: Sun and other London fire office registers

Henry Billinghurst. He insured his workshop at 67 Aldersgate Street for £300 in 1769, as well as stock and utensils valued at £455.[268] By 1820 George Clark, who described himself as a watch manufacturer, insured his workshop at 3 Cherrytree Court, Aldersgate Street, for £100 and in it watchmaker's lathes valued at £850, and stock and utensils valued at £1500.[269] William Rowland was a specialist watch case and dial maker who insured his workshop at 33 Lower Smith Street, Northampton Square, for £350 in 1825. He also insured stock, utensils and goods for £1000.[270] However, much more typical of the hundreds of small specialised Clerkenwell watchmaking firms was John Lervis, a watch gilder, who insured his workshop at 7 Albermarle Street for £100 in 1820, as well as stock, utensils and goods valued at £40. Even he had to supplement his income by running a chandler's business.[271]

Although the large majority of firms were located in Clerkenwell and St Luke's – 58 per cent in the 1770s and 64 per cent in the 1820s – there were substantial numbers also to be found in the East End and around Holborn, the latter especially in the 1770s.

London's Other Major Manufacturing Trades

Shipbuilding   There were, of course, many other substantial London manufacturing trades. Shipbuilding was not only still a major London industry in the period 1775–1825, but it was central to a great number of both specifically peripheral and less directly related trades. In the first category came anchorsmiths, sailcloth and sailmaking, rope-making, manufacture of mathematical and optical instruments and chronometers and the trade in ships' stores through ship chandlers and dealers in marine stores; among the second category were the enormously important activities of ship owners and agents, shading off into those of international merchants.

Over the period 1775–1825, shipbuilding tended to move down river and beyond the boundaries of the metropolis proper. Nevertheless, until about 1850 shipbuilding along the Thames as a whole was still expanding. Its reputation was high and demand was steady, not least from the Admiralty which ordered at least 60 per cent of its outside building from London yards. London's supremacy prior to the decline which set in after about 1850 has been well described as 'a symbol of the predominance of the merchants of London over those of the outports'.[272]

Pigot listed 217 shipbuilders in 1826–27. The fire office registers record 15 separate trades which include bargebuilders, block makers, caulkers, lighter builders, mast makers, oarmakers, riggers and ship carvers, joiners and breakers. In addition, Pigot listed 28 anchorsmiths, 64 sailmakers, 105 ropemakers and 122 makers of mathematical and optical instruments. There was also a substantial pleasure boatbuilding industry exemplified by the firms of Rawlinson and Lyon and R. and T. Roberts. The former had their yard on the Surrey side of Westminster Bridge. They circulated a trade card around 1800 which stated that they would 'Build all sorts of Pleasure Boats, for Rowing or Sailing'. In addition: 'Pleasure Boats Bought, Sold & taken care of. Also repair'd and fitted up ... Boats to Let for Rowing or Sailing.'[273] The latter had a yard in Lambeth and a few years earlier circulated a trade card to inform 'the Nobility and Gentry' that they 'continue to LET the genteelest Pleasure Boats for Rowing or Sailing ... a very neat Pleasure Barge to Let. Pleasure Boats of all Sorts BUILT, bought, sold and taken Care of, also repair'd and fitted up.'[274]

Although there were substantial numbers of smaller firms, especially in the 1770s, the industry was dominated by larger firms. Over two-thirds of all businesses in the 1770s insured capital valued at £500 or less, and these accounted for 27 per cent of all capital insured in the industry. By the 1820s the proportion of such firms had fallen to 43 per cent, and they accounted for only 8 per cent of all capital insured in shipbuilding. The average value of capital insured more than doubled from £563 to £1154 between the 1770s and the 1820s,

TABLE 4.20 Shipbuilding

Capital insured (£)	No. of firms 1770s	Percentage of total	No. of firms 1820s	Percentage of total
100 and under	29	22.1	8	15.7
101–500	61	46.6	14	27.5
501–1000	20	15.3	11	21.6
1001–2999	19	14.5	12	23.5
3000 and over	2	1.5	6	11.8
Total	131	100.0	51	100.0

Source: Sun and other London fire office registers

when 12 per cent of firms could be described as large. Table 4.20 shows the full breakdown by value of capital insured.

Among the more substantial firms in the 1770s were Joseph and Hugh Woolcombe. They described themselves as shipbuilders and breakers and insured their warehouses, sheds and crane house in East Lane, Rotherhithe, for £1250 in 1775, as well as stock and utensils valued at £1500.[275] Larger still was another Rotherhithe shipbuilder, Peter Mestaer. In 1775 he insured three warehouses in Shipwright Street for £200, a sawpit and reed loft for £75, another warehouse and sheds for £50 and a dock and wharf, with gates and fencing, for £1000. In addition, he insured docks, wharves and slips at King and Queen's Stairs for £700, sawpits, lofts and a crane house for £50, another sawpit and treenail loft for £150, and his counting house, iron house and the fencing around them for £100. He also insured stock, utensils and goods valued at £1785.[276] Forty-six years later, after his death, Cornelius Truefitt had taken over Peter Mestaer's business. In 1821 he insured a mould loft with sawpits, a wheel crane and a deal house for £2500 at King and Queen's Dock, sawpits, treenail lofts and a wheel crane house for £400, a blacksmith's shop for £600, two warehouses with lofts over for £200 each, docks, wharves, slips and the gates and fencing for £1500, the yard for £200, and fencing and palings for £250.[277] This means that the valuation put on the King and Queen's Stairs yard rose from £1250 in 1775 to £4850 in 1821, an increase of 288 per cent. However, Peter Mestaer had also insured similar facilities in Shipwright Street for another £1325.

Ward and Milner were major specialist mast, block and oarmakers.

In 1821 they insured their workshops and counting house in Wapping for £300, the machinery in the workshops for £350, a warehouse for £1000, and other workshops, buildings and the cover for their yard for £850. They also insured stock and utensils for £3650.[278] Sometimes fire insurance policies valued ships under construction. Thus, for example, John Grant, a shipbuilder of Gun Lane, Limehouse, insured a ship for £2000 in 1824.[279] The following year, George Searle, a Lambeth bargebuilder insured a barge under construction for the Stationers' Company for £500, a ship under construction for £200, his boat house for £400, and stock, utensils and goods for £400.[280]

Shipbuilding firms were almost equally divided between the north and south banks of the Thames to the east of the City, that is to say Wapping, Limehouse, Shadwell and Poplar, and Rotherhithe and Bermondsey, with a few small boatbuilders in Chelsea.

Scientific Instrument Making One of the trades both closely associated with shipbuilding and within which London was particularly predominant was the making of scientific instruments, usually known to contemporaries as 'mathematical, philosophical and optical instruments'. Pigot listed 144 makers in 1826–27. Few London trades have as assiduous an historian as Anita McConnell. She sums it up very succinctly,

> A hierarchy of makers can be detected: at the top were the famous 'names', to whom buyers from government departments, institutions, and elite British and foreign customers went for all types of instruments and globes ... Below these leading houses were reputable makers specialising in certain instruments, or supplying one class of buyer ... Below again, the makers who seldom dealt with the public but served the firms above them. At the base, those numerous makers of second-class goods for which there was a growing market.[281]

Dickens described a 'Ship's Instrument Maker' in *Dombey and Son*: 'The stock in trade of this old gentleman comprised chronometers, barometers, telescopes, compasses, charts, maps, sextants, quadrants, and specimens of every kind of instrument used in the working of a ship's course, or the keeping of a ship's reckoning, or the prosecuting of a ship's discoveries.'[282] Dickens was writing in 1846 but an important change had taken place about a hundred years earlier. With increasing demand major firms began to specialise, either as retailers of a wide range of smaller apparatus or as manufacturers of larger apparatus to order. Nevertheless, the range of instruments produced by any one manufacturer could be very large. Thus, Edward Nairne of 20 Cornhill, who lived from 1726 to 1806, issued a trade card which described his products, many his own inventions, at very great length under the separate headings of spectacles, magnifying glasses, telescopes, microscopes, camera obscuras, air pumps, barometers, apparatus for electrical experiments, thermometers, hydrostatic balances, quadrants, compasses, sundials, globes, rulers, drawing pens, theodolites, pencils and drawing instruments, drawing boards and all sorts of measuring devices.[283] Even so most firms employed very modest sums of capital. The average capital insured in the 1770s was £269 and it rose only to £359 in the 1820s. In both periods, over 80 per cent of all businesses insured for £500 or less. Benjamin Cole, a mathematical instrument maker of 136 Fleet Street was quite exceptional in insuring stock and utensils valued at £825 in 1769.[284] There were also a few larger manufacturers in the 1820s like John Tuther, a mathematical and optical instrument maker who insured his workshop at 221 Holborn for £50, as well as stock and utensils valued at £1580.[285]

Other areas of precision instrument making in London were measuring equipment and surgical instruments. Very few were to be found in the 1770s, most of the latter being indistinguishable from ordinary cutlers. However, one surgical instrument maker, William Pepys of 22 Poultry, took out a policy for stock and utensils valued at £250 in 1774 and was still trading in 1821 when he valued his stock and utensils at the eight times larger sum of £2000.[286] It has been estimated that there were about 200 firms producing surgical instruments in the 1820s, though most were general cutlers.[287] Pigot listed 35 specialist surgical, medical and optical instrument makers in 1826–27, 32 truss makers and 12 other firms, including 3 makers of artificial arms and legs and one artificial eye maker. The technological sophistication of the trade is shown by the 1827 advertisement of J. Robinson of 35 Northumberland Street. He stated that he had been supplying artificial legs and hands for 'upwards of twenty years' and that he made 'Artificial Legs, above or below the knee ... also from the Finger to a whole Hand ... Knee-joint Pin Legs, for ease in sitting down ... Common Pin Legs of every description; False Calves for wasted or deformed Legs'.[288] In fact, over 60 years earlier, in 1763, Holmes and Laurie of Bartholomew Close circulated a trade card which described themselves as 'Workmen to St Bartholomew's, St

Thomas's, Guy's, St George's, the Middlesex and Foundling Hospitals, and the London Infirmary. Make & Sell Steel Springs & all other kinds of Trusses, Collars, Neck-Swings, Strait Stockings, Steel Bodice, with various instruments for the Lame, Weak and Crooked'.[289] Nevertheless, most firms were very small. Over 72 per cent insured capital valued at £500 or less in the 1820s and the average was only £466.

There were a few larger manufacturers of measuring equipment like Samuel Crosley. He was a gas meter manufacturer who insured his manufactory in Cottage Lane, City Road, for £1000 in 1824 and stock and utensils valued at £1750 in 1825.[290] Pigot listed 12 such firms in 1826–27. The fire office registers also contain policies for barometer, thermometer, hydrometer and weighing machine makers.

Gunmaking Another trade in which London was pre-eminent was gunmaking. Pigot listed 109 firms in 1826–27, 90 of which were described as gunmakers and the rest as either the gun lock, stock or barrel makers who supplied them. There were also a few very substantial shotmakers. As early as 1747 Campbell described the trade's specialisation: 'The Gun Smith is a Compound of the Joiner and Smith; he works both in Wood and Iron: The Gun or Pistol Barrel is none of his making; they are made at the Foundry, and he buys them in Parcels, makes Locks for them and mounts them.'[291] However, a trade card circulated over 60 years later in 1810 by one Blake, a gunmaker and sword cutler of 168 Fenchurch Street, stated that he 'Makes & Sells all sorts of Fowling Pieces, Rifle and Air Guns, Pistols of all sorts, Small Swords and Navy Harpers, Patent Shot and best double strong Gun Powder'.[292]

Few firms were very large, though their size increased dramatically over the period 1775–1825, the average value of capital insured rising more than three-fold from £456 in the 1770s to £1507 in the 1820s. In the 1770s nearly 79 per cent insured capital valued at £500 or less; this halved to 40 per cent in the 1820s. Conversely, the proportion of 'large' firms insuring £3000 or more increased from 2 per cent to 19 per cent. By the 1820s gunmakers were insuring collectively for over £164,000, less than 4 per cent of which was accounted for by firms insuring £500 or less. In the 1770s it had been over 30 per cent. Table 4.21 shows the full breakdown by value of capital insured.

One of the foremost London gunmakers in the 1770s, indeed until his death in 1790, was John Twigg. In 1773 he insured his workshop

TABLE 4.21 Gunmaking

Capital insured (£)	No. of firms 1770s	Percentage of total	No. of firms 1820s	Percentage of total
100 and under	14	29.8	6	18.8
101–500	23	48.9	7	21.9
501–1000	4	8.5	9	28.1
1001–2999	5	10.6	4	12.5
3000 and over	1	2.1	6	18.8
Total	47	100.0	32	100.0

Source: Sun and other London fire office registers

at 30 Cornhill for £200. Two years earlier he had insured stock and goods valued at £2000.[293] Among a number of very substantial makers in the 1820s was James Purdey. His clientele included, as has the firm's ever since, some of the most fashionable in the land. He had moved to 4 Princes Street, Leicester Square, in 1814 and by 1825 his stock, utensils and goods were valued at £2600.[294] There were several very much larger gunmakers, such as Thomas Barnett and Son who insured their warehouse at 134 Minories for £1000, and stock, utensils and goods for £7900 in 1825.[295] Another long-established London gunmaker was Joseph Manton. He established his business in 1795 and by 1820 he was insuring several workshops at 11 Hanover Square and 314 Oxford Street for £1700 as well as stock and utensils valued at £2000. However, six years later he was bankrupt, having achieved an annual average profit of no less than £3074 over the previous 30 years.[296] Mention must also be made of the firm of Thomas Beaumont who was a shot manufacturer on a very large scale. In 1825 he insured his manufactory at 7–8 Tooley Street for £2500, two steam engines for £2400, and a counting house, warehouse and shot tower for £4000.[297]

Engineering Pigot also listed 277 manufacturers of general mechanical equipment in 21 separate trades. Included among these were general engine and machine makers, fire and garden engine makers, pump and rose engine makers, beer engine makers, scale and scale beam makers, cock founders, and press, mill and printing machine makers. Most numerous were general engine makers or turners, sometimes simply known as 'engineers', of whom Pigot listed 80, and scale makers, of which 47 were listed. Between them they insured capital valued at over £240,000 in the 1820s.

Most of the surviving trade card material is for makers of water pumping machinery. Typical was the description contained on an invoice sent out in 1829 by George Turner of 65 Dorset Street: 'Single & Double Barrell Pumps, to Let or Hire. Ship Pumps of every description.' He described himself as smith and iron founder as well as engine manufacturer.[298] A wider range of products was set out in a trade card circulated in 1827 by T. Eddy of 354 Oxford Street. He made and supplied 'Patent Horizontal Mangles, Washing Machines, Table-Cloth Presses, Churns ... Vapour Baths, Garden-Engines [and] Weighing Machines'.[299] Rather more technologically advanced was the product range of William Russell of 44 St John Street. He described himself as an engineer in a handbill he circulated in 1830 and his manufactures as 'Fire Pumps ... Hydraulic Presses, Air and Gas Condensing Machines, and Soda Water Machines'. Some of these firms were manufacturing substantial pieces of machinery.[300]

Most firms were small; exactly three-quarters insured capital valued at £500 or less in the 1770s and two-thirds in the 1820s. There was also very little change in the average value of capital insured; in the earlier period it was £757 and in the later £878. This was despite the great advances made in engineering technology over the last quarter of the eighteenth century and the first quarter of the nineteenth. A typical firm was William Bynon, who described himself as a millwright when he insured his workshop, counting house, shed and a lean-to in Vine Street, Lambeth, for £170 in 1777, and stock and utensils for £400.[301] However, there were some large firms. In the 1770s, 4 per cent insured for £3000 or more and by the 1820s the proportion had risen to over 9 per cent. John Bristow, who described himself as an engine maker and whose trade card showed that he manufactured 'all sorts of Engines for Extinguishing Fires, or Watering Gardens', insured a counting house, warehouse and workshop adjacent to his house in Ratcliffe Highway for £600 in 1771, another warehouse, lofts and sheds for £210, another counting house in Cloth Fair for £300, an adjoining warehouse and workshop for £200, a warehouse and workshop there for £250, a warehouse over the stables for £350 and a stable loft for £70. He also insured stock and utensils valued at £5940.[302]

It has been claimed that Joseph Bramah (1748–1814) was the founder of the metropolitan school of mechanical engineers. In 1778 he invented an improved water closet and he also developed and manufactured beer engines and various types of locks. In 1789 he took on Henry Maudslay (1771–1831) and they worked together until 1807, most significantly on a hydraulic press which was later used by both Robert Stephenson, on the Britannia railway bridge across the Menai Straits, and Brunel on the *Great Eastern*. Then Maudslay went into business for himself and developed the first screw cutting machinery as well as other revolutionary machine tools. Between 1803 and 1809 he manufactured 44 ship's block manufacturing machines for the Admiralty for use at Portsmouth Dockyard, some of which were still in use in the first decade of this century. In 1810 he moved from Wells Street, off Oxford Street, to Lambeth. There he trained many of the later nineteenth century's most famous engineers as well as carrying out a great deal of work for Brunel.[303] He always described himself as an 'engineer' in his fire insurance policies and in 1825 he insured a steam engine house in Cheltenham Place, Lambeth, for £1000, a smith's shop for £2000, an iron foundry for £600, a turnery room for £210, his counting house for £150, a porter's lodge for £90, and stock, utensils and goods for £4850.[304] Less highly capitalised were Hopwood and Tilley, engine makers in Blackfriars Road. An 1819 invoice stated that they manufactured 'all sorts of Engines and Pumps [to supply] Mansions, Houses and Towns with Water, and also for Public Bodies and Shipping [and] Patent valve Cocks, for Canals and Water Works'.[305] They manufactured 11 models of pumping engines, some of which required 22 men to operate them. Yet, their manufactory was valued at the comparatively modest figure of £600 in 1820.[306] All these firms are worth quoting in some detail as examples of the major role London played in the engineering industry throughout the period 1775–1825, and as an illustration of how far its importance increased in the second half of that period.

Glass, Glassware, Ceramics and Non-metallic Mineral Products   Another group of industries which were of comparatively small importance to London individually, but of some significance taken together, may be considered under the joint headings of glass, glassware, ceramics and other non-metallic mineral products. Pigot listed 356 firms engaged in these trades and they insured capital valued at £516,000 in the 1820s. Pigot listed 18 glass manufacturers, 14 manufacturers of glassware and 71 ceramics manufacturers. The latter included 24 potters and 10 water closet manufacturers. There were also 29 brickmakers and 22 Roman cement makers. However, the largest group were statuaries and stone workers who numbered 164. The fire office registers record no less than 35 separate trades. In addition to the above they include plaster of Paris, ornamental composition, slate, emery and glass paper, watch glass, plate glass, looking glass, lamp glass, cut glass, bottle, lustre, tile, glass bead and general china, glass and earthenware manufacturers.

Across such a wide group of manufacturing industries, it is possible only to illustrate the many trades by a few examples. Of course, most firm were small. In these trades as a whole, over 72 per cent insured capital valued at £500 or less in the 1770s. Fifty years later the proportion was still nearly 60 per cent. The number of glasshouses in London was declining drastically from about the middle of the eighteenth century. In 1696 there had been 24 in London; by 1833 there were only three left. However, those that remained were very large indeed, making the full range of lead crystal or white glass, green glass for bottles (a London speciality) and plate glass for windows.[307] In 1821 Reed and Wainwright insured their warehouses and a glass house in Upper East Smithfield for £7290, a steam engine for £1400, the steam engine house for £600, a number of other industrial buildings for £4000, stock and utensils for £10,800 and glass for £4200.[308] This was one of the very largest manufacturing firms in London. A substantial firm of glass bottle manufacturers was Vigne, Neave, Winscote and Walker. In 1774 they insured a manufactory in Gravel Lane, Southwark, for £900, their stock of glass for £200, and other stock and utensils for £3500.[309]

Most ceramics manufacture was outside the metropolis. Even Bow was on the other side of the River Lea and Chelsea was in its final days by 1775. Although very little was left in London by the first quarter of the nineteenth century, there were a few substantial potters in the 1770s. Thomas Wilkinson, for example, insured for £5900 in both 1771 and 1775 at 258 Wapping New Stairs.[310] The Chelsea works was insured for £8560 in 1775 and Bow had been valued at £2500, 15 years earlier.[311] By the 1820s all that was left in London were potters like Henry Bingham who insured his clay shed in Princes Street, Lambeth, for £100 in 1825, as well as stock and utensils valued at £200.[312]

The most important area of manufacture of non-metallic mineral products was artificial stone making, usually known as 'Roman cement' in this period. For the most part the raw material was to be found only in Essex and Kent and London dominated the industry until at least the 1830s. Much the most famous manufacturer was Eleanor Coade, perhaps the most remarkable businesswoman of her era. Born in Exeter in 1733, she came to London in 1766 and set up as a linen draper. Two years later she was describing herself as a merchant but by 1771 she was advertising herself as the proprietor of the business at King's Arms Stairs in Lambeth making artificial stone ornaments. In 1775 she bought another factory in Knightsbridge but sold it four years later. The firm made architectural ornaments, statues, fountains, urns and commemorative and funerary monuments of every kind and was employed by every eminent architect of the day. Its work was exported to the Americas and all over Europe and the Russian Empire. The firm flourished from 1769 to 1833, although she herself died in 1821. She first published her famous *Descriptive Catalogue of Coade's Artificial Stone Manufactory* in 1784 and by 1799 the fame of her products was such that she could open Coade's Gallery in Westminster Bridge Road and publish a guide to its 'Exhibition of Artificial Stone'.[313] In the year she established the business, the stock and utensils in her warehouse in Narrow Wall, Lambeth, were valued at £700. Two years later they were valued at £1400.[314] Interestingly, Daniel Pincot, who had first acquired the business, insured for only £300.[315] Unfortunately, no policy survives for any of her manufactories.

Three other firms worth mentioning are Arnold Goodwin, a plaster of Paris manufacturer,[316] David Hill, a stone potter,[317] and Robert Davis, an emery manufacturer.[318] The first insured two manufactories at 67 Great Guildford Street for £600, as well as stock, utensils and livestock for £550; the second valued a warehouse, storehouse and manufactory in Vauxhall at £850 in addition to stock and utensils insured for £1150; and the third insured his mill and warehouse in Joiner Street, Southwark, for £150, and stock and utensils for £500. All three took out their polices in 1819. There were also a few small brick and tile makers like William Weston. In 1771 he insured his tile kilns in Grays Inn Lane, as it then was, for £100, and stock and utensils for £200.[319]

Musical Instruments Another luxury trade centred on London was the making of musical instruments. There was a huge increase in musical activity in London from about the middle of the eighteenth century and a growing market both for fine instruments of all sorts and also for cheaper versions for children and students, the latter often made by outworkers who supplied the bigger names in the trade.[320] Of 203 British violin and related instrument makers trading in the period 1765–1830, 87 or nearly 43 per cent were to be found in London. Interestingly, London's predominance lessened as time went on; 56 per cent were to be found in London in the period 1765–80, but only 33 per cent in 1815–30.[321] Organbuilding was also pre-eminently a London trade. Thirty were to be found in 1807.[322] Pigot listed 180 makers of musical instruments in 1826–27, of which pianoforte makers were the largest group with 74. Also listed were 23 organbuilders and 22 flute makers. The 19 specialist trades found in the fire office registers include bow and bowstring, drum, French horn, guitar, harp and harp string, harpsichord, metronome, wind instrument, pianoforte key and string, violin and violoncello makers. In the 1820s musical instrument makers insured capital valued at £180,000 in total.

Organbuilding involved a particularly wide range of specialised operations. J. C. Bishop, later to become Bishop and Sons and to trade into the 1850s, founded the firm in Marylebone in 1807. Although he made his own wooden pipes, he relied on specialist makers of metal pipes and on specialist cabinet makers such as George Tooke of 23 Judd Street for the cases. Cheaper organs were made for the trade, the more expensive ones only on commission, most usually for churches. The scale of the trade can be seen from the fact that individual organs were priced up to about £26 in the 1820s, although the cheaper organs supplied to retailers had a wholesale price of only £2 12s 6d to £6 in 1815.[323] However, the archetypal trade was pianoforte making. By the end of the first quarter of the nineteenth century, it had become the most widely owned musical instrument in the world, a symbol of both respectability and solvency, if rarely played. The trade was described in 1824 as 'very lucrative ... 70 guineas being frequently paid for a good article of the kind'. Certainly, three were advertised for sale in 1820 priced at 75, 38 and 24 guineas.[324]

There was a dramatic increase in the size of firm between the 1770s and the 1820s. The average value of capital insured rose by 237 per cent, from £297 to £1003. This was mainly the result of the emergence of a small number of much larger firms since median values of capital insured increased only 28 per cent, from £235 to £300. Over 80 per cent of businesses insured for £500 or less in the

TABLE 4.22 Musical instruments

Capital insured (£)	No. of firms 1770s	Percentage of total	No. of firms 1820s	Percentage of total
100 and under	17	30.4	11	22.9
101–500	28	50.0	22	45.8
501–1000	11	19.6	3	6.3
1001–2999	0	0	7	14.6
3000 and over	0	0	5	10.4
Total	56	100.0	48	100.0

Source: Sun and other London fire office registers

1770s and it was still nearly 69 per cent in the 1820s. The proportion of total capital in the trade insured by firms valuing their risk at £500 or less fell from over 54 per cent in the earlier period to 14 per cent in the later. At the other end of the scale, no firm insured for £3000 in the 1770s; 50 years later over 10 per cent came into the 'large' category by insuring for £3000 or more. Table 4.22 shows the full breakdown by value of capital insured.

Much the largest firms tended to be general manufacturers of musical instruments, although there were also a few larger-scale manufacturers of particular instruments. The increase in size of firm over the period 1775–1825 is illustrated by the fact that a very large business in the 1770s was John and James Simpson, general musical instrument makers in Swithin's Alley.[325] They insured for £1000 in 1769, whereas half a century later in 1819 Astor and Co of 79 Cornhill were insuring for £8500.[326] A large specialist instrument maker, of harps, was Jacob Erol. He insured his manufactory at 23 Berners Street for £500 in 1825, as well as stock and utensils valued at £2800.[327] One pianoforte manufacturer, John Walter of Leicester Street, averaged profits of £520 for the seven years prior to his bankruptcy in 1827.[328] Trading on a much smaller scale was Samuel Keat of 3 Fisher Street, Red Lion Square, who insured for £200 in 1824.[329]

Jewellery There was no more long-established London luxury manufacturing trade than jewellery, nor one where it is more difficult to distinguish between bespoke production and general manufacturing. Nevertheless, it is possible to identify innumerable trades which were clearly related to the manufacture of gold, silver, jewellery, pewter and related products as distinct from the retail gold, silver and jewellery trades. Pigot listed 533 businesses and these insured capital valued at over £350,000 in the 1820s. However, much the largest firms were to be found in the retail sector where Pigot listed 375 firms, and policies contained in the surviving fire office registers suggest £578,000 was insured. There was a large degree of specialisation in the manufacturing sector. Pigot listed 22 separate trades of which working jewellers, working silversmiths, chasers and embossers, and gold and silver beaters were the most numerous with 184, 79, 68 and 49 entries respectively. There were even 13 specialist gold seal and chain makers. The fire office registers contain an even greater degree of detail with 49 separate trades represented. These include specialist gold chain makers, gold, coral and jet setters, gold and silver button and flower and court trimming makers, silver plate manufacturers, silver buckle and button makers and makers of motto rings, necklaces, pearl beads and buttons, pendants and gold watch chains. That this was wholesale manufacturing for sale to retailers is shown by a trade card circulated by William Hunt and Sons of Cheapside, who described themselves as gold workers in the latter years of the eighteenth century. It stated that 'Merchants & Dealers may be Supply'd on the most Reasonable Terms' and described their product range as 'Rich Work in Gold, & Curious Stones. Viz. Watch Chains, Etwees, Snuff Boxes, Sword Hilts, Cane heads, Buckles and Motto Rings: with variety of Trinketts'.[330] It is worth noting that where the trade overlapped with the manufacture of 'toys', in the contemporary sense of trinkets, it had mainly moved to Birmingham.[331] Certainly, the fire office registers contain only four toymakers in the 1770s and three in the 1820s.

Unsurprisingly for an industry of so many specialist trades, few firms were very large. Nearly 96 per cent insured capital valued at £500 or less in the 1770s, 65 per cent at £100 or less. These proportions were still 75 per cent and 38 per cent 50 years later. The average value of capital insured was only £150 in the earlier period, though this did rise more than four-fold to £657 in the later. The comparable figures for the retail trade were £554 and £1541 respectively. However, even in a trade so dominated by small firms, the proportion of total capital accounted for by businesses insuring £500 or less was only just over 17 per cent in the 1820s and 4 per cent of all firms could be described as large. Table 4.23 shows the full breakdown by value of capital insured.

TABLE 4.23 Jewellery

Capital insured (£)	No. of firms 1770s	Percentage of total	No. of firms 1820s	Percentage of total
100 and under	102	64.6	38	38.0
101–500	49	31.0	37	37.0
501–1000	6	3.8	14	14.0
1001–2999	1	0.6	7	7.0
3000 and over	0	0	4	4.0
Total	158	100.0	100	100.0

Source: Sun and other London fire office registers

One very specialised trade in which London predominated was coffin plate making. Abraham Atterbury of 71 Snow Hill insured his business for £1400 in 1771.[332] Another was silver flatting and Mary Godley insured her flatting mill at 18 Aldersgate Street for £350 in 1777, as well as plate valued at £60 and stock and utensils at £300.[333] Substantially larger firms were to be found in the 1820s. Eley and Co described themselves as working silversmiths in 1824 and 1825 when they insured their workshop and warehouse in Lovell's Court, Paternoster Row, for £500, the machinery in the workshop for the same sum, and stock, utensils and fittings valued at £11,550.[334] Similarly, Rundell and Co of Ludgate Hill insured their manufactory for £500 in 1822, a steam engine and other machinery for £500, and stock, utensils and goods valued at £10,000 three years later.[335]

London's Smaller Manufacturing Trades There were many other numerically smaller London manufacturing trades which do not belong to any of the major standard industrial classifications. Pigot listed 411 such firms in 26 separate trades in 1826–27 and the fire office registers record 32 distinct trades. Some of the major trades listed in Pigot are fishing tackle makers (with 28 firms), pen, pencil and quill manufacturers (63), feather makers (88), comb makers (32) and tobacco pipe makers (47). One firm of fishing rod and tackle makers, Bowness and Son of 14 Bell Yard, Temple Bar, claimed in 1838 to have been established for 80 years. They advertised 'Artificial Flies dress'd to any pattern for England, Scotland, Ireland & all parts of the Continent & from the different Treatises on Angling. Every article manufactured by themselves'.[336] Also represented in the fire office registers were billiard table, doll, inkstand, ivory and bone, shirt button, teapot handle and jewel case makers, bird and beast stuffers, whalebone cutters and plaster and wax and clay modellers.

Dodd exaggerated when he wrote that children's toys 'give rise to no inconsiderable amount of manufacturing enterprise. The ball and the bat, the whistle and the drum, the rocking-horse and the mimic cart, the hoop, the doll, the humming-top, the skipping rope – all are sold so very largely as to render the employment of a considerable number of persons.'[337] In fact, Pigot listed only seven doll makers, seven makers of backgammon boards, five rocking-horse makers, one cricket bat maker and two bow and arrow makers. One of the latter was Thomas Waring of Caroline Street, Bedford Square. An invoice of 1809 illustrates how specialised such firms were; he stated that his business was the manufacture of 'Bows, Arrows, Targets, &c'.[338]

The overwhelming majority of such businesses were small although Kirby, Beard and Tovey, pen makers of 46 Cannon Street, insured their business for £3000 in 1822,[339] and a feather manufacturer, Joseph Defriez of 3 Houndsditch, his for £2850 two years later.[340] Nearly 50 years earlier, in 1775, William Rogers, a tobacco pipe manufacturer, insured his kiln house and workshops at 2 Hermitage Bridge for £250, the kiln for £80, a warehouse for £210, and stock and utensils valued at £1300.[341] Much more typical in the 1770s were Benjamin Crayer, a doll carver at 132 Golden Lane, who insured stock and utensils for £200 in 1773;[342] Charles Lacey, a combmaker in Great Turnstile, who insured stock and utensils for £340 in 1777;[343] and the exotically named Onesimus Ustonson, who was a fishing tackle maker at 205 Fleet Street and insured for £550 in 1773.[344] Examples from the 1820s were John Chamberlain, a billiard table maker of 15–17 Sherborn Lane, who insured for £350 in 1822;[345] Anthony Bazzoni, a wax and composition doll maker at 23 Kingsgate Street, who insured for £270 in 1824;[346] and Joseph Rhoades, an ebony inkstand maker, who insured his manufactory at 5 James Street for £150 the previous year as well as stock and utensils valued at £240.[347]

Employment in Manufacturing

The 1841 Census showed that just over a third of London's working population was employed in manufacturing. It has been

TABLE 4.24 Employment in trade or manufacturing, 1811–31

Year	Total number of families	Number engaged in manufacturing	Percentage engaged in trade or manufacturing
1811	242,040	151,487	62.6
1821	287,101	184,239	64.2
1831	347,556	196,620	56.6

Source: 1831 Census

suggested that this demonstrates the comparatively small part played by manufacturing in the economy of the metropolis. In a recent study it is said of London that 'at no time during the nineteenth century did industry provide the bulk of its employment'.[348] This is to misunderstand the structure of industry both in London and other parts of Britain. In fact, no nineteenth-century Census showed the proportion of manufacturing to total employment as more than 38 per cent for Britain as a whole. In 1881 it was as low as 33 per cent. In 1841 the comparable figures for London and Britain as a whole were 34 per cent and 35 per cent. However, the national figure includes many thousands, possibly tens of thousands, of people, women in particular, who were engaged in bespoke production and should more properly be classified under retailing. This would probably bring the national proportion of employment in manufacturing to below the London percentage. Either way, the point is that there was little significant difference between London and the rest of the country in manufacturing employment.

Unfortunately, the statistical evidence is both sparse and inconsistent for the period 1775–1825, indeed virtually non-existent prior to 1800. Nevertheless, it is possible to put together an outline picture for the first three decades of the nineteenth century and to attempt a much fuller analysis of the 1841 Census than has previously been deemed practicable. With regard to the 1811–31 Censuses, a breakdown is included of 'families in trade or manufacture'. Unfortunately, no attempt is made in the 1811 and 1821 Censuses to distinguish between 'trade', by which is meant the distributive trades, and 'manufacture'. After an increase between 1811 and 1821, from 62.6 per cent to 64.2 per cent, the proportion decreased to 56.6 per cent in 1831 (see Table 4.24). Such a large decrease is difficult to explain although it should be noted that the proportion of families shown to be engaged in either no form of employment or in the professions rose from 34.8 per cent in 1821 to 42.5 per cent in 1831. Although increasing wealth could have accounted in part for such a dramatic shift, it is far more likely that it is the result of statistical and methodological inconsistencies between the Censuses of 1821 and 1831, especially since those of 1811 and 1821 are so close.

The 1831 Census was the first to attempt a detailed breakdown of employment in London, albeit only for males aged 20 and over. The total count was 180,755 of which 53,687, or 30 per cent, were in manufacturing trades. Because the count omitted both males aged under 20, who comprised about 20 per cent of the male population, and women, who accounted for over a quarter of total employment, it is impossible to draw conclusions from the figures for particular trades since some employed more young people than others, for example those particularly associated with apprenticeship, and employment of women was concentrated in the textile and clothing industries. Most heavily represented in the count are manufacture of metal goods (with about 10,000 employees), furniture (7000), paper, printing and publishing (5000), leather and leather goods (4000), coachbuilding, shipbuilding and textiles (3000 each).

It has been fashionable to dismiss the analysis of employment in the published 1841 Census statistics as of little value. However, this is mainly because of an inadequate count of people employed in domestic service. Certainly, there is little to suggest that the picture it presents of employment in manufacturing is significantly inaccurate. The original editors recognised that

> The residue of the population whose occupations are entirely unaccounted for ... would at first appear to be a large proportion. It must however be remembered that this comprehends both sexes and all ages ... only 2½% are males above 20 years of age ... The number of women above 20 years of age ... consists generally of unmarried women living with their parents, and of the wives of professional men or shopkeepers, living upon the earnings but not considered as carrying on the occupations of their husbands.[349]

The 1841 Census identified 135,667 persons employed in manufacturing in London, 32.6 per cent of the total (415,617) which can be identified with specific industrial sectors. Table 4.25 shows the breakdown by manufacturing sector.

TABLE 4.25 Employment in manufacturing in 1841

Manufacturing sector	Number of employees	% of total	% of firms 1826–27	% of capital 1820s
Metals	944	0.7	0.4	0.2
Non-metallic products	2757	2.0	2.5	3.0
Chemicals	1414	1.0	2.7	4.4
Metal goods	18,042	13.3	8.5	6.7
Engineering	7095	5.2	2.7	2.3
Shipbuilding	3770	2.8	1.5	1.6
Coachbuilding	6646	4.9	3.9	4.6
Watchmaking	4440	3.3	4.3	1.3
Precision instruments	656	0.5	1.8	0.6
Food, drink and tobacco	3133	2.3	4.3	17.1
Textiles	21,334	15.7	8.4	13.3
Leather	10,246	7.6	6.8	7.9
Clothing	10,682	7.9	7.8	7.5
Timber	13,687	10.1	16.0	5.4
Furniture	13,457	9.9	11.8	6.9
Printing and publishing	11,876	8.8	8.9	12.9
Other manufacturing	5488	4.0	7.7	4.1
Total	135,667	100.0	100.0	100.0

Source: 1841 Census; Pigot and Co, *London and Provincial New Commercial Directory for 1826–27*; and Sun and other fire office registers

The Census also identified 86,476 people who cannot be associated with any specific manufacturing trade. The majority were described as 'labourers (unspecified)', of whom there were 50,209; 'clerks', of whom there were 20,417; and 'unspecified employees', of whom there were 6974. A large proportion of these would have been employed in the manufacturing trades, particularly those which were highly labour intensive such as metal goods, engineering, ship- and coachbuilding and manufacture of food and drink. It is reasonable to estimate that around 40 per cent of such people were employed in manufacturing, that is about 35,000. This would bring total employment in manufacturing in London to about 170,000, just over one-third of all employment.

The question mark over the accuracy of the 1841 Census with regard to employment arises from the fact that for Britain as a whole male employment was 27.4 per cent of the total population compared with a little over 31 per cent in 1851, 1861 and 1871. This does suggest a small but significant degree of under-counting, although not one which would invalidate the broad orders of magnitude to be found for employment in London. Overall, Table 4.25 shows that the major areas of manufacturing employment were to be found in textiles (21,000), metal goods (18,000), the timber trades (14,000), furniture (13,000), printing and publishing (12,000), and leather and clothing (10,000 each). The numbers of employees to be found in clerical and general labouring occupation would add an average of about 25 per cent to these figures. This latter consideration makes it difficult to attempt any analysis of individual trades by degrees of labour or capital intensity. However, in very broad terms, the most labour intensive trades were metal goods (where employment was 13.3 per cent of the total and insured capital 6.7 per cent), engineering (5.2 per cent compared with 2.3 per cent) and the timber trades (10.1 per cent compared with 5.4 per cent). The most capital intensive were food, drink and tobacco (2.3 per cent compared with 17.1 per cent), printing and publishing (8.8 per cent compared with 12.9 per cent) and chemicals (1.0 per cent compared with 4.4 per cent). Again, this illustrates how diverse were London's manufacturing trades.

In many ways, it is easier to analyse the 1841 Census employment data for individual specialised trades than it is for broad industrial sectors. For many trades it is possible to compare directly the Census employment data with a count of firms in the London *Post Office Directory* for 1841. This listed just under 47,000 businesses, much the same as Pigot's total for 1826–27. Table 4.26 shows selected examples of numbers of firms and employees where there was likely to have been both comparatively low numbers of self-employed persons and of general labourers and clerical staff.

These examples show the very small scale of firms in terms of numbers employed. Overall, of 96 discretely identifiable manufacturing trades where numbers of employers and employees can be directly compared in 1841, 35 employed 5 people or less, 30 employed 6 to 10, 26 employed 10 to 20 and only 5 more than 20. The only major industry within which average numbers employed exceeded 30 was shipbuilding. The average was just over ten, or nearly thirteen if general labourers and clerical staff are included. These figures are perfectly consistent with the 1851 Census, when a count was made

TABLE 4.26 Numbers of employers and employees in selected trades, 1841

Manufacturing trade	Employers	Employees	Average no. of employees
Blue	11	52	4.7
Blacking	38	102	2.7
Glue and size	14	54	3.9
Filemaker	13	99	7.6
Guns	109	1109	10.2
Mast and block	38	395	10.4
Barometers	25	85	3.4
Math. instruments	61	395	6.5
Trusses	28	74	2.6
Soda water	45	259	5.8
Floorcloth	43	178	4.1
Rope and twine	94	1192	12.7
Trunks	96	1024	10.7
Backs	11	39	3.5
Bed and mattress	56	330	5.9
Looking glasses	48	134	2.8
Card	16	174	10.9
Pencils	35	157	4.5
Fishing tackle	31	102	3.3
Tobacco pipes	30	118	3.9

Source: 1841 Census; and *Post Office London Directory*

of employment by individual firm. This revealed that 86 per cent of people in London were employed in firms with ten employees or less, 75 per cent with firms employing five or less. Only 1.6 per cent were employed by firms with over 50 employees.

There are also a few tantalising glimpses of employment in individual firms throughout the period 1775–1825 which, if they scarcely amount to anything like a full picture of manufacturing employment in London, at least throw light on a few examples which are likely to be not untypical of the metropolis as a whole. A few exemplify the overwhelming majority of small firms, such as James Taylor, a typefounder in Old Bailey, who employed two people in 1827; Charles Thompson, a bookbinder in Blackfriars, who employed three apprentices in 1831; Frederick Martin, the silk ribbon manufacturer, who employed eight in the same year; Spratley and Johnson, coach axle manufacturers in Long Acre, who employed 12 in 1827;[350] and Bishop and Son, organbuilders in Marylebone, who employed 15 in 1825.[351] However, there are examples of very much larger firms too: Christy's the hatmakers employed 1500 at their factory in Bermondsey in 1843;[352] Green and Wigram the shipbuilders employed between 600 and 800 at their Blackwall yard in the early part of the nineteenth century;[353] Harwood and Co, wallpaper manufacturers, employed 600 at their Cumberland Place factory in 1813;[354] Seddons the cabinet makers employed 400 in 1786;[355] and in the same year Hatchett and Boyes the coachmaker were described as employing 'several hundred workmen'.[356] Details also survive of several medium-sized employers such as Henry Maudslay the engineer, who employed 80 people in his Lambeth works in 1810;[357] Thwaites and Reed, the Clerkenwell clockmakers, who employed 35 to 40 between 1828 and 1830;[358] and Dowdings, who were coopers in Wapping and employed 50 to 60 people between 1796 and 1799.[359]

CHAPTER 5

The Construction Trades in London

In his classic study *Georgian London*, first published in 1948, Sir John Summerson described twin 'foundation stones' for the building of the metropolis between 1714 and 1830: taste and wealth.[1] Undoubtedly both played a major role, especially in the evolution of the great squares to the west of the city. However, with regard to the metropolis as a whole, the single major factor was the huge growth in population. Over the period 1775–1825, the population of London grew by at least 600,000, from perhaps three-quarters of a million to over 1,350,000. In the first half of the eighteenth century, London's population had been static at around 675,000, although the evidence is that its housing stock may have risen from about 60,000 to 75,000. The first four Censuses reveal a further huge growth in housing stock; from 121,189 in 1801 to 141,732 in 1811, 164,681 in 1821 and 196,666 in 1831. This was an increase of 62 per cent between 1801 and 1831, and of the order of 160 per cent between the 1750s and 1831.

The last quarter of the eighteenth century and the first quarter of the nineteenth saw enormous changes in the organisation of the construction industry, especially in London. What did not change was that at the heart of the construction trade, especially for cheaper housing, was the speculative builder. In Summerson's evocative words:

> the mainspring of London's expansion for three hundred years, has always been a person of the most various characteristics. Sometimes he has been a lord, sometimes little more than a labourer; sometimes a substantial capitalist, sometimes a craftsman, with only his skill and time to adventure; sometimes an architect, sometimes a bricklayer or carpenter; sometimes a lawyer, a mechanic, a schoolmaster, a quack, an actor – indeed, almost any class, trade or profession.[2]

Summerson might also have added that the speculative builder could be of either sex. One of the major London builders in the 1770s was Elizabeth Harrison of Drury Lane. She described herself as a 'carpenter' in the fire insurance policy she took out in 1771 to cover 34 houses valued at £2380. She also insured a workshop for £20 and stock and utensils for £50. The following year she insured nine houses for £1660.[3] She was by no means unique. In 1774 Mary Grisson of 14 Billiter Lane, who described herself as a 'bricklayer', insured two houses under construction for £800.[4]

Another factor which did not change over the period 1775–1825 was the distinction between the 'financier' who might speculate in both land and the houses built on it, and the building craftsman who was far more likely to speculate in houses alone. However, the way this was organised did change. Traditionally, small speculators continued to take a building lease of one or more plots on somebody else's land where they built their houses and sold them with the lease. This method was adopted by building craftsmen working in groups, each contributing its own trade, so that very little capital was required. These small master craftsmen were most usually bricklayers or carpenters, but might also be joiners, painters, masons, plumbers or glaziers. They employed only those in their own trade and confined themselves to their own trade. It was very much in their interests to build the tall, narrow, terraced 'Georgian' town house to maximise the numbers to be got on to the site. There were also master builders who in addition directly sub-contracted other trades. Much of Georgian London was built without any clear line of demarcation between the two. However, increasingly from the last quarter of the eighteenth century onwards, group working disappeared and a clear distinction began to emerge between 'master craftsmen', who had become 'employers' of labour in their own trade and sub-contractors of skills in other trades, but who nevertheless took responsibility for the whole building, and 'master builders' who employed both skilled men from every trade and unskilled labourers. As early as 1763 Thomas Mortimer noted:

> Of late years the capital masters of carpentry have assumed the name of Builders ... for this reason, because they make an estimate of the total expense of a House and contract for the execution of the whole for the amount of their estimate; for they take upon themselves the providing of all materials and employ their own Masons, Plumbers, Smiths, etc. where-

as formerly it was the custom for gentlemen and merchants to apply to the several masters in each branch and employ them in executing their Plans: this indeed is sometimes the case at present, but very rarely, particularly with regard to Houses, whole streets having been of late erected by Builders.[5]

The master builders might emerge from any of the construction trades. The fire office registers contain policies for construction firms describing themselves variously as builders, carpenters, joiners, bricklayers, plasterers, plumbers, painters, glaziers, slaters and masons. In many instances the same firm describes itself differently in different policies, sometimes even in the same year. For example, John Matthews of Hercules Buildings, Lambeth, took out three policies in 1771; in two of these he described himself as a plasterer, but in the third as a builder.[6] Half a century later even Thomas Cubitt sometimes described himself as a builder and at other times as a carpenter.

Summerson described house building in London throughout the eighteenth and into the first third of the nineteenth centuries as coming 'in waves', two of which were the period from about 1760 onwards and the decade or so following the Napoleonic war, with very little activity during the war years themselves from 1793 to 1815.[7] The latter assertion seems doubtful since the Census shows that London's occupied housing stock increased by over 20,000, or 17 per cent, between 1801 and 1811. What cannot be in doubt is that after the war there was what has been described as 'an almost unbroken boom in building'.[8] Between 1811 and 1831 the number of occupied houses in London increased by 55,000 or 39 per cent. This boom extended far beyond domestic housing; there were larger numbers than ever before of contracts for buildings of great size and cost such as docks, bridges, churches, theatres, and barracks commissioned by the government, public authorities or joint stock companies. Competitive tendering became widespread. Nevertheless, most of the work was still the building of domestic houses and the period 1775–1825 saw Somers Town and Camden Town emerge from former agricultural land and Islington evolve as the healthier alternative to the City. Between 1801 and 1831 the populations of Chelsea, Kensington, Hackney and Bethnal Green increased by over 150 per cent and those of St Pancras, Poplar, Newington and Lambeth more than trebled.

Buildings were estimated to comprise about 15 per cent of national capital in 1812 with very little change over the next twenty years.[9] Self-evidently the building industry occupied a prominent position in the national economy throughout the period 1775–1825, not least as a source of 'products' which helped underpin economic growth. The construction trades were also huge consumers of both raw materials and the finished products of other trades, especially timber, bricks, tiles, pipes, paint, wallpaper, plaster and lime. They were also major users of transport services.

Even though the industry was subject to so many political, economic and seasonal fluctuations, both the surviving fire office registers and London trade directories do provide the means of establishing its size with some accuracy in the 1820s. Pigot in 1826–27 listed 201 builders and 667 bricklayers and plasterers. There were also 1197 carpenters. Analysis of the fire office policy registers suggests that in the 1820s just under 38 per cent were involved in the construction industry, the rest being general carpenters. On this basis about 450 were involved in the building trade. Pigot also listed 1013 painters, plumbers and glaziers, 110 paperhangers, 31 slaters, 23 lath renders and 11 paviours. In total this was over 2500 firms, more than 5 per cent of all London businesses.

Unlike many other trades, increasing demand for its products was met in the construction industry by a proliferation of small firms rather than by increases in the size of firm or improvements in productivity. Also unlike almost every other industry in London, there was no increase either in the average size of firm or in the numbers of larger firms over the period 1775–1825. Few advances were made in technology and the industry remained highly labour intensive. This can be measured in a number of ways. Even in the general building sector, which was much larger in firm size than the sector concerned with installation of fixtures and fittings and building completion work, the average size of capital insured remained virtually unchanged at £1120 in the 1770s and £1113 in the 1820s. While few builders were very small in size, only 7 per cent insured for £100 or less in both the 1770s and 1820s, most insured for between £100 and £1000, 63 per cent in the 1770s and 61 per cent in the 1820s. The proportion of 'large' firms insuring for £3000 or more declined from 9 per cent in the 1770s to 5 per cent 50 years later. Table 5.1 shows the full breakdown by value of capital insured.

Another measure of the continuity of size of firm is that in both

TABLE 5.1 General building and construction

Capital insured (£)	No. of firms 1770s	Percentage of total	No. of firms 1820s	Percentage of total
100 and under	38	7.2	24	7.3
101–500	190	35.8	108	32.8
501–1000	143	26.9	94	28.6
1001–2999	113	21.3	86	26.1
3000 and over	47	8.9	17	5.2
Total	531	100.0	329	100.0

Source: Sun and other London fire office registers

the 1770s and the 1820s just over 11 per cent of all capital insured by general builders was accounted for by small firms individually insuring for £500 or less. The fire insurance registers also reveal that there was no change in the average value of individual houses insured over the period 1775–1825. Usually the fire insurance policies specified that these were unfinished or empty. A random 15 per cent sample covered 80 firms in the 1770s and 50 in the 1820s. In the earlier period 506 houses were insured for £122,900; in the later 342 for £83,270. Remarkably, this gives an average value of £243 in both periods, although it must be noted that building costs were falling, certainly for the more humble dwelling. It has been estimated that their unit cost fell from 3¾d per cubic foot in 1815 to 2½d in 1830.[10] Obviously, many properties under construction were of considerably greater value than the average: in 1777 Edward Gray, who described himself as a bricklayer, insured five unfinished houses in Grosvenor Square for £8300.[11] Nearly half a century later in 1825, James Sim, a builder at 24 Little Torrington Street, insured 15 houses valued at £18,450.[12] At the other end of the scale were the six houses insured for £300 by Joseph Downey in Mare Street, Hackney.[13]

It has been observed that London builders rarely worked more than a mile or two from their yards and that most erected fewer than ten properties a year.[14] Again the fire office registers throw considerable light on this. Table 5.2 shows that nearly 77 per cent built five houses or less in 1775 and only 9 per cent erected more than ten; 50 years later these proportions were little changed at 74 per cent

TABLE 5.2 Numbers of houses built by individual builders in 1775 and 1825

Number of houses built	1775	Percentage of total	1825	Percentage of total
5 and under	109	76.7	68	73.9
6–10	20	14.1	18	19.6
10 and over	13	9.2	6	6.5
Total	142	100.0	92	100.0

Source: Sun and other London fire office registers

and 7 per cent. The fire office registers also show that the median value of capital insured was £600 in the 1770s and £700 50 years later. It has already been seen that the average value of house insured was £243; this suggests that the median number of houses under construction by individual builders was between two and three in both the 1770s and the 1820s. Little changed in the next generation: in North Kensington it took 31 firms to erect 137 houses in 1845, with only two builders responsible for more than 11 each. Indeed, as late as 1872 three-quarters of building firms built six houses or less in a year.[15]

Nevertheless, there were larger firms. Jonathan Mann, who described himself simply as a carpenter, insured 23 houses in and around Berkeley Square, 15 of which were specified as unfinished, for the enormous sum of £16,100 in 1775.[16] The previous year Thomas Nicholl had insured six unfinished houses for £5500; three years later he insured his workshops at 16 Margaret Street for £900, and stock and utensils for £800.[17] In 1820 Seth Smith insured 13 houses, seven of them unfinished, for £7900. He also insured his extensive workshops in Davies Street for £2400, and stock, utensils and livestock for another £1000.[18] A few building firms flourished over a very long period, such as the Burnells. John Burnell of 25 Fleet Market insured a number of houses and other buildings under construction in the 1770s, in 1772 alone valuing them at £4400. By the 1820s he had been succeeded by his son George who insured four houses for £5300 in 1819, as well as a workshop at 21 Bartlett's Buildings, Holborn, for £350, and stock and utensils for the same amount. George insured two more houses in 1821 and three in 1824.[19]

There could be considerable variation from year to year in the workload carried out by individual firms, especially the very largest. The development of Somers Town on the old Brill Farm took place between about 1780 and 1830.[20] One of the major developers was John McGill of 34 Middlesex Street. He insured five houses for £5000 in 1819, eleven for £11,400 in 1821, four for £3200 in 1822, seven houses and other work in hand for £8700 in 1824 and four coach houses under construction for £1000 in 1825.[21] The great Thomas Cubitt insured 32 houses for £29,400 with the Sun between 1821 and 1825.[22] These properties represented only a small part of his work in the area of his huge building yard and workshops in Grays Inn Road. From the 1820s until his death in 1855 he worked on a large scale at Highbury Park in Islington, on the south side of Tavistock Square, in Woburn Place, Endsleigh Street and Gordon Square, in Pimlico and in Belgrave and Eaton Squares. The records of his bankers, Smith's in Lombard Street, show that he used an advance of £10,000 to build four houses in Eaton Place in 1828 and ten years later deposited deeds with them for properties valued at £264,120.[23] The scale of Cubitt's activity was unique. Nevertheless, James Burton erected 900 houses on the Foundling Hospital and Bedford estates between 1793 and 1803 and a century earlier Nicholas Barbon had worked on a similar scale in developing Lincoln's Inn Fields, the Strand and Soho.[24] In the area of public buildings, Alexander Copland built Covent Garden Theatre, St Katharine's Docks and a number of military barracks from about 1800 till his death in 1834. It was estimated that his government contracts for barracks alone totalled £1.3 million in the period 1796–1806.[25]

In addition to the many firms engaged in the actual construction of buildings there were large numbers engaged in the complementary trades involved in installation of fixtures and fittings and in building completion work. It has already been noted that Pigot listed 1013 plumbers, painters and glaziers and 110 paperhangers in 1826–27. Many firms combined several of these trades. A trade card circulated about 1820 by Elizabeth Procter of 50 Shoe Lane described the business as plumber, glazier and painter and promised 'Writing, Graining, Marbling and Gilding. Water Closets and Hydraulic Pumps, Fixed and Repaired'. About the same time another trade card was circulated by one Lindsay of 7 St Martin's Lane. He called himself painter, glazier and plumber and undertook 'Writing, Gilding, Transparencies

TABLE 5.3 Installation of fixtures and fittings and building completion work

Capital insured (£)	No. of firms 1770s	Percentage of total	No. of firms 1820s	Percentage of total
100 and under	108	46.2	67	36.8
101–500	79	33.8	72	39.6
501–1000	23	9.8	24	13.2
1001–2999	20	8.5	18	9.9
3000 and over	4	1.7	1	0.5
Total	234	100.0	182	100.0

Source: Sun and other London fire office registers

&c., Forced Pumps and Water Closets, Beer Engines &c. Ornamental Paper Hanging in all its Branches – Colouring in Distemper &c'.[26]

Although these were predominantly much smaller businesses, they none the less accounted for capital insured in the 1820s to the value of nearly half a million pounds. In both the 1770s and the 1820s the average value of capital insured was £406, only about a third of that for the building trade proper. In the earlier period, 80 per cent of businesses insured for £500 or less, 46 per cent for £100 or less. Fifty years later these proportions were little changed at 78 per cent and 40 per cent. Very few firms insured capital valued at £3000 or more. Only 10 per cent insured for £1000 or more in either period and most of these would have also been directly involved in construction work in addition to their main trades. Thus, for example, James Lawrence, a plumber, painter and glazier in Hatton Garden, insured for £3200 in 1775, but this included 12 houses valued at £2700.[27] Small firms, insuring £500 or less, accounted for well over a third of all capital insured in these trades in the 1770s and this decreased very little to 29 per cent by the 1820s. Table 5.3 shows the full breakdown by value of capital insured.

Among specialist firms, William Willson, a lath render at 14 Cleveland Street, Fitzroy Square, insured stock and utensils for £1150 in both 1819 and 1823,[28] and Thomas Wiltshire and Sons, paperhangers in Ball Alley, insured stock and utensils for £1500 and fittings for £300 in the latter year.[29] Four years earlier a plumber, Edward Ottey, insured his workshop in Cartaret Street, Westminster, for £400, and stock and utensils for £750.[30]

Bankruptcy files do not suggest that profit levels were particularly high, either in the building or in the fixtures, fittings or completion trades. For 15 firms the average start-up capital was £1424 and average annual profits just £364, the latter representing 25.6 per cent of the former. One moderately large firm of builders was Ackroyd and Rowles in King Street, Long Acre. Over an 11-year period prior to their bankruptcy in 1828 they averaged annual profits of £783. Typical of firms in the other trades were Teeling Cusins, a paperhanger in Little Brook Street, John Fiander, a plumber in Dover Street and John Lamb, a glazier in Newington Causeway. The first two were declared bankrupt in 1830 and the third in 1824. Their average profits were £228 (over five years), £356 (ten and a quarter years) and £400 (six and a half years).[31]

Employment in the Construction Trades

Employment in building and construction was very large throughout this period. The 1831 Census recorded 15,222 men aged 20 and over employed in nine trades under the general heading 'builder'. A further 2431 were shown under the separate headings of plumbers, glaziers and paperhangers and over 5000 of those shown as carpenters are also likely to have been in the building trade. With a few others in trades such as lath rending, the total was about 23,000. However, the 1831 Census made no provision for general labourers. The 1841 Census is the first which enables any definitive estimate to be made of employment in the construction trades. The total count for the various separately identified building occupations was 39,300. To this must be added about 20,000 persons shown as general labourers, giving a total of nearly 60,000, which was 12 per cent of total employment in London. The major occupations were:

Painters, plumbers and glaziers	11500
Carpenters	6900
Bricklayers	6700
Masons	4100
Plasterers	2600
Builders	1800
Plasterers	600
Lath renders	200

Reliable estimates exist for employment by a number of London's major builders during the period 1775–1825. Thomas Cubitt is variously estimated to have employed between one and two thousand men once he had opted to employ direct labour in and working out of his huge 11-acre yard in Grays Inn Road. Rather earlier, at the turn of the century, Alexander Copland employed 700 men. Thomas Burton, who succeeded James Burton, employed an average of 170 between 1825 and 1832, mainly for repairs and alterations work in the City and West End.[32]

. . . .
London and the Consumer Revolution

By 1826–27 nearly half of London's 49,000 businesses were involved in wholesale or, more particularly, retail distribution. These accounted for 35 per cent of all capital insured in the 1820s and 37 per cent of employment. In total there were 22,671 firms, which insured nearly £26 million and employed over 188,000 people. Although no such precise estimate can be made for the last quarter of the eighteenth century, it is probable that by the 1770s there were already at least 14,000 businesses engaged in wholesale and retail distribution. They insured capital valued at nearly £7 million, which was about one-third of all commercial capital insured in London.

These figures alone, derived from the fire office registers and London trade directories, form a new and definitive background to any discussion of whether or not a consumer revolution took place in eighteenth-century England, and, if it did, what part London played. This chapter discusses trade by trade the enormously complex and very highly sophisticated wholesale and retail distribution infra-structure which had evolved in London by the period 1775–1825.

Neil McKendrick powerfully summarised the thesis developed by Brewer, Plumb and himself:

> There was a consumer boom in England in the eighteenth century. In the third quarter of the century, that boom reached revolutionary propor-tions. Men, and in particular women, bought as never before ... the later eighteenth century saw such a convulsion of getting and spending, such an eruption of new prosperity, and such an explosion of new production and marketing techniques, that a greater proportion of the population than in any previous society in human history was able to enjoy the

pleasures of buying consumer goods. They bought not only necessities, but decencies, and even luxuries ... the same unmistakable breakthrough occurred in consumption as occurred in production ... Just as the Industrial revolution ... marks one of the great discontinuities of history [so] does the matching revolution in consumption. For the consumer revolution was the necessary analogue to the industrial revolution, the necessary convulsion on the demand side of the equation to match the convulsion on the supply side.[1]

Chapter 4 demonstrated clearly the extent to which London itself contributed to both the 'explosion of new production ... techniques' and the 'unmistakable breakthrough ... in production'. Indeed, no feature of this consumer revolution would have been possible without London. On the one hand, its unrivalled size enabled it to become the showcase for and arbiter of fashion, and the means whereby consumer behaviour throughout the entire kingdom could be influenced, not only in the clothing market, but in every other; on the other hand, and again in McKendrick's words:

> small items of household consumption offered the lure of profit for those who flocked to make and sell them. There was a vast and growing market clamouring to buy. For those with the skills to manufacture and to market, the opportunities were legion. It was not for nothing that the first industries to blossom in the Industrial Revolution were more characteristically to be found in the consumer sector than in the heavy industrial sector. The beauty of smallness had not been recognised in the eighteenth century, but the profitability of such unconsidered trifles as pans and nails, buttons and forks, knobs and knockers, pots and pans, hats and coats, gloves and shoes certainly had.[2]

The contribution to and significance of all these trades, and many others, great and small, luxury and necessity, for the consumer revolution are quantified below. Two of the other major contributors to the debate about retailing in England, the Muis and David Alexander, have rather missed the point of much of what was happening in eighteenth-century London. Although the Muis attempt to define the channels through which goods reached the consumer, they do not fully understand the nature of retailing in this period. Nevertheless, they do recognise the intricate network and great variety of shops which had emerged by the middle of the eighteenth century.[3] David Alexander did acknowledge that eighteenth-century retailing 'focused on the London market', but mistakenly believed that 'shopkeepers drew most of their trade from a small class of highly paid workers, tradesmen, farmers, gentry and aristocracy'.[4] This may or may not have been true of the typical small market town; but that it most certainly was not the case in London will be shown in a number of trades where large-scale retailers of comparatively luxurious goods were to be found in the very poorest districts. As an example, Shadwell High Street in 1817 had 16 grocers, tea dealers and cheesemongers, nine boot- and shoemakers, six haberdashers and hosiers, four linen drapers, three wine merchants, three tailors, two booksellers, two stationers, two oil and colourmen and a silversmith. Certainly, when the old St James's Market was demolished to make way for the building of Regent Street between 1813 and 1820, Nash took great care to ensure that a new market area was provided between Regent Street and Haymarket and that it was surrounded by 'domestic' shops specifically to serve the local population.[5]

By the second half of the eighteenth century London's shops were the wonder of the world:

> High-grade retailing was becoming the province of stylish shops. Superior streets in both the West End and the City gloried in all manner of quality suppliers: upholsterers, glovers, goldsmiths, stationers, cartographers, mathematical-instrument-makers, music publishers, tailors, milliners, perfumiers, jewellers, chemists, druggists, tea and coffee merchants, wine and spirit merchants, pastry cooks, porcelain, china and glass shops, woollen- and linen-drapers, boot- and shoemakers, tobacconists, gold and silver lacemen, carpet manufacturers, parasol makers, furriers, seedsmen and florists, lampmakers – and scores more.[6]

Retailing in London had progressed far beyond the generalisation made for the eighteenth century by Dorothy Davis in her *History of Shopping* that 'no two manufactured articles could be relied on to be exactly alike. About their materials, their design, their workmanship, the buyer could only guess.'[7] This was by no means true of London by the last quarter of the eighteenth century.

Shopping as a leisure activity was born in Georgian London. Georg Christoph Lichtenberg recorded in his *Visits to England* an account of a stroll along Cheapside and Fleet Street in January 1775:

> On both sides tall houses with plate glass windows. The lower floors consist of shops and seem to be made entirely of glass, many thousand candles light up silverware, engravings, books, clocks, glass, pewter,

paintings, women's finery, modish and otherwise, gold, precious stones, steel work and endless coffee-rooms and lottery offices. The street looks as though it were illuminated for some festivity: the apothecaries and druggists display glasses filled with gay-coloured spirits … The confectioners dazzle your eyes with their candelabra and tickle your nose with their wares … In these hang festoons of Spanish grapes, alternating with pineapples, and pyramids of apples and oranges … All this appears like an enchantment to the unaccustomed eye.[8]

On the other hand, retailers catering for customers at the other end of the social spectrum were nothing like so grand. For them 'most shops were small and dark, their wares stacked behind the counter in piles which reached as high as the ceiling. Some of them were little more than shacks propped up against the side of houses'.[9] There was nothing 'to discourage anyone who occupied the ground floor of a house and could get a few goods together, from keeping a shop'.[10]

Of course, all these accounts, either contemporary or modern, are necessarily impressionistic. But now, for the first time, analysis of the fire office registers enables a quantitative assessment to be undertaken. Again, the over-riding background factors are London's enormous size and wealth. These determined that, as in manufacturing, clothing and household goods would predominate in both the wholesale and retail sectors, and that within each there would be an important luxury element.

Wholesale Distribution

No more in the eighteenth and nineteenth centuries than in the twentieth is it possible to be sure whether a great many firms were wholesalers or retailers. In practice they were very often both. Thousands of surviving trade cards, shopbills, handbills, newspaper advertisements and invoices use the words 'wholesale and retail'. Very often, and particularly in the clothing and textile trades, there was another element to the distinction in that London houses often sold retail within the metropolis and wholesale to provincial retailers. However, for the purposes of this book firms are assumed to be predominantly retail unless there is good evidence in the fire office registers to the contrary.

Although there were a great many food, drink and tobacco

wholesalers in London (Pigot listed 806 in 1826–27), comparatively few policies survive in the fire office registers. Wholesale tea dealers and meat and fruit wholesalers located at the various markets comprised the largest numbers. Pigot listed 120 wholesale tea dealers and 58 wholesale grocers. Some operated on a very considerable scale and as early as 1750 London's wholesale cheesemongers monopolised the trade in Cheshire cheese, importing nearly 4200 tons a year into the capital.[11] The average value of capital insured by food wholesalers rose from £3668 in the 1770s to £4701 in the 1820s; median values trebled from £1000 to £3000. Most individual firms were substantial in size. In the 1770s nearly half insured capital valued at £1000 or more, and 50 years later the proportion had risen to nearly three-quarters. The percentages of really large firms insuring for £3000 or more were 35 and 52 respectively.

One of the largest wholesale grocers in the 1770s was Davison and Newman at 44 Fenchurch Street. Founded in 1650, they insured for £16,000 in 1772[12] and when Abraham Davison died in 1799 his estate was worth £600,000.[13] The term 'wholesaler' is used far more commonly in the 1820s, although Joseph Travers and Sons, who were in business from about 1666 to the latter part of the twentieth century, described themselves as 'wholesale dealers in groceries' from 1728. In 1820 they insured their warehouse at 19 St Swithin's Lane for £2000 and its contents for £12,000. Seven years later a single order was valued at over £5000.[14] In 1823 Kymer and Co, wholesale grocers at 38 Mincing Lane, insured stock, utensils and goods valued at the immense sum of £30,000.[15] In the same year Francis and Child, tea and coffee dealers at 13 Nag's Head Court off Gracechurch Street, insured for £21,000.[16] Harben and Larking were very large cheesemongers. Their warehouse at 8 Whitechapel was insured for £2150 in 1824, and stock, utensils and goods for £18,000.[17] Many fruit wholesalers were to be found in and around Botolph Lane. One firm, Joshua and Joseph Williamson at number 16, traded on a very substantial scale. In 1820 they insured nuts alone for £17,000, as well as other stock and utensils valued at £2000. The following year they insured their warehouse for £1000.[18] There were also wholesale bacon merchants, fishmongers and butchers. An example of the large profits to be made is provided by Denis Lambert and Co, who were wholesale grocers in Upper Thames Street. Over a 17-year period prior to their bankruptcy in 1829 they averaged £3149 a year.[19] By the 1820s well over 70 per cent of food and tobacco wholesalers were located in the City. This was especially true of wholesale grocers, for whom Eastcheap was the centre of the trade: 46 were to be found there in 1836.[20]

In many ways the archetypal London wholesale trade was clothing and textiles. The London 'warehouseman' straddled the divide between wholesale and retail distribution in these key London trades. Some were involved in the classic pattern of wholesaling to both London and provincial retailers while also retailing directly to London customers; others were virtually entirely wholesale. At least one house which survived into the second half of the twentieth century, Cooks of St Pauls, started out as retailers and rapidly switched to wholesaling. In this particular case, young William Cook had arrived in London in 1807 and apprenticed himself to a linen draper in Clerkenwell. By astutely marrying a wealthy City alderman's sister, he was able to buy out his former master and set up in the wholesale trade in Cheapside in 1818 as a wholesale linen draper and warehouseman, taking advantage of the post-war boom.[21] By 1823 he was insuring with two fire offices for £11,000.[22] Yet another long surviving house, Williams and Son of Bread Street, started out as manufacturers of ladies' dress trimmings in Bethnal Green before becoming City warehousemen under the son of the original William Williams who founded the firm in 1819.[23]

Together with clothing and textile retailers, warehousemen were of crucial importance in those trades where London fashions dictated demand from the entire country. In the words of one of the few historians to study the London warehousemen, Stanley Chapman, although textile manufacturing largely deserted London during the Industrial Revolution, 'one of the apparent anomalies of economic history is the continued development of London as a major centre of the textile trade through the eighteenth and nineteenth centuries ... The textile sector of the City of London, the narrow streets between Wood Street and St Paul's Churchyard, evidently retained a momentum of its own, both in its particular forms of enterprise and its relations with the provinces.'[24] Over-production and consequent falling prices in the post-Napoleonic war depression gave a group of London drapers, led by James Morrison, an opportunity to buy cheap and sell through high turnover warehouses at modest profit margins.[25] A classic description of a warehouseman appeared in the 1830 Bankruptcy Commission file of John Millar, inevitably of Wood Street:

TABLE 6.1 Clothing and textiles

Capital insured (£)	No. of firms 1770s	Percentage of total	No. of firms 1820s	Percentage of total
100 and under	3	2.3	7	2.1
101–500	26	20.2	22	6.6
501–1000	33	25.6	37	11.1
1001–2999	42	32.6	64	19.3
3000 and over	25	19.4	202	60.8
Total	129	100.0	332	100.0

Source: Sun and other London fire office registers

'buying of Irish Cloth, Calicoes, Checks, Cottons, Sheetings and Bed Ticks in the Wholesale and selling the same to retail houses.'[26]

The 1826–27 edition of Pigot does not use the term 'warehouseman'. However, the fire office registers record policies for 129 firms in the 1770s and 332 in the 1820s. The latter insured capital valued at £2.65 million, over 3.6 per cent of all commercial capital insured in London. Apart from those firms calling themselves simply 'warehousemen', there were also those which described themselves in more specialist terms as Manchester, Norwich, Scotch, cotton, woollen or worsted warehousemen. In addition there were wholesale shoe warehouses and wholesale hosiers, glovers, mercers and linen drapers.

Most firms were very substantial in size. In the 1770s the average value of capital insured was £2111; half a century later it had trebled to £6265. Just over half of all firms in the 1770s insured capital valued at £1000 or more and nearly 20 per cent came into the 'large' category, insuring £3000 or more. By the 1820s the proportion insuring capital valued at £1000 or more had risen to 80 per cent, and over 60 per cent came into the 'large' category. Even more spectacularly, over a third of all firms insured for £5000 or more and 13 per cent for £10,000 or more. One wholesale glover traded throughout the period 1775–1825, increasing the value of the risk they insured over fivefold. The firm traded as Thomas Nalder at 6 Bucklersbury in 1771 and insured capital valued at £1800; by 1823 it was trading as Francis and Thomas Nalder at 40 Cheapside and insured capital valued at £10,000.[27] Table 6.1 shows the full breakdown by value of capital insured.

Among the largest firms in the 1770s were Nash, Eddowes and Pelice at 89 Cheapside. The term 'warehousemen' was less used in the 1770s than in the 1820s and they described themselves as wholesale linen drapers when, in 1777, they insured stock, utensils and goods valued at £25,500 with three different fire offices.[28] The size of firm had become very much larger by the 1820s with 7 per cent insuring for £20,000 and more. In 1822 Samuel Thorp and Sons of 14 Aldgate, who called themselves wholesale linen drapers and warehousemen, insured goods valued at £50,500.[29] Joseph Morrison, referred to above, was managing partner of Joseph Todd and Co of 105–6 Fore Street, Cripplegate. They insured for £26,000 in 1822 and the range of goods they dealt in is shown by the description of themselves in their policy as 'haberdashers, glovers, hosiers, lacemen, mercers, furriers and dealers in woollens, stuffs and fancy trimmings'.[30] Their turnover had risen from £65,000 in 1813 to over £1.5 million by 1822.[31] One specialised wholesale house, John Bassett of 34 Wood Street, described his firm as baize, blanket and flannel warehousemen when he insured for £13,600 in 1825.[32] The great firm of Bradbury Greatorex and Co had started out in a small way in 1820 when John Bradbury and Jeremiah Greatorex left Manchester to try their fortune in London. As former Manchester commercial travellers, they specialised in Manchester cotton piece goods, sheets and towels. In 1824 they insured for £50,000 and just over twenty years later a fire at their warehouse in Aldermanbury destroyed stock valued at £300,000.[33] The value of the 'warehouse' itself in the 1820s is shown in the policy of Joseph Watson, a Manchester warehouseman. He insured his at 8 Watling Street for the very considerable sum of £8000 in 1824 and 1825.[34] The level of profits is illustrated by John Dickson, a wholesale haberdasher in Fish Street Hill, who achieved profits of over £9300 in the three and a half years prior to his bankruptcy in 1825.[35] Increasingly, the overwhelming majority of firms were to be found in the City, around Wood Street, 76 per cent in the 1770s and 95 per cent 50 years later.

Two other major wholesale sectors were timber and building materials and agricultural and textile raw materials. The several construction booms in the period 1775–1825 created a massive demand for timber and other building materials. Pigot listed 344 firms engaged in their wholesale supply in 1826–27. Most were either timber merchants (256) or dealers in building materials (21), although there were also such specialist trades as brick and sand merchants, lath

TABLE 6.2 Timber and building materials

Capital insured (£)	No. of firms 1770s	Percentage of total	No. of firms 1820s	Percentage of total
100 and under	2	2.3	4	4.2
101–500	19	22.1	31	32.3
501–1000	20	23.3	19	19.8
1001–2999	34	39.5	23	24.0
3000 and over	11	12.8	19	19.8
Total	86	100.0	96	100.0

Source: Sun and other London fire office registers

dealers, plate glass dealers and marble merchants. There was some overlap with coal merchants. Individual firms, such as Hall and Co of Croydon, founded in 1824, traded in coal in the winter when the construction trades were slack and in building materials in the summer when construction was busy and demand for coal was slack. In this way the use of both employees and transport facilities was optimised.[36]

It was possible to trade in these commodities on a comparatively modest scale. In the 1770s nearly a quarter of all firms insured capital valued at £500 or less; half a century later this had actually risen to over a third. Nevertheless, the average value of capital insured nearly doubled, from £1657 to £3185. This was because of the emergence of a number of very large timber merchants in particular in the 1820s. The number of large firms insuring for £3000 or more rose from 13 per cent in the 1770s to 20 per cent in the 1820s. Indeed, in the latter period 10 per cent of all firms insured for £5000 or more and over 5 per cent for over £10,000. In total, timber merchants and dealers in other building materials insured capital valued at £1.1 million. Table 6.2 shows the full breakdown by value of capital insured.

Most firms were located near the river for easy access to the cheapest form of transport, either in the City or to the east or southeast. Many of the largest were located in Blackfriars, especially timber merchants. In 1774 Matthew Yerroway insured the cranes in his yard at 5 New Street for £350, and the scaffolding, stock, utensils and goods therein for £9650.[37] By the 1820s there were at least three

TABLE 6.3 Agricultural and textile raw materials

Capital insured (£)	No. of firms 1770s	Percentage of total	No. of firms 1820s	Percentage of total
100 and under	8	8.4	4	5.4
101–500	27	28.4	17	23.0
501–1000	27	28.4	16	21.6
1001–2999	15	15.8	15	20.3
3000 and over	18	18.9	22	29.7
Total	95	100.0	74	100.0

Source: Sun and other London fire office registers

enormous timber firms in Blackfriars: Sewell and Necks[38] and Boulton and Co,[39] both in Chatham Place, and George Norman at 23 Earl Street.[40] The first two insured for £58,500 and £41,000 in 1819 and 1820 respectively; the third for £45,000 in 1819. This placed all three among the largest one-third of 1 per cent of all businesses in London in terms of value of capital insured. Steam power was widely used by timber merchants in the 1820s: Winter and Barton, for example, insured their steam engine, together with its engine house and the sawpits and workshops it powered in St Martin's Lane, for £1000.[41] Substantial profits were to be made. Thomas Jenkins in Castle Street, Finsbury, averaged annual profits of £972 over the seven and a half years prior to his bankruptcy in 1826, although his start-up capital had been only £700.[42]

Pigot also listed 376 wholesalers of agricultural and textile raw materials, 158 of them dealers in corn and 62 in hops. In the 1820s they accounted for capital insured for nearly £1.4 million. Represented in the fire office registers are wholesale distributors of 29 agricultural and textile raw materials. These include hops, corn, malt, seed, yeast, horses, hogs, pigs, cattle, sheep and asses, leather and skins, cotton, hemp, flax and horsehair, feathers and horn. Most firms were of a substantial size. The value of capital insured more than doubled between the 1770s and 1820s, rising from £1596 to £3620. Nearly 19 per cent of all firms insured for £3000 or more in the 1770s; 50 years later it was 30 per cent. In the later period 18 per cent insured for £5000 or more and 8 per cent for over £10,000. Table 6.3 shows the full breakdown by value of capital insured.

Throughout the period 1775–1825, the largest firms were hop merchants. Timothy Yeats of 2 St Mary Hill insured for £8000 in 1771[43] and Ismay and Creed insured their five warehouses at 79 Borough alone for £5000 six years later.[44] By the 1820s there were a number of very large firms indeed. Tavernor and Co insured their warehouse at 21 Borough for the enormous sum of £10,500 in 1823 and 1824, as well as stock and utensils valued at £19,000,[45] and Armstrong and Co of Fish Street Hill insured for £28,000 in 1820.[46] Among the wholesalers of other commodities were Messrs Lucas, corn and flour dealers at 18 Millbank, who insured their warehouse for £1700 in 1823, barges for £150 and stock and utensils for £5500,[47] and Francis Alvin, a feather merchant at 9 Walbrook, who insured merchandise valued at £7000 in 1819.[48] Most firms were located in the City. However, the hop trade was mainly located in and around the Borough where the hops would arrive from Kent to be supplied to the many breweries in the area.

There were also many London wholesale dealers in a wide range of very different commodities. Pigot listed 181 dealers in fuels, ore, metals and industrial materials. Among them were 58 drysalters, 37 iron merchants, 36 lime merchants and 24 lead merchants. Represented in the fire office registers are wholesale distributors of dyes, copper, iron, lead, gum, lime, clay, pitch, tar, glazier's diamonds, coal and coke. Most of London's coal merchants were primarily retailers and are dealt with as such below. However, the establishment of the Coal Exchange in 1769 led to the so-called 'first buyers', who bought up whole cargoes when ships arrived from the Durham and Northumberland coalfields, becoming predominant in the trade. In fact, the tonnage of coal imported into London more than trebled from 677,000 tons in 1750 to 2,079,000 in 1830 and by the 1820s there were 6000 arrivals a year into the port of London. Indeed, it was noted as early as 1791 that 200 ships would arrive simultaneously from Newcastle. The 'first buyers' sold on either to 'loaders', who distributed beyond London, or to 'dealers' who supplied domestic households, or to 'retailers', who sold in small amounts from such retail premises as chandler's shops. It was estimated in the 1780s that capital of £10,000 was required by a 'first buyer'.[49] Forty years later in 1820, one firm of coal merchants, Wood and Phillips, insured their counting house at Northumberland Wharf for £500, various coal yard buildings for £2200, and stock, utensils and livestock for £2650.[50]

It had been estimated in 1813 that the number of coal factors in London had risen to about 30, from 19 in the 1770s. It was also estimated that the 30 averaged profits of about £1500 a year.[51]

Wholesalers rarely circulated trade cards and few invoices have survived. An exception is an invoice sent out in the 1820s by Thomas Jarvis, a lead and oil merchant at 10 Little Knightrider Street. His stock included 'refined Pig Lead, Milled Sheet Lead, Cast Sheet Lead, Patent Shot, Cast Lead Pipes, in Rolls and Lengths, Pump Barrels, Heads and Handles, Patent Pipes of all Sizes, Sealed Solder and Soldered Pipes, Tin in Blocksor Ingots, Church and Common Window Lead, Red and White Lead'.[52] Robert Graham, an iron merchant of Trigg Lane, Upper Thames Street, insured for £3250 in 1822, and Savill and Janian, copper merchants at the Steel Yard, insured cake and sheet copper valued at £2000 two years earlier.[53]

The range of stock of two bankrupt drysalters in the 1820s, James Cosler of Spitalfields and John Henderson of Lawrence Poutney Lane, included logwood, fustic, ebony, cochineal, shuma, indigo and lac-dye.[54] The capital insured by them could be very large indeed. In 1775 William, Henry and James Hanson insured their warehouses at 27 Miles Lane for £1000 and the contents for £12,000.[55] Lime was another commodity dealt in on a substantial scale; in 1823 Thomas Forrest of Puddle Dock insured for £2950.[56] The bulk of most of these commodities meant that most firms were located near the river for ease and cheapness of transport, a large proportion in the City.

Pigot also listed 415 other wholesalers, the largest numbers being stationers (94), druggists (54), ironmongers (53), dealers in marine stores (53) and perfumers (28). Dickens described the principal items of stock of a 'dealer in all kinds of Ships' Provisions' as 'ships' biscuit, dried meats and tongues'.[57] The fact that there was sufficient business in London for 28 wholesale perfumers is itself ample illustration of the sophistication of the London retail trades by the 1820s. The fire office registers suggest that few such wholesale firms had emerged by the 1770s although there were several very large druggists such as Richard Staveley of Mincing Lane who insured stock and utensils valued at £9000 in 1775.[58] Staveley was also a dealer in rum. In 1801 Ching and Butler, who described themselves as 'medicinal ware-houseman' and 'wholesale dealers' in their handbill, advertised 84 named patent medicines, ranging from Bateman's Pectoral Drops to Ching's Worm Lozenges.[59] Some examples of very large wholesalers trading in the 1820s were Dutton and Willats, wholesale stationers at 4 Queenhithe, who insured stock, utensils, goods and livestock for £13,700 in 1822;[60] Clode and Richards, phial and bottle merchants, who insured their warehouse in Crispin Street, Spitalfields, for £200 in 1820 and its contents for £8500;[61] Samuel and Thomas James, wholesale oil and colourmen of 17 Great Trinity Lane, who insured stock, utensils and goods for £5000 in 1819;[62] and Thomas Van, a dealer in marine stores, who insured his warehouse at 18 Tooley Street for £2500 in 1821, as well as stock and utensils valued at £4300.[63]*

Retail Distribution

Any attempt at a definitive count of numbers of retailers in London has to face the difficulty of distinguishing them from both wholesalers and from smaller-scale manufacturers who sold to wholesalers, retailers and directly to the individual customer. Bespoke production is treated as retailing proper. However, the nature of their trades suggests that up to about ten thousand of those firms predominantly involved in manufacturing would also have been involved in retailing directly to the customer, at least from time to time or as opportunity arose. This was also true of a large number of wholesalers, certainly in the textile trades. There would certainly have been at least a thousand such firms. Similarly, such very different trades as catering, pawn-broking and hairdressing, dealt with separately in this study, also had a significant retail element; there were at least five thousand of these too. If all these are counted, the number of businesses in London involved in retailing as at least one of its significant activities, if not necessarily its major activity, was of the order of 36,000 by the 1820s.[64]

However, this section deals only with those businesses for which the sole or major activity was retailing. Pigot listed just over 20,000 in 1826–27. They insured capital valued at nearly £16 million, 22 per cent of all commercial capital insured in London. It is worthy of

---

* The Muis used excise counts to identify 21,603 'retail shops' in London as early as 1759 and this figure appeared to be confirmed by the younger Pitt's inquiry of 1797 which identified 22,017. On the face of it both these figures seem very high for such early dates but undoubtedly both counts included *any* business involved in retail sales and must therefore be compared with the estimate made in this book of 36,000 in the 1820s.

note that 145 bankruptcy files for the 1820s show average annual profits of £628; this is 8 per cent higher than the average for all businesses.

Food, Drink and Tobacco Nothing illustrates the bewildering complexity, wide range and high sophistication of London's network of retail shops better than the most basic of all consumer products: food and drink. The 1826–27 edition of Pigot listed 8454 retailers involved in 29 separate trades, more than one in six of all businesses in London. They are equally well represented in the fire office registers, with over 2500 in both the 1770s and 1820s in 66 separate food and drink trades. Pigot also listed 226 retail tobacconists. In the 1820s food, drink and tobacco accounted for capital insured for almost £4.5 million, 28 per cent of capital insured in the retail trades and 6 per cent of capital insured by all London businesses.

There are 1519 butchers, poulterers and retailers of other meat products alone listed in Pigot. Apart from butchers, the most prominent trade was that of poulterers, of whom Pigot listed 70. Fire insurance policies also survive for tripemen, sausage dealers and dealers in sheep's heads. Most were very small. The average value of capital insured was £117 in the 1770s and half a century later it had risen only to £144. The median value was £100 in both periods. Contemporary estimates from 1747 through to 1837 suggested that £100 or less was all that was required to set up in business as a butcher. Less still was required for a sausage maker and £5 to £50 was thought to suffice for a tripeman. The overwhelming majority of businesses insured capital valued at £500 or less, well over 95 per cent throughout the period 1775–1825. However, the proportion insuring for only £100 or less did fall from nearly 79 per cent in the 1770s to 61 per cent in the 1820s. Those very smallest businesses, insuring for £100 or less, accounted for 35 per cent of all capital insured in the 1770s and for over 27 per cent 50 years later. Even so, the meat trade was considerable in size overall. Annual meat consumption in the United Kingdom was 86.8 lb per head in the decade 1831–40 and remained virtually unchanged until the 1870s.[65] However small the individual business, the trade as a whole insured capital valued at well over £200,000 in the 1820s. Table 6.4 shows the full breakdown by value of capital insured.

Among the few larger butchers was Richard Kilbinton who insured

TABLE 6.4 Meat and poultry

Capital insured (£)	No. of firms 1770s	Percentage of total	No. of firms 1820s	Percentage of total
100 and under	220	78.6	199	60.9
101–500	51	18.2	116	35.5
501–1000	6	2.1	11	3.4
1001–2999	3	1.1	1	0.3
3000 and over	0	0	0	0
Total	280	100.0	327	100.0

Source: Sun and other London fire office registers

a slaughterhouse in Wapping Wall for the considerable sum of £800 in 1775, as well as stock, utensils and goods valued at £400.[66] More typical was Maria Pitt. In 1823 she insured her slaughterhouse at 25 Wapping Wall for just £25, and stock and utensils for £200.[67] John Emblin, who described himself as a tripeman, insured his tripe house at 67 Leather Lane for £400 in 1820, and stock and utensils for £450.[68]

There were even more bakers than butchers. Pigot listed 1858, over 9 per cent of all London retailers and nearly 4 per cent of all businesses in London. Although most were very small, capitalisation did increase significantly. In the 1770s the average value of capital insured was £160; 50 years later it had nearly doubled to £306. Median values rose from £150 to £250. The major difference was that in the earlier period the large majority of bakers (61 per cent) insured for £100 or less; by the later the proportion had fallen to 14 per cent and nearly three-quarters were insuring for between £100 and £500. Less than 1 per cent insured for over £500 in the earlier period; in the later it was nearly 10 per cent. By the 1820s the total value of capital insured by the retail bakery trade was nearly £570,000. Contemporary estimates of start-up capital were never higher than £100 or £200 and in 1786 just £5–£10 was thought sufficient for a muffin baker. Table 6.5 shows the full breakdown by value of capital insured.

Bake houses were sometimes insured for quite substantial sums; in 1771 James Sheridan insured his at 39 Marylebone High Street for £300, as well as stock and utensils valued at £250.[69] By the 1820s there were a few businesses insuring substantially larger risks such as

TABLE 6.5 Bakers

Capital insured (£)	No. of firms 1770s	Percentage of total	No. of firms 1820s	Percentage of total
100 and under	133	38.2	69	14.3
101–500	212	60.9	365	75.9
501–1000	3	0.9	40	8.3
1001–2999	0	0	7	1.5
3000 and over	0	0	0	0
Total	348	100.0	481	100.0

Source: Sun and other London fire office registers

Nathan Negus who insured his warehouse, bake house, stock, utensils and goods at 44 Petticoat Lane for £1960 in 1822 and 1825.[70]

There were no very great differences in the value of capital insured in the different districts of London in the 1770s; 50 years later there were. The highest capital values insured were in the west central area, the City and the West End, £353, £337 and £303 respectively. The average was exactly the same in the East End as the West End but in the districts south of the river it was only £277, in and around Islington £263 and in the new district of Somers Town £229.

There were considerably fewer fruiterers and greengrocers than retailers of most other foodstuffs. Fruit and vegetables, and also fish, were still most often sold by hawkers and costermongers, especially in poorer areas. Much of the produce was supplied by market gardeners in and just beyond the outer suburbs. In 1824 it was noted that 'there are supposed to be about 5000 acres of land constantly cultivated for the supply of the London markets with garden vegetables, exclusive of about 800 acres cropped with fruit of various kinds, and about 1700 acres cultivated for potatoes'.[71] The evidence of the fire office registers suggests that fruiterers' and greengrocers' shops were becoming far more common by the first quarter of the nineteenth century. The number for which insurance records survive rose by 125 per cent over the period 1775–1825. Even so, the total value of capital insured was little more than £50,000 in the 1820s. Pigot listed 299 in 1826–27. The average value of capital insured was £137 in the 1770s and 50 years later it had risen only to £170. In the former period nearly three-quarters insured for £100 or less and most of the re-

TABLE 6.6 Fruit and vegetables

Capital insured (£)	No. of firms 1770s	Percentage of total	No. of firms 1820s	Percentage of total
100 and under	43	72.9	75	56.4
101–500	13	22.0	49	36.8
501–1000	2	3.4	7	5.3
1001–2999	1	1.7	2	1.5
3000 and over	0	0	0	0
Total	59	100.0	133	100.0

Source: Sun and other London fire office registers

mainder for £500 or less; even in the latter period it was still 56 per cent and 37 per cent respectively. Table 6.6 shows the full breakdown by value of capital insured.

By the 1820s there were a few substantial businesses. In 1821 Jeremiah Bigg, who described himself as a fruiterer, insured his shop at 11 Little Russell Street for £1000, as well as stock, utensils and goods for £700.[72] Four years later John Johnston and Son, orange merchants at 32 Pudding Lane, insured stock and utensils for £1100.[73] Orange merchants were among the largest of such firms and were often both wholesalers and retailers. Indeed, it was estimated in 1761 that £1000 was required to set up in business.[74] A trade card circulated in 1803 by William Parnell of Botolph Lane stated that he sold 'Lemons and Oranges, Lemon and Orange Juice, Nuts, Chestnuts, & Almonds, Wholesale and Retail'.[75] Dried fruit was another common commodity. Samuel Hanson of 47 Botolph Lane was trading in oranges and lemons from Spain and Cyprus, figs, sultanas and raisins from Greece and almonds from the Balearic Islands in 1747. In 1770 he insured stock and utensils valued at £1000.[76] Throughout the period many potato merchants and greengrocers dealt also in coal because of the common bulk transport requirements. Of 98 businesses dealing in potatoes in the 1820s, nearly half (48) dealt also in coal.

There were more fishmongers than fruiterers and greengrocers. Pigot listed 411 in 1826–27. Again, there was a tendency for the number of retail shops to increase; the number in the fire office registers nearly trebled between the 1770s and the 1820s. Even so, they were usually very small. The average value of capital insured was only £85 in the earlier period and it rose to no more than £153 half a century later. Most contemporary sources estimated that little more than £50 or at most £100 was required to set up in business. A number of surviving trade cards exemplify the variety of fish retailed. One circulated about 1810 by Palmer and Jay of Hungerford New Market advertised 'Barrelled Oysters & Shell Fish of every description, Pickled Salmon, Yarmouth Bloaters, Anchovies, Prawns &c.' More specialised was J. Edmonds of 83 Snow Hill; his 1830 trade card described the business as an 'Oyster and Pickled Salmon Warehouse'.[77] Another oyster warehouse keeper, Mary Ann Norbury in Birchin Lane, insured for £200 in 1821.[78] A very large business was that of John Lucy at 17 Thomas Street who insured for £600 in 1824.[79]

By far the largest, most diversified and wealthiest of all the London retail food trades was grocery and provisions. Pigot listed 3284 businesses, nearly 7 per cent of London businesses and 16 per cent of all retailers. The fire office registers alone contain policies for 1435 in the 1770s and 1363 in the 1820s. By the latter period retailers of grocery and provisions insured capital valued at nearly £1.5 million. This was an increase of about 40 per cent compared with the 1770s. Contemporaries recognised three overlapping groups of trades: grocers and cheesemongers; chandlers; and retailers of other provisions, of which tea and coffee dealers and oilmen were the most common. These were, in fact, the self-descriptions of their businesses most frequently found in the fire office registers. In practice many individual businesses described themselves as involved in a number of these trades, such as Mary Dawson of Wapping who described herself as a 'grocer, cheesemonger and chandler' in 1821.[80] Scores more described themselves as 'grocer and cheesemonger'. However, much the most significant distinction was size; this in turn most frequently depended on the degree of specialisation. At the very bottom of the scale came the chandler. Campbell's dismissive description of 1747 would be echoed for the next century and more: 'The Chandler's-Shop deals in all Things necessary for the Kitchen in small Quantities: He is partly Cheesemonger, Oil-Man, Grocer, Distiller, etc. This last Article brings him the greatest Profit, and at the same time renders him the most obnoxious Dealer in and about London.'[81] The 1751 Act removed the worst of the evils caused by unrestricted sale of gin but the chandler remained the supplier of staple provisions – bread, small beer, cheese, milk, tea, soap, candles and coal – to the poorest Londoners throughout the period 1775–1825. Interestingly, the fire office registers show that nearly one in ten of all chandlers in the 1820s was also engaged in non-retail trades, for example as carpenters. This suggests that retailing was only one of a number of ways of making a living at the subsistence level for the individual or family concerned. It was estimated in 1786 that as little as £5 was sufficient to set up in business as a chandler. Forty years earlier £500 had been suggested by Campbell as the minimum capital required to set up in business as a grocer.

Campbell was equally dismissive of the oilman, if rather more flattering towards the cheesemonger: 'The Cheesemonger [is] a Retailer of Cheese, Butter, Eggs, Bacon and Ham. His Skill consists in the Knowledge of the Prices and Properties of these Kind of Goods … The Oil-Shop is furnished with Oils, Pickles, Soap, Salt, Hams … He is a mere Retailer.' The overlap can be seen from his description of the grocer who deals in 'Tea, Sugar, Coffee, Chocolate, Raisins, Currants, Prunes, Figs, Almonds, Soap, Starch, Blues … Oils, Pickles'.[82] This overlap is further illustrated by many contemporary trade cards and handbills. Thus, Edward Cockerton of 36 Ludgate Street, who described himself as an oilman in 1779, listed his stock in trade as 'oils, pickles, hams and tongues, vinegar, pepper and spices, ketchup, ginger, herbs, mustard etc'.[83] John Smith, a grocer and tea dealer in Fore Street, invoiced a customer in 1767 for loaves, sugar, currants, raisins, rice, starch, blue, candy, saltpetre, salt, beeswax, hartshorn shavings, caraway seeds, pearl barley, pepper, nutmeg, mace, cloves, cinnamon and ginger.[84] Nearly sixty years later in 1825, the catalogue of Lawes and Co of 115 Regent Street listed no fewer than 217 product lines. These included 36 types of preserves, 29 of confectionery, 28 sauces and pickles, 23 foreign fruits and 14 varieties of tea.[85] On the other hand, represented in the fire office registers are 27 areas of specialised retail trade. These include vinegar, butter, cocoa, spices, coffee, sugar, salt, pease, oil and pickles, honey, milk and cream, eggs, flour, lemon juice and mineral waters. One branch of the trade was the Italian warehouseman. An advertisement placed in 1820 by Price's Old Italian Warehouse at 3 Haymarket offered 'true Honeycomb Parmasan Cheese, of very superior quality' as well as macaroni, vermicelli, olives and capers.[86]

Demand in all these trades was booming. Tea consumption alone nearly doubled in the last 15 years of the eighteenth century, an increase seven times that of the growth in population.[87] Even so, most businesses were very small. Nearly 45 per cent insured capital valued at £100 or less in the 1770s, and another 43 per cent insured for between £100 and £500; 50 years later fewer insured for £100 or less (28 per cent), but more for between £100 and £500 (nearly 52 per cent). In the 1770s nearly 45 per cent of all capital insured was accounted for by businesses insuring for £500 or less and 10 per cent by those insuring for £100 or less; by the 1820s these percentages had fallen to 37 and 4 respectively. However, virtually every chandler insured for £500 or less, and most for no more than £100. Their importance declined over the period 1775–1825: in the 1770s they accounted for 13 per cent of all capital insured by retailers of provisions; 50 years later only for 8.5 per cent. The average value of capital insured by chandlers was £91 in the 1770s and £123 in the 1820s compared with £471 and £557 for grocers and cheesemongers. In 1826 an inventory of the fixtures and fittings of the grocery shop of a Mr Gregory at 183 Shoreditch valued them at just £299 19s.[88] On the other hand, 'an old established' grocer in the West End had fixtures valued at under £100 yet had a weekly turnover of £30 to £40.[89]

Although most other retailers of provisions were also small – exactly half of all grocers and cheesemongers insured for £500 or less in the 1820s – there were exceptions. Over 8 per cent insured for over £1000 in the 1770s and this proportion rose to 12 per cent 50 years later. Indeed, 2 per cent and 3.5 per cent respectively were 'large' firms insuring for £3000 or more. Table 6.7 shows the full breakdown by value of capital insured.

Throughout the period the very largest firms were likely to be cheesemongers such as Moore and Strange of 2–3 Bishopsgate who insured for £8000 in 1770.[90] They were undoubtedly wholesalers as well as retailers, as would have been Garrett and Taddy, tea dealers at 7 Thames Street, who insured stock and utensils valued at £4500 two years later.[91] Over 50 years later in 1824, Whalley and Warther of 14–15 Aldgate High Street described themselves as cheesemongers when they insured stock, utensils and goods valued at £7000.[92] Already among the largest grocers were Fortnum and Mason at 182–3 Piccadilly and in the same year they insured stock and utensils valued at £4150.[93] By this time the firm was already 117 years old and had been well established at the luxury end of the market for at least 60

TABLE 6.7 Grocery and provisions

Capital insured (£)	No. of firms 1770s	Percentage of total	No. of firms 1820s	Percentage of total
100 and under	643	44.8	383	28.1
101–500	610	42.5	702	51.5
501–1000	114	7.9	172	12.6
1001–2999	54	3.8	75	5.5
3000 and over	14	1.0	31	2.3
Total	1435	100.0	1363	100.0

Source: Sun and other London fire office registers

years. A recent history of the firm notes: 'By 1788 they were selling boned portions of poultry and game in aspic jelly, decorated with lobsters and prawns; potted meats; hard-boiled eggs in forcemeat; eggs in brandy-soaked cake with whipped cream, mince pies; savoury patties and fruits fresh and dried.'[94] Another firm which survived into the twentieth century was Fitch and Co. They were established as cheesemongers by James Fitch in 1784 and by the 1820s, with James's nephew George as proprietor, they were making daily deliveries of butter, cheese, bacon, sausages, ham, tongue and eggs to every part of London.[95]

Retailers of grocery and provisions were to be found in large numbers throughout London. There was, however, one interesting trend. In the 1770s the proportions of chandlers on the one hand and grocers and cheesemongers on the other varied little between different parts of the capital. For example, 25 per cent of grocers and cheesemongers were to be found in the City, and 25 per cent of chandlers also. Similarly, 20 per cent of grocers and cheesemongers were to be found in the west central area and 22 per cent of chandlers. In the East End the proportions were 20 per cent and 18 per cent respectively. By the 1820s a marked difference had appeared. While 25 per cent of grocers and cheesemongers were located in the City, only 19 per cent of chandlers were. Conversely, over one-third of chandlers were found in the East End compared with under a quarter of grocers and cheesemongers. This is further evidence of a widening social distinction between the trades. At the upper end of the market most of the trade in the 1770s concentrated around Gracechurch

Street for the City, Aldgate High Street and Shoreditch for the East End, St Martin's Lane for the West End and Borough High Street for Southwark. Half a century later, the trade had moved outwards with the new expanding suburbs and the City trade had concentrated around Eastcheap. By the 1830s, in addition to 46 wholesale grocers, there were 18 retail grocers, 69 tea and coffee merchants and 16 pickle and Italian warehousemen.

Mention must also be made of the specialised trade in milk. It has been claimed that milk contributed little to the national diet before about 1850. Most purchases were casual and the most common means of distribution was still the milkmaid, working either for the urban cowkeeper or for the larger-scale suburban supplier. Islington was very much the centre for the latter in the eighteenth century. Not until the late 1820s did shop-based dairymen begin to outnumber traditional cowkeepers. The 1832 edition of Pigot listed 645 London milk tradesmen, at which time it was estimated that there were about 200 dairies and cowsheds. Certainly, the urban cowshed was still an essential part of the trade as late as 1871.[96] A century earlier in 1776, a trade card circulated by Martha Prokter and Lydia Edwards of Marylebone Lane stated 'Asses Milk to be Sold. Also Fine Red-Cow's Milk & Goat's Milk.'[97] A minor commercial tragedy is described in a handbill circulated in 1783 by W. Gibbons, a cowkeeper in Swan Yard, Southwark. He complained: 'by reason of a Combination enter'd into by several Milk-Carriers, his Servant has been taken into custody, and had before the Sitting Magistrates at Guildhall, for suffering his Cows to get upon the Foot pavement, which at Times it is impossible to prevent, and on that Account he finds himself under the disagreeable Necessity of discontinuing the bringing his Cows into the City.'[98]

The average value of capital insured by cowkeepers was only £273 in the 1770s, although it nearly doubled to £536 fifty years later. Even so, there were a few larger firms. As early as 1775 John Moul of Limehouse insured capital valued at £1160.[99] Fifty years later, and a sign of things to come in the milk trade, the Great Western Dairy insured for £6250.[100] The range of fixed capital required for cow keeping on a more substantial scale is exemplified by the fire insurance policy of William Cossey. He insured one cowshed in Gough Street, Grays Inn Lane, for £60 in 1825, a dairy for £30, a measuring house for £50, a group of cowsheds, stables, hay lofts and sheds for £1000 and stock and utensils for £1060.[101]

Trading on a different scale to suppliers of most edible foodstuffs were the retailers of wine, beer and spirits. Pigot listed 853 and they insured capital valued at over £1.7 million in the 1820s. The huge increase in demand for and output of domestically produced alcohol has already been noted. The increase in consumption extended equally to imported wines and spirits. Over 23,000 pipes of port were imported in 1823 alone.[102] The typical range of drinks sold by a London wine merchant is exemplified by an invoice sent out in 1802 by John Foulds from his Wine and Brandy Vaults opposite London Bridge Waterworks. It was for the supply of 'wines, brandy, rum, shrub and Holland's Geneva'.[103] Other firms were much more specialised. Thus, C. Palk circulated a handbill from his premises at 31 Mill Lane, Tooley Street, in 1820 which promised 'Real Devonshire Cyder sold here. Superior Bottled Perry'.[104] The contemporary *Wine and Spirit Merchant's Companion* listed the properties and characteristics of well over one hundred types of alcoholic drink.[105]

Businesses increased markedly in size over the period 1775–1825. The average value of capital insured by wine, beer and spirit merchants rose from £813 in the 1770s to £2009 fifty years later. One wine merchant, John Wild of St Martin's Lane, increased his turnover from £200 in 1777 to £10,000 in 1790.[106] While nearly two-thirds of all firms insured for £500 or less and only 16 per cent for over £1000 in the 1770s, by the 1820s these proportions were less than 25 per cent and over 57 per cent. The number of 'large' firms insuring for £3000 or more increased from under 5 per cent to over 15 per cent. Table 6.8 shows the full breakdown by value of capital insured.

One very large brandy merchant in the 1770s was Timson and Jones at 6 Little Tower Street. They insured for the huge sum of £19,000 in 1774.[107] Two years earlier, Hilditch and Danne, beer and cider merchants at 11 Morgan Street, Southwark, insured stock, utensils and goods valued at £3000.[108] At this time non-specialist retailers described themselves as 'dealers in spirituous liquors' and one, Thomas Bramwell of Greek Street, insured stock and utensils for £1800, also in 1772.[109] Half a century later in 1819, William Mandall, a wine and brandy merchant at 39 St Mary at Hill, insured stock, utensils and goods valued at £25,000.[110] Indeed, by the 1820s, 3 per cent of all wine and spirit merchants insured for over £10,000. However, more typical was George Killick who insured his counting house at 2 Brabant Street for £300 in 1825, other commercial buildings

TABLE 6.8 Wine, beer and spirits

Capital insured (£)	No. of firms 1770s	Percentage of total	No. of firms 1820s	Percentage of total
100 and under	50	12.8	3	1.8
101–500	192	49.1	38	22.6
501–1000	85	21.7	31	18.5
1001–2999	45	11.5	70	41.7
3000 and over	19	4.8	26	15.5
Total	391	100.0	168	100.0

Source: Sun and other London fire office registers

for £150, and stock and utensils for £1500.[111] Ale and beer merchants were usually considerably smaller, although William Allan of 32 Seething Lane insured for £1200 in 1820.[112]

Bankruptcy files show enormous differences in the scale of profits made in the retail food and drink trades. At one extreme Thomas Dracon, a City grocer and tea dealer in Skinner Street, showed average annual profits of £2331 over a 13-and-a-half-year period prior to the failure of his business in 1826,[113] and Miles and Frisby, wine merchants in Mark Lane, averaged £2111 a year for the three years prior to their bankruptcy in 1827;[114] at the other, Alan Cornfoot, a baker at 18 Houndsditch, showed a profit of only £180 in the year previous to his bankruptcy in 1823,[115] and the average annual profits over 16 years previous to the failure of William Downer's business as a poulterer in Leadenhall Street in 1828 was £449.[116] On a start-up capital of £600 George Cross, a butcher in Clare market, showed a profit of £700 in 1820. This reduced to £350 in 1824 but increased to £400 in both 1825 and 1826. He ceased trading in the latter year.[117] The average annual profit for 31 food and drink retailers in the 1820s was £527.

There was also a substantial trade in tobacco and snuff. As early as the mid-eighteenth century, annual per capita consumption averaged 1.33 lb,[118] and by 1826–27 Pigot was listing 226 tobacconists in London. Most were very small. The average value of capital insured changed only from £591 in the 1770s to £559 fifty years later. Although there were a few large firms insuring capital valued at £3000 or more, 4 per cent in the 1770s and 5 per cent in the 1820s, much more

TABLE 6.9 Tobacco and snuff

Capital insured (£)	No. of firms 1770s	Percentage of total	No. of firms 1820s	Percentage of total
100 and under	30	31.9	32	38.1
101–500	45	47.9	32	38.1
501–1000	7	7.4	7	8.3
1001–2999	8	8.5	9	10.7
3000 and over	4	4.3	4	4.8
Total	94	100.0	84	100.0

Source: Sun and other London fire office registers

typical were four out of five insuring for £500 or less. Table 6.9 shows the full breakdown by value of capital insured.

Among the handful of large tobacconists were Sales, Pollard and Yates at 71–2 Aldersgate Street. They insured their stock and utensils for £13,500 in 1777.[119] Forty-seven years later in 1824, Jabez Beynon of 10 Gracechurch Street insured for £5000.[120]

Clothing and Footwear Unsurprisingly, the number of retailers supplying the metropolis with clothing and textiles was second only to the number supplying food and drink. Pigot listed 5370 retailers of clothing and textiles, over a quarter of all London retailers and one in nine of all firms. In the 1820s they insured capital valued at nearly £5.5 million , 7.5 per cent of the total for all businesses in London.

There were four groups of businesses: those involved mainly in bespoke production, usually on a very small scale, such as tailors, dressmakers and milliners, staymakers and shoemakers; those involved in the sale either of small, more expensive, ready-made articles of dress or the textiles from which they would be made, often in a substantial way of business, such as haberdashers, hosiers, mercers and drapers; those involved in the sale of cheap ready-made clothing, both new and second-hand, mostly on a very small scale but in a few cases on a very large scale indeed; and, those involved in both sale of ready-made items and in bespoke production, such as hatters and glovers. In practice, of course, all these categories overlapped and innumerable businesses were involved in several such activities and trades. Nevertheless, it has to be noted that the majority of firms, 64 per cent in the 1820s, described themselves in the fire office registers in terms of a single trade such as tailor, dressmaker, haberdasher, linen draper, hosier, hatter or slopseller. This still means that there were large numbers of, for example, drapers and mercers or hosiers and glovers, and self-descriptions such as 'haberdashers, hosiers, lacemen, mercers, furriers and dealers in woollen cloths and fancy trimmings' (in a fire insurance policy taken out in 1822 by Creed and Keen of 10 Fore Street, Cripplegate). Typical also is the heading of an invoice sent out in 1820 by Fry and Co of 111 Long Acre. They describe themselves as dealing in haberdashery, silk mercery, linen drapery, hosiery, gloves, lace &c.'[121]

For Neil McKendrick, the outward spread of fashion in clothes from London to every part of the kingdom was both one of the most important engines of the eighteenth-century consumer revolution, and one of its foremost identifying features. This phenomenon rested ultimately on thousands of tailors, dressmakers, milliners and other similar small businesses, as well as on the great master tailors:

> All those tiny London satellites to the Lancashire cotton mills – the tailors, dressmakers, milliners and mantua makers – would produce enough minor variations on the prevailing fashions to satisfy the market, keep its interests alive and allow the factories to churn out stripes or muslins or whatever was required – whether prevailing material or dominant colour – until the next major change was introduced – if possible stage-managed and timed to suit the needs of commerce.[122]

The edifice resting on this foundation was the world of high fashion, satisfying the requirements of what Alison Adburgham called the 'well-dressed Englishwoman'.[123] For men Savile Row began its long reign of supremacy in 1806.[124]

George Dodd was always prone to exaggeration but his description of the trade in 1843 is recognisable in the cold statistics of the trade directory and the fire office registers. He remarked that 'although scarcely any woven fabrics are produced in London ... the arrangements for working up these materials into garments are here developed to an extraordinary extent. Tailors and dressmakers are to be reckoned, not by thousands, but by tens of thousands.'[125] In fact, tailors and dressmakers, the latter more usually described as mantua makers in the eighteenth century, were among the commonest of London trades. Pigot listed 2340 in 1826–27, nearly 5 per cent of all businesses in London. In the 1820s they insured capital valued at nearly £700,000.

As well as tailors and dressmakers there were also specialised gown makers, habit makers, robemakers, saque makers, fancy dressmakers and child's coat makers. A typical invoice from the upper end of the trade was sent out by Plumpton and Baker, tailors at 40 Cheapside, in 1815. They described themselves as tailors and made or supplied 'Ladies' Habits, Children's Dresses, Liveries, Naval & Military Uniforms ... Patent India Rubber & Camlet Cloaks. And Capes in great variety.'[126] An advertisement placed in *The Times* five years later by Radford and Co in Fleet Street gives a clear indication of prices at the upper end of the market:

> Elegant Coats, cut and made in a very superior manner, of the best superfine cloth, from £3 3s to £3 12s; walking and great coats, faced with silk, from £3 3s to £4 4s; fashionable waistcoats, from 8s to 15s; best double-milled kersey-mere breeches, £1 4s; blue or fashionable trowsers [*sic*], from £1 1s to £1 12s; Ladies' beautiful habits, by experienced workmen, from 4 to 5 guineas; suit of livery complete £4 10s; Ladies' and Gentlemen's travelling-coats, boat-coats, and chaise-coats, from £2 2s to £5 5s ... A suit of clothes made in 5 hours.[127]

An interesting example of the clear distinction between what was made to individual order and what was sold ready-made is provided by an invoice sent out in 1779 by Pritchard's Warehouse at 39 Tavistock Street. This stated: 'Made, The Robe de Cour, Suits, Saques, Masquerade Dresses ... Sold, Riding Habits and Coats, Stays, Hoops and Quilted Coats.'[128]

Although there were a number of large master tailors, most firms were small. The average value of capital insured doubled between the 1770s and the 1820s, but only from £146 to £291. In the former period 95 per cent insured for £500 or less, 70 per cent for £100 or less; in the latter, these proportions were still 88 per cent and 46 per cent. Master tailors were a very small proportion of the trade – only 2 per cent of tailors insured for over £1000 in the 1770s and 6 per cent in the 1820s. However, by the 1820s they accounted for 36 per cent of all capital insured in the trade. Table 6.10 shows the full breakdown by value of capital insured.

One substantial master tailor was Nellewill and Nugent at 10 Goldsmith Street. They insured stock and goods valued at £4000 in

TABLE 6.10 Tailors and dressmakers

Capital insured (£)	No. of firms 1770s	Percentage of total	No. of firms 1820s	Percentage of total
100 and under	458	70.5	210	46.5
101–500	165	25.4	190	42.0
501–1000	16	2.5	27	6.0
1001–2999	10	1.5	24	5.3
3000 and over	1	0.2	1	0.2
Total	650	100.0	452	100.0

Source: Sun and other London fire office registers

1769.[129] In the same year John Winter insured his workshop in St James's Street for £400, and stock, utensils and goods for £1500.[130] Exactly 50 years later, Edward and James Smith of 47–8 Houndsditch insured stock and utensils valued at £5600,[131] and Messrs Burns insured their workshop at 5 Nassau Street for £300 in 1823, as well as stock, utensils and goods valued at £1500.[132] There were even a few large dressmakers such as Ann Smith of 9 Waterloo Place who insured for £2500 in 1821.[133] A typical dressmaking workshop, at 1 Lisle Street, was valued at £70 by Jane Mackintosh in 1777.[134] Although found in all parts of London, tailors and dressmakers were concentrated in the City, the West End and the west central area, especially the master tailors.

Pigot also listed 174 staymakers. Very few insured capital valued at more than £500 and the average sums insured were only £124 in the 1770s and £212 in the 1820s. But even in this trade there were exceptions, such as Saltzman and Croft in Henrietta Street who insured stock, utensils and goods for £1950 in 1771.[135] An invoice sent out in 1794 by one Holt, a staymaker at 45 Mortimer Street, was for a pair of stays supplied to a Miss Turner at the considerable cost of £1 11s 6d. Holt made 'Corsets, French, Italian, and all Sorts of Stays in the compleatest Manner'.[136]

Much the wealthiest of all London retail trades were the dealers in fine cloth, textile fabrics and fancy articles of apparel at the upper end of the market. Of these, the drapers and mercers were wealthiest of all. Pigot listed 890, the large majority being linen (442) or woollen drapers (171). There were also 91 silk mercers and 89 furriers. In the

1820s they insured capital valued at nearly £2.25 million, over 3 per cent of all commercial capital insured in London. No trades were more central to London's role as a centre of fashion and in 1824 *The Book of English Trades* breathlessly described the trade of a linen draper, stressing that in London it was quite distinct from that of a silk mercer:

> We believe that there is no trade in England, in which more efforts are made to captivate the public, and more especially the ladies, by a display of goods: and in London, this display is carried to a most costly and sumptuous extent. In most of the principal streets of the metropolis, shawls, muslins, pieces for ladies' dresses, and a variety of other goods, are shown with the assistance of mirrors, and at night by chandeliers, aided by the brilliancy which the gaslights afford, in a way almost as dazzling to a stranger, as many of those poetical fictions of which we read in the Arabian nights' entertainment ... Some of the retail Linen-Drapers in the metropolis, transact daily, so much business as almost to exceed belief ... We have known persons in this line, whose receipts have averaged £500 per day ... In such a shop, 20 or 30 persons, or more, are constantly employed.[137]

Fifty years earlier the wide range of stock kept by a linen draper was set out in a trade card circulated by Timothy Adams of Gravel Lane, Houndsditch:

> all Sorts of the finest Childbed Linnen, fine quilted Bed-gowns, Baskets and Cushions, Satin Mantles, Dimity Mantles, Blankets, Rowlers, with all sorts of the finest Small Linnen, Children's Dimity Coats, Flannel Coats, white and colour'd Frocks, Shoes, Stockings, Work'd Petticoats, with cambricks, Muslins, Calicoes, Bagg Hollands, and Isinghams, Irish, Garlick and Russia, Clouting Diapers, and Damask, printed Linnens, Striped Cottons, all Sorts of white and striped Flannels, white and colour'd baize.[138]

These were the most highly capitalised of London's retail textile and clothing trades. Even in the 1770s over 45 per cent of all firms insured capital valued at over £1000; by the 1820s this had risen to over 61 per cent. 'Large' firms insuring £3000 or more comprised over 12 per cent of the total in the earlier period; by the later the proportion had more than doubled to nearly 27 per cent. In the 1820s, over 2 per cent of firms insured for more than £10,000. The average value of capital insured rose from £1482 in the 1770s to £2450 half a century later. Table 6.11 shows the full breakdown by value of capital insured.

TABLE 6.11 Drapers and mercers

Capital insured (£)	No. of firms 1770s	Percentage of total	No. of firms 1820s	Percentage of total
100 and under	27	6.2	26	4.9
101–500	102	23.3	91	17.2
501–1000	111	25.3	87	16.4
1001–2999	145	33.1	185	34.9
3000 and over	53	12.1	141	26.6
Total	438	100.0	530	100.0

Source: Sun and other London fire office registers

The great size of some of London's drapers and mercers as early as the 1770s is exemplified by Rogers and Greaves, linen drapers at 131 Cheapside, who insured their stock, utensils and goods for the enormous sum of £16,000 in 1777.[139] Seven years earlier, William Barlow, William Ashburne, Richard Ellison and George Nelthorpe, who described themselves as mercers, insured stock and utensils valued at £10,000 in their premises in King Street, Covent Garden.[140] One very large woollen draper, Stephen Goddard in Crown Court, Pulteney Street, insured stock and utensils for £5750 in 1772.[141] By the 1820s, some were very much larger still, such as Halling, Pearce and Stone, linen drapers in Regent Street, who insured for £31,000 with nine fire offices in 1820.[142] Three years later John Harvey, describing himself as a linen draper and haberdasher, insured stock and utensils at his premises at 15–17 Ludgate Hill valued at £25,500.[143] Later the firm was to become Harvey Nicholls. One retail furrier, George Smith in Gough Square, insured for £10,400 in 1823,[144] and in 1825 Broughton and Evered, men's mercers at 382 Oxford Street, insured for £10,000.[145] There were, of course, many smaller businesses catering for the less wealthy, but satisfying the same consumer demand for fashion as the huge West End and City shops, such as Thomas Rogers, a linen draper in Red Lion Street, Spitalfields, who insured for £400 in 1822.[146]

A few fire insurance policies separately specify the value of a shop or showroom. An Oxford Street showroom, in this case at number 75, was insured for £350 in 1819 by James Ince, a silk mercer,[147] and in the same year Robert Salmon, a linen draper, insured his shop at 112 High Holborn for £200.[148]

There were interesting variations in the average value of capital insured in different districts of London. In the 1770s it was £1006 in the East End but £1814 in the City, a difference of 80 per cent. Fifty years later the differences were still more marked. In the East End the average was £1164 compared with £2915 in the City, £2936 in the West End as a whole and £3283 in and around the new shopping district of Regent Street. However, it has to be noted that in the 1820s one in seven linen drapers and mercers in the East End insured capital valued at £3000 or more so there was a substantial enough demand for large retail businesses to flourish even in the least wealthy areas of the capital.

Second in the retail clothing and textiles trades' pecking order to drapers and mercers were London's numerous haberdashers and related retailers. There were 465 listed in Pigot and in the 1820s they insured capital valued at £570,000. Pigot listed 325 firms described principally as haberdashers. There were also 50 retail lace dealers, 32 specialist gold and silver lacemen and 36 button and trimming sellers. There was a huge trade in mourning wear, in which haberdashers were in the forefront with black crêpe being a particularly profitable line of merchandise. Typically, John Breach advertised that his shop at 1 Aldgate sold 'Every Article for Mourning'[149] and the firm which was to become the modern Debenham's, established by William Franks in 1778 and trading as Clark and Debenham from 1813, made a speciality of its family mourning service.[150]

The average value of capital insured rose from £753 in the 1770s to £1224 in the 1820s, an increase of 63 per cent. Most businesses were quite small with 61 per cent insuring for £500 or less in the 1770s and over half 50 years later. Nevertheless, 20 per cent insured for over £1000 in the earlier period and this increased to 29 per cent in the later. A small proportion were among London's 'large' firms, insuring for £3000 or more, 4 per cent in the 1770s and nearly 11 per cent in the 1820s. Table 6.12 shows the full breakdown by value of capital insured.

As early as 1770 James Mawhood, John Paulin and John Coates were partners in a haberdashers with stock and utensils in Tavistock Street valued at £12,000,[151] and Wilson, Burley and Etty described themselves as lacemen when they insured their stock and utensils at 31 Lombard Street for £4000 five years later.[152] These firms would also have been wholesalers, as were Ellis and Brown of 16 Ludgate Street, who insured for £19,900 in 1819.[153] Swan and Edgar survived

TABLE 6.12 Haberdashers

Capital insured (£)	No. of firms 1770s	Percentage of total	No. of firms 1820s	Percentage of total
100 and under	52	18.8	42	22.5
101–500	118	42.6	61	32.6
501–1000	52	18.8	30	16.0
1001–2999	45	16.2	34	18.2
3000 and over	10	3.6	20	10.7
Total	277	100.0	187	100.0

Source: Sun and other London fire office registers

as a major London department store until the 1980s, but in 1820 still described themselves simply as 'haberdashers' when they insured stock and utensils at 10 Piccadilly valued at £7000.[154] By the following year George Swan, who founded the firm in 1814, was dead and his former assistant George Edgar had taken over and had achieved a turnover of £80,000.[155]

Hatters, hosiers and glovers were also numerous in London throughout this period; Pigot listed 226 hatters and 232 retail hosiers and glovers in 1826–27. It was only in the 1820s that 'milliners' became particularly identified with hats and bonnets; earlier they had been regarded as dealers in fancy articles of dress in general; Pigot listed 507. The total value of capital insured was over £330,000 in the 1820s. A comprehensive description of the stock of a hosier and glover is contained in an invoice sent out in 1763 by Thomas Jones of Holborn Bridge: 'all Sorts of Stockings, White & Colour'd Baize, Flannels, Linseys, & Swan-skins, Pieces for Waistcoats & Breeches, Worsteds, Swaithes, Gloves and Mittens, &c.'[156] Seventy years later the catalogue of the stock of a hatter, sold at auction in Lombard Street on 19 February 1834, included 58 beaver hats or bonnets, 69 caps, variously made of cloth, velvet, horse-hair, India rubber, leather, merino, seal-skin, oil-skin, fur and felt, 3 straw hats, 10 silk hats and 12 other hats.[157] The value of such a stock may be computed from an advertisement placed a few years earlier by Godfrey's Commission Hat-Warehouse at 14 Blackmoor Street which priced 'gentlemen's superfine best town-made beaver hats' at a guinea and waterproof silk hats at 16 shillings.[158]

TABLE 6.13 Hats, hosiery and gloves

Capital insured (£)	No. of firms 1770s	Percentage of total	No. of firms 1820s	Percentage of total
100 and under	136	22.7	64	23.6
101–500	300	50.2	98	36.2
501–1000	106	17.7	52	19.2
1001–2999	50	8.4	44	16.2
3000 and over	6	1.0	13	4.8
Total	598	100.0	271	100.0

Source: Sun and other London fire office registers

Few businesses were very large in any of these trades. The average value of capital insured was £494 in the 1770s and, although it doubled by the 1820s, it was still only £928. Nearly 73 per cent insured for £500 or less in the earlier period and 50 years later it was still 59 per cent. Indeed, nearly a quarter insured for £100 or less in both periods. A very small number (9 per cent) insured for over £1000 in the 1770s; by the 1820s this had risen significantly to 21 per cent. By then 5 per cent were insuring for £3000 or more. Table 6.13 shows the full breakdown by value of capital insured.

Among the larger retailers of hats, hosiery and gloves were Pleston and Fuller, hosiers at 76 Houndsditch, who insured for £8100 in 1769,[159] and Thomas Davies, a hatter at 83 New Bond Street, who insured for £4000 four years later.[160] However, by 1819 James Robertshaw, a hosier at 99–100 Oxford Street, was insuring for £19,700,[161] and two years later Borrodale, Sons and Ravenhill, hatters at 34 Fenchurch Street, insured goods valued at £8000.[162] A large specialist glover was Thomas Wing at 20 Great Newport Street. He insured stock, utensils and goods for £1600 in 1825.[163]

Beverley Lemire has amply demonstrated in recent years how, as part of the preoccupation with material betterment that characterised the eighteenth century, an increasing demand for clothing that was both cheap and fashionable led to the manufacture of ready-made clothing on an extensive scale, and to a network of retail dealers for its distribution, both new and second-hand.[164] Pigot listed 85 slop-sellers and another 251 dealers in ready-made clothes, and by the 1820s the trade as a whole insured capital valued at over £150,000. In fact, the second-hand trade had flourished from a very early date. In Beverley Lemire's words: 'Used apparel was available in the market place and, along with new garments, answered the needs of a significant segment of society, ranging from the middle ranks to labourers.'[165] Campbell put it very succinctly as early as 1747: 'The Salesmen deal in Old Cloaths, and sometimes in New.'[166] There were dealers in both new and used clothing and the existence of a large and widespread market for second-hand articles suggests that people were used to buying clothes already made-up.[167] The extent of the market in second-hand garments, and the original connection of the trade with supply of naval apparel, is exemplified by a trade card circulated in the 1760s by Charles Jones of 2 Sharps's Buildings, Rosemary Lane. He advertised 'all sorts of Men and Boys' Cloaths, Both New and Second-hand, and all Sorts of Sea Cloaths, great Choice of women's Apparel, Both New and Second-hand ... The greatest Price given for Left-off Cloaths'.[168] So large was the market that the term 'salesman' was synonymous with 'clothes salesman' throughout the later eighteenth century and into the nineteenth.

Hosiery and knitwear were produced in standard sizes from the eighteenth century and shirtmaking was a sweated industry in London in the early nineteenth. It has already been noted that in 1771 Bromley's linen and shirt warehouse in Charing Cross were advertising ready-made shirts to be supplied in any quantity, costing from 5s 6d to 21s.[169] Over forty years later in 1814, C. H. Herman described his premises at 25 Cockspur Street as a 'Ready Made Shirt and Handkerchief Warehouse'.[170] On a much wider scale, Thomas and Co at 193 Fleet Street advertised in 1820 'pelisses, mantles, or wrapping cloaks, dresses, spencers, bonnets, caps, turbans, super Leghorn and straw hats' to be selected from ' a stock of great multitude, which is kept in all sizes for instant accomodation'.[171] Although the great days of the huge ready-made clothing retailers like Hyam and Co, and most especially Moses and Son, did not arrive until the middle of the nineteenth century, their precursors were well known in the eighteenth and three members of the Moses family itself (Henry, David and Moses) were involved in the trade by the 1820s. All three described themselves as slopsellers.[172]

Throughout this period London was the undisputed centre of the ready-made clothing trade. By the 1820s the trade was international. In 1827, for example, John and William Dixon, slopsellers at 50

TABLE 6.14 Retailers of ready-made clothing

Capital insured (£)	No. of firms 1770s	Percentage of total	No. of firms 1820s	Percentage of total
100 and under	57	31.0	63	27.0
101–500	90	48.9	118	50.6
501–1000	29	15.8	31	13.3
1001–2999	8	4.3	16	6.9
3000 and over	0	0	5	2.1
Total	184	100.0	233	100.0

Source: Sun and other London fire office registers

Fenchurch Street, invoiced for jackets, coats waistcoats, beaver hats, breeches and cloaks, describing the order as 'Negro Clothing for Exportation'.[173] Thomas Mortimer was quite wrong when he wrote in 1823 that 'Ready-made clothes ... have recently become an article of considerable interest in commerce'.[174] They had long been so. Unsurprisingly, the large majority of retailers of ready-made clothing were very small indeed. The average value of capital insured was only £335 in the 1770s, and it rose very little to £454 by the 1820s. Throughout the period 1775–1825, four out of five dealers insured capital valued at £500 or less. In the 1770s, only 4 per cent insured for more than £1000 and this proportion little more than doubled over the next 50 years. Table 6.14 shows the full breakdown by value of capital insured.

Among the few larger businesses in the 1770s was George Purdon of 97 Lower Thames Street. He described himself as a slopseller and undoubtedly was still supplying the naval market in 1770 when he insured for £1600.[175] By the 1820s there were several much larger businesses. Dixon and Co insured stock and utensils for £4000 in 1821,[176] and three years later Mosedon and Crockett of 7 Minories, who described themselves as clothes salesmen, insured for £3050.[177] Already there were numerous Jewish-owned businesses in the ready-made clothing trade, some on a substantial scale like Isaac and Mark Israel of 69 Lower East Smithfield, who described themselves as slopsellers and salesmen when they insured their stock and utensils for £1550 in 1821.[178] The two major locations for the trade in used clothing were around Rosemary Lane and the Minories to the east of the City and in and around Monmouth Street in Seven Dials to the west; two-thirds of all such dealers were to be found there throughout the period 1775–1825.

The other great area of consumer demand for ready-made articles of apparel was shoes. Pigot listed 1672 boot- and shoemakers and in the 1820s they insured capital valued at nearly £500,000. As early as 1738, and probably before that, the London shoemaking trade acknowledged clear distinctions between bespoke production and retail sale of ready-made products and by 1770 the retail trade in ready-made shoes was well established.[179] A trade card circulated by Charles Bottrell of Newgate Street stated that he 'Makes & Sells all sorts of Men's Shoes, Boots & Pumps, Likewise all sorts of Women's & Children's Shoes & Clogs, Wholesale & Retail'.[180] An advertisement placed in 1828 by W. Figg for his 'Cheap Shoe Warehouse' at 29 Stonecutter Street shows that the practice of selling retail to London customers and wholesale to country shopkeepers was not confined to textiles. It read: 'Schools and Charities of every description served on the lowest terms. A great choice of Ladies' Fashionable and Strong Boots and Shoes of every description, Gentlemen's Strong and Light Shoes of every kind, Pattens and Clogs of every description made to order. Country Shopkeepers supplied.'[181] Retail business was also carried out side by side with an export trade. Collyer had described in 1761 how 'The master shoe-makers in London keep shop and employ many workmen and workwomen. Some of them export great quantities to our Plantations.'[182]

As in most of the clothing trades, the large majority of businesses were very small. The average value of capital insured was £174 in the 1770s; 50 years later it had increased only to £296. In the earlier period over half of all London shoemakers insured for £100 or less and almost all the rest for between £100 and £500. Fifty years later more than a third were insuring for £100 or less and over half for between £100 and £500. Table 6.15 shows the full breakdown by value of capital insured.

A rare larger business in the 1770s was that of John Hayter of King Street, Westminster. He insured stock and utensils valued at £1100 in 1770.[183] A few firms described themselves as 'shoe warehousemen' and were exclusively retailers of ready-made boots and shoes. One, William Dorsett, insured stock and utensils valued at £800 in his Piccadilly 'warehouse' in 1769.[184] By the 1820s there were

TABLE 6.15 Shoemakers

Capital insured (£)	No. of firms 1770s	Percentage of total	No. of firms 1820s	Percentage of total
100 and under	137	52.9	100	34.2
101–500	106	40.9	156	53.4
501–1000	15	5.8	23	7.9
1001–2999	1	0.4	12	4.1
3000 and over	0	0	1	0.3
Total	259	100.0	292	100.0

Source: Sun and other London fire office registers

a small number of larger shoemakers such as John and Henry Gamble of 33 Fish Street Hill who insured for £3800 in 1823.[185] Some bespoke shoemakers insured their workshops, for example John Blacklock who insured his at 21 Everett Street, Russell Square, for £100 in 1819.[186]

The average annual profit for 37 clothing, textiles and footwear retailers was £770 in the 1820s. There were considerable variations. Over the six years prior to cessation of trading in 1826, William and Henry Hart, linen drapers in High Holborn, averaged profits of £2269 a year.[187] However, another firm of linen drapers, Davies and Morris of Crawford Street, showed an average of only £615 over the four years prior to their bankruptcy in 1828.[188] Smaller again were the profits of Thomas Milligan, a haberdasher who ceased trading in 1825, Thomas Farrar, a slopseller of 46 Shadwell High Street, who ceased trading in 1826 and Joseph Farrant, a tailor at 420 Strand, who was declared bankrupt in 1822. They showed annual average profits of £627 over five years and nine months, £557 over three and a half years and £467 over three years and nine months respectively.[189] Samuel Woolston, a boot- and shoemaker in Bloomsbury High Street, showed a profit of 20 per cent (£542) on an annual turnover of £2745 over a three-year period prior to ceasing trading in 1826.[190]

Hardware and Household Goods Pigot listed 2528 businesses supplying Londoners with hardware, ironmongery and household goods. This was nearly 13 per cent of all London retailers, and over 5 per cent of all firms in the metropolis. They insured capital valued at over £2.5 million in the 1820s, nearly 16 per cent of all capital insured in the retail sector. It is a measure of the increasing importance of these trades that the number of 'large' firms, insuring for £3000 or more, more than trebled between the 1770s and the 1820s, from 2 per cent to 6 per cent.

Hardwaremen and ironmongers were no longer craftsmen-shopkeepers by the late eighteenth century but retailers of products which were as likely, if not more likely, to have been made in Birmingham as by the hundreds of small London manufacturers of finished metal and other household goods. Pigot listed 859 in 1826–27. The commonest trade was retail ironmonger, of which there were 383, although many firms described themselves as both ironmongers and hardwaremen. Within the trade as a whole more than one million pounds was insured in the 1820s. A comprehensive description of the ironmonger's trade was set out in the trade card of Edward and William Martin of Foster Lane. In 1776 they stocked:

> all sorts of Files and Tools for Goldsmiths, Jewellers, Engravers, Clock and Watchmakers; also for Blacksmiths, Gun-makers, Braziers, Tin-men, Upholsterers, Carpenters, Joyners, Carvers, Turners, Coopers, Bricklayers, Shoemakers, and all other Artificers; Curriers' Knives & Implements for Gardening, all Sorts of Nails, Locks, Hinges and Brass-work for cabinets &c, Furniture for Coffins; all sorts of Brass & Iron Wire, Spinnet and Harpsichord ditto, Watch-keys, Glasses, Springs, Pinion-wire & other Materials for Watchmakers ... Melting Pots of all Sorts, Emmery, Pumice & Rollen Stones, Turkey Oil-stones ... Steel of all sorts, Houghs, Bills, Axes & other Iron Work for ye Plantations.[191]

A rather different range of stock was kept by Warner and Cooke of New Bond Street in 1772: 'Locks, Hinges, Nails and Brass Cabinet Goods, Fine Grates, Bath-stoves, Kitchen-ranges, Smoke and windup-Jacks ... Copper Utensils ... Plated Goods. Japanned- waiters, Table Knives & Forks & Gentlemen's Tool Chests.'[192]

Few ironmongers or hardwaremen were very small and the average value of capital insured was at the higher end of the range for London's retail trades: £796 in the 1770s and £1250 in the 1820s. Just under a half of all businesses insured capital valued at between £100 and £500 in the 1770s; half a century later this had reduced to just over a third. One in five insured for more than £1000 in the earlier period, one in three in the later. Another measure of the increasing capitalisation of the trade over the period 1775–1825 was the three-fold increase in the proportion of 'large' businesses, insuring for £3000

TABLE 6.16 Hardware and ironmongery

Capital insured (£)	No. of firms 1770s	Percentage of total	No. of firms 1820s	Percentage of total
100 and under	16	13.0	17	11.6
101–500	59	48.0	53	36.1
501–1000	23	18.7	28	19.0
1001–2999	20	16.3	31	21.1
3000 and over	5	4.1	18	12.2
Total	123	100.0	147	100.0

Source: Sun and other London fire office registers

or more, from 4 per cent to over 12 per cent. Table 6.16 shows the full breakdown by value of capital insured.

Among the very large firms in the trade in the 1770s were Townsend and Crossley of 3 Gracechurch Street, who insured stock, utensils and goods for £9000 in 1770.[193] Nearly half a century later in 1819, Morris Emanuel of 1 Bevis Marks described himself as a hardwareman when he insured stock and utensils valued at £7000.[194] The retail trade was heavily concentrated in the City, where about half of all ironmongers and hardwaremen were to be found throughout the period 1775–1825, and the west central area, where nearly a third were to be found. However, one of the largest firms of general ironmongers was Holmer, Martyr, Moser and Manson at 165 Borough High Street. The firm was founded by Thomas Dunnett in 1787 and by 1790 he was in partnership with William Holmer and George Pix. The initial capital had been £1000. By 1814 their stock was valued at £9000 and in 1823 at £11,600. Their profits rose from £1700 in 1815 to £3000 in 1823. By about 1830 the firm was valued at £28,800 and was under the sole proprietorship of Richard Moser. Under this name the firm survived into the present century.[195]

Another comparatively highly capitalised trade was china, glass and earthenware. Pigot listed 466 retailers, of which 340 called themselves dealers in china, glass and earthenware. Eight were specialist dealers in imported china and porcelain. Another 91 were dealers in glass. In the 1820s the total value of capital insured was over £530,000. The trade involved complex relationships between supplier and retailer. John Wylie established his cut glass manufactory and Staffordshire

TABLE 6.17 China, glass and earthenware

Capital insured (£)	No. of firms 1770s	Percentage of total	No. of firms 1820s	Percentage of total
100 and under	57	39.9	33	23.4
101–500	47	32.9	62	44.0
501–1000	21	14.7	16	11.3
1001–2999	13	9.1	18	12.8
3000 and over	5	3.5	12	8.5
Total	143	100.0	141	100.0

Source: Sun and other London fire office registers

warehouse at 7 Smock Alley, off Widegate Street, in 1792 and the firm survived into the 1850s. By the 1820s it was buying from no fewer than 45 Staffordshire makers, with annual purchases varying in the period 1794–1825 from as little as £101 to as much as £1443. Purchases of glass were about £800 a year.[196] In 1767 Maydell and Windle of the Strand, who described themselves as 'Glass Makers to his Majesty', sent an interesting invoice to Sir Cotton Lynch. It was for 14½ dozen assorted wine, ale and water glasses costing £7 0s 6d and was not settled until 18 May 1769, two years after they had been supplied.[197]

The average value of capital insured more than doubled between the 1770s and 1820s, from £589 to £1146. In the earlier period nearly 73 per cent insured for £500 or less and 50 years later this had fallen only to 67 per cent. However, by the 1820s more than 21 per cent were insuring capital valued at over £1000. Table 6.17 shows the full breakdown by value of capital insured.

A small number of firms were large enough to insure for £3000 or more. In 1770 Akerman and Scrivenor insured stock and utensils at 3 Fenchurch Street for £10,000.[198] A showroom at 69 Fleet Street was insured for £500 by William Parker in 1769, its contents for £5500 three years later.[199] By the 1820s the largest retail outlets were mostly the London showrooms of the great Staffordshire potters. In 1824 James Davenport and Co also insured a warehouse for £500 in Fleet Street, at number 82, but its contents for the vast sum of £24,500.[200] In the same year Josiah Wedgwood insured for £14,000 in York Street, St James's. There was nothing new about this. In 1771, the first Josiah

Wedgwood, calling himself a Staffordshire warehouseman and aware of the value of a London showroom in providing access to a market accustomed to 'fine prices', had insured stock and utensils for £3000 at his retail premises in Great Newport Street.[201] Earlier still, in 1752, the Chelsea works had a showroom in Pall Mall where stock was insured for £2000.[202]

In addition to the 1718 cabinet makers and related trades described above, Pigot listed 478 retail dealers in furniture and general household goods in 1826–27. Most were known as 'brokers' in the 1770s and 'brokers of household goods' half a century later. There was a very real social distinction between the cabinet maker and the broker, illustrated in Thackeray's *The Newcomes*: 'The fine house in Tyburnia was completed by this time, as gorgeous as money could make it. How different it was from the old Fitzroy Square mansion with its ramshackle furniture, and spoils of broker's shops, and Tottenham Court Road odds and ends.'[203] Indeed, many of the general brokers and the more specialised dealers in, for example, bedsteads, writing desks and looking-glasses were dealing in second-hand articles. The trade card of Joseph Hubbard, a broker at 10 Marshall Street, Carnaby Market, stated in 1779 that he 'Appraises, Buys and Sells all manner of Household Furniture'.[204] Over forty years later another trade card, circulated by James March of 15 Coburg Place, Southwark, who described himself as a furniture broker, promised 'A fair price given for all sorts of Household Furniture'.[205]

Most businesses were very small. In the 1770s only 2 per cent insured for over £1000 and 92 per cent for £500 or less, 33 per cent for £100 or less. Even 50 years later 74 per cent insured for £500 or less. The average value of capital insured increased only from £253 to £493. Table 6.18 shows the full breakdown by value of capital insured.

While there were virtually no larger businesses in the 1770s, by the 1820s there were a few. One broker of household goods, Peter Jackson, insured his warehouse at 1 Harp Alley, Fleet Market, for £300 in 1819, and its contents for £5100.[206] Four years later William Kinsey, who described himself as a printed furniture warehouseman at his fashionable premises at 125 New Bond Street, insured stock and utensils for £4500.[207]

Separately listed by Pigot were 144 specialist dealers in carpets, household textiles and furnishing fabrics, 73 of them described as 'carpet warehouses'. Some of the latter were quite substantial.

TABLE 6.18 Furniture and general household goods

Capital insured (£)	No. of firms 1770s	Percentage of total	No. of firms 1820s	Percentage of total
100 and under	54	32.7	35	18.3
101–500	97	58.8	110	57.6
501–1000	10	6.1	28	14.7
1001–2999	4	2.4	13	6.8
3000 and over	0	0	5	2.6
Total	165	100.0	191	100.0

Source: Sun and other London fire office registers

William Tomlinson, for example, in St Helen's Place, insured for the very large sum of £6000 in 1819.[208]

There were also large numbers of retailers of oils, candles and paints. Pigot listed 376 and they accounted for capital insured for nearly £300,000 in the 1820s. Most were either oil- and colourmen or wax and/or tallow chandlers. A typical statement of the former's trade is contained in an invoice sent out in 1830 by Henry Smith of 146 Shoreditch High Street: 'Colours prepared in Oil or water for Painting, Painter's Brushes & Varnishes of every description, Pitch, Tar, Resin, Oils, Turpentine'; the latter by a trade card circulated in 1794 by James Elmer of 69 Cannon Street who sold: 'Soap, Starch & Blues ... Mould and Stove Candles.'[209] Most firms were of middling size, 69 per cent insuring for between £100 and £500 in the 1770s and 54 per cent in the 1820s. The proportions insuring for over £1000 were 9 per cent and 15 per cent. The average value of capital insured increased only from £514 to £727. Table 6.19 shows the full breakdown by value of capital insured.

Among the small number of 'large' firms in the 1770s was Moore, Smith and Sack, oil- and colourmen at 99 High Holborn. They insured for £10,800 in 1775.[210] Forty-five years later Mayor, Mayor and Yates at 52 Little Britain insured for the nearly identical figure of £11,000.[211] A very large tallow chandler was Thomas Merrigan at 53 Burr Street who insured for £3200 in 1771.[212]

There were smaller numbers of other retailers of household goods as well. For example, Pigot listed 175 retailers of cutlery and plated goods, 98 dealers in pictures and prints and 76 dealers in music or

TABLE 6.19   Oils, candles and paints

Capital insured (£)	No. of firms 1770s	Percentage of total	No. of firms 1820s	Percentage of total
100 and under	14	6.1	14	6.3
101–500	158	69.0	121	54.0
501–1000	36	15.7	55	24.6
1001–2999	17	7.4	28	12.5
3000 and over	4	1.7	6	2.7
Total	229	100.0	224	100.0

Source: Sun and other London fire office registers

musical instruments. Cutlery was typical of the retail trades in household goods in that the articles sold were less and less likely to have been made in London, either by the shopkeeper himself or by a London manufacturer. As early as 1747 Campbell had noted that cutlery manufactured in Birmingham and Sheffield was as good as anything made in London, and much cheaper.[213] The 1770 invoice of W. Riccard, a cutler in Castle Street, Leicester Fields, mentions that he made as well as sold 'razors, knives, scissors, lancets, etc'.[214] However, by the 1840s Dodd was drawing attention to the fact that such articles were merely finished in London.[215] A typical trade card from a retailer at the upper end of the market survives from 1796. Like fine china, it comes from the fashionably located London showroom of a provincial manufacturer. John Bright's Sheffield Plate Company Warehouse in Bruton Street advertised: 'Dinner Services in Dishes, Covers Plated, Water Plates, Turners, Epergues, Bread-Baskets, Candlesticks & Branches, Tea-Equipages, Vases, Kettles & Lamps, Tea-Pots, Coffee-Pots.'[216] One major City cutler, George Machin of 60 Leadenhall Street, insured stock and utensils for £3400 in 1820.[217]

Considerable sums were also insured by a few printsellers such as Hurst, Robinson and Co of 90 Cheapside who insured for the huge sum of £20,000 in 1819.[218] In a much smaller way of business were a number of dealers in pictures and curiosities, such as Montague Levoi who in 1820 insured his stock, utensils and goods at 52 Greek Street for £600.[219] Finally, note should be made of London's music and musical instrument sellers. In practice most dealers were primarily musical instrument makers but there were a small number of substantial music sellers. Peter Welcher of Gerrard Street insured stock specified as 'printed music' for no less than £2200 in 1773.[220] On a different scale to any other firm in the trade were Birchall, Lonsdale and Mills at 140 New Bond Street. They described themselves as music and musical instrument sellers in 1821 when they insured their stock, utensils and goods for £9500.[221]

Bankruptcy Commission files for 23 retailers of household goods show an average annual profit of £517. A little higher than this was the figure for Henry Downer, an ironmonger in the Strand. He averaged £635 for the nine years prior to his bankruptcy in 1826.[222] Another ironmonger, John Paterson of New Bridge Street, commenced trading with a capital of £1000. He increased profits nearly ten-fold between 1820 and 1823, from £160 to £1510. But then they fell away to £716 in 1825 and £236 in 1826. He ceased trading in 1827.[223] Much lower annual profits were shown over seven- and nine-year periods prior to their bankruptcies in 1827 and 1825 respectively by Philip Raphael, a dealer in glass, china and earthenware in Hosier Lane (£320),[224] and Thomas Lane, an oil and colourman in Chandos Street (£270).[225]

Coal and Fuel Another basic necessity of life was coal and fuel. As far as the retail sector is concerned, Pigot listed 593 coal merchants in 1826–27. In addition, many chandlers and other small retailers also dealt in small amounts of coal. Interestingly, this latter trade diminished over the period 1775–1825: in the 1770s the fire office registers contain policies for 161 per cent more chandlers and other retail businesses which described their secondary activity as dealing in coal as there were actual coal merchants; fifty years later there were only 83 per cent more. The large majority of retail coal merchants were very small. In the 1770s nearly 97 per cent insured for £500 or less and half a century later it was still 95 per cent. Table 6.20 shows the full breakdown by value of capital insured.

Typifying the trade throughout the period was Thomas White. He described himself as a dealer in coals and insured his coal shed at 152 Whitecross Street for £60 in 1777, his carts for the same amount, the stables for his horses for £50, and his stock and utensils for £540.[226]

Books and Stationery The last quarter of the eighteenth century and the first quarter of the nineteenth saw Britain become a society

TABLE 6.20 Coal and fuel

Capital insured (£)	No. of firms 1770s	Percentage of total	No. of firms 1820s	Percentage of total
100 and under	66	45.5	66	61.7
101–500	74	51.0	36	33.6
501–1000	3	2.1	4	3.7
1001–2999	1	0.7	1	0.9
3000 and over	1	0.7	0	0
Total	145	100.0	107	100.0

Source: Sun and other London fire office registers

dependent on the written word as never before. It has already been noted that London was the centre of the printing and publishing trades and that these were among the most important in the metropolis, and growing steadily more important. The scale of the bookselling trade became enormous. James Lackington of Chiswell Street, who claimed to be 'the cheapest bookseller in the world' was selling 100,000 new and second-hand volumes a year in the 1790s and making annual profits of £5000, although he started in business with just £5. As early as 1784 he issued a catalogue of 12,000 titles, with another containing 20,000 a few years later.[227] In practice it is far from easy to distinguish booksellers from publishers, printers and bookbinders on the one hand, and stationers on the other. Many firms in the trade described themselves as both booksellers and stationers: 18 per cent in the 1770s and 15 per cent in the 1820s. Pigot listed 685 booksellers and 501 stationers who between them insured capital valued at just under two million pounds.

Bookselling was one of the most highly capitalised of London's retail trades. The average value of capital insured more than doubled from £980 in the 1770s to £2386 fifty years later. Nevertheless, many booksellers were quite small. Over half insured capital valued at £500 or less in both the 1770s and 1820s. Such firms accounted for 14 per cent of all capital insured in the 1770s, but for under 6 per cent 50 years later. The major difference between the 1770s and the 1820s was the increase in the proportion of larger firms. Those insuring for £1000 increased from under 22 per cent to 34 per cent. Even more significantly, the proportion of 'large' firms, insuring for £3000 or

TABLE 6.21 Booksellers

Capital insured (£)	No. of firms 1770s	Percentage of total	No. of firms 1820s	Percentage of total
100 and under	12	10.0	23	11.5
101–500	51	42.5	82	41.0
501–1000	31	25.8	27	13.5
1001–2999	17	14.2	30	15.0
3000 and over	9	7.5	38	19.0
Total	120	100.0	200	100.0

Source: Sun and other London fire office registers

more, rose from 7.5 per cent to 19 per cent. Table 6.21 shows the full breakdown by value of capital insured.

Firms such as Longman's, John Murray, Joseph Butterworth and Sons, Thomas Kelly and George Whitaker and Co described themselves as booksellers throughout this period even though they had evolved into what would later be thought of as very large publishing houses. All insured for five-figure sums in the 1820s. However, there were booksellers proper on a substantial scale in both the 1770s and 1820s. In 1769 Robinson and Roberts insured stock, utensils and goods at 25 Paternoster Row for £5500.[228] Half a century later in 1825, Howell and Stewart of 295 High Holborn insured stock and utensils valued at £5600.[229] However, more typical of London booksellers in general were Benjamin White of 63 Fleet Street, who insured his stock for £500 in 1769, and Priscilla and Agnes Nicol of 3 Great Newport Street, who insured for £400 in 1820.[230] Profits could be very high. William and John Baynes of Paternoster Row made over £1160 in the nine months prior to their bankruptcy in 1828 alone.[231] However, the average for 13 firms declared bankrupt in the 1820s was £484 and William Anderson of Waterloo Place averaged only £395 in the six years before ceasing trading in 1830.[232]

The activities of London's stationers overlapped not only with the book trade, but also with paper manufacturing. Thus, Bloxham and Fourdrinier described themselves as both retail and wholesale stationers in the 1770s when they insured their warehouse at 11 Lombard Street for £3000 and its contents for £9000 in 1777. By 1825 they had become large-scale paper manufacturers but were still insuring stock

TABLE 6.22 Stationers

Capital insured (£)	No. of firms 1770s	Percentage of total	No. of firms 1820s	Percentage of total
100 and under	20	18.0	24	15.9
101–500	56	50.5	84	55.6
501–1000	23	20.7	21	13.9
1001–2999	10	9.0	17	11.3
3000 and over	2	1.8	5	3.3
Total	111	100.0	151	100.0

Source: Sun and other London fire office registers

and fittings as stationers valued at £2000.[233] Of the 501 stationers listed by Pigot, 127 were specialist law stationers and 17 were described as fancy stationers. Unlike the book trade, there was very little change in average capitalisation between the 1770s and 1820s; it increased only from £627 to £640. Over 70 per cent insured for £500 or less in both periods and these smaller firms accounted for over a quarter of all capital insured. A newspaper advertisement in 1820 referred to premises at 7 St Agnes Place, Old Street Road, and read 'to be disposed of, the stock and fixtures of a small shop in the stationery line ... Any person who has from £50 to £100 at command will find it worth his attention'.[234] Less than 2 per cent could be regarded as 'large' firms in the 1770s and only just over 3 per cent 50 years later. Table 6.22 shows the full breakdown by value of capital insured.

In 1820 William Dobson of 166 Strand insured for £6100,[235] and five years later a law stationer, Lucas Houghton, insured stock, utensils and goods for £2000 in his two branches at 30 Poultry and 119 Chancery Lane in 1825.[236] James Arthur traded as a stationer in Garlick Hill. His original start-up capital was £980. Profits rose each year between 1823 and 1828, from £297 to £646. However, he was then declared bankrupt even though his stock was valued at the substantial figure of £1668. Somehow he had managed to run up debts of £4753.[237]

Jewellery The comprehensive list of London's goldsmiths, jewellers, bankers and pawnbrokers from 1200 to 1800 compiled by Sir Ambrose Heal includes 566 firms involved in the retail jewellery trade between

1760 and 1780. The overlap with other trades is considerable. Besides working gold- or silversmiths, there were cutlers, spoon makers, toymen, hardwaremen, watch and watch case makers, plate workers, gold lacemen, necklace makers, diamond merchants, pawnbrokers and, at very different ends of the spectrum, artificial teeth makers and bankers.[238] It is very difficult to distinguish between firms involved in bespoke work, those retailing the work of other manufacturers and those engaged purely in manufacturing. Many firms were involved in all three. However, the fire office registers do enable those businesses mainly involved in either bespoke work or retail sales to be identified. Pigot listed 375 and they insured capital valued at nearly £600,000 in the 1820s.

There were predominantly retail businesses as early as the first half of the eighteenth century. A trade card from the period 1739–62 shows a well-stocked retail shop interior in St Paul's Churchyard.[239] In 1830 an advertisement for S. Alderman, a jeweller, silversmith and cutler with shops at 41–2 Barbican and 16 Norton Folgate, infers that jewellery stocked at his 'Extensive Showroom and Warehouse at the back of the Premises' was mainly manufactured by them but cutlery and plate by others.[240] The firm was established in 1796 and in 1825 insured capital valued at £3500.[241]

The retail jewellery trade grew substantially in size between the 1770s and the 1820s: the average value of capital insured nearly trebled from £554 to £1541. Two-thirds of all businesses insured for £500 or less in the 1770s but half a century later this had fallen to under 43 per cent. More importantly, the number of 'large' firms insuring for £3000 or more rose from only 1 per cent to over 16 per cent. Table 6.23 shows the full breakdown by value of capital insured.

In the 1770s the largest jewellers were to be found in the City. Two examples, both in Cornhill, were Henry Shephard at number 85, who insured stock, utensils and goods for £5500 in 1772,[242] and Bird and Branston at number 39, who insured for £3000 two years later.[243] By the 1820s the largest and most fashionable jewellers were located in the West End, such as Harker and Wiltshire at 6 Old Bond Street who insured their general stock and utensils for £7500, and jewels, precious stones and diamonds for £5200 in 1825.[244] Garrard's, at this period in Panton Street and under the proprietorship of Robert, James and Sebastian, insured for £9000 in 1822.[245] William Asprey had already founded his firm in Bond Street by 1781.[246] Some idea of the

TABLE 6.23 Jewellery

Capital insured (£)	No. of firms 1770s	Percentage of total	No. of firms 1820s	Percentage of total
100 and under	28	18.5	13	7.2
101–500	73	48.3	64	35.6
501–1000	31	20.5	34	18.9
1001–2999	17	11.3	40	22.2
3000 and over	2	1.3	29	16.1
Total	151	100.0	180	100.0

Source: Sun and other London fire office registers

grandeur of the West End jeweller can be gathered from the fire insurance policy of Francis Lambert. He insured the window glass alone in his shop front at 11–12 Coventry Street for £200 in 1819, as well as stock and utensils valued at £3100, gold valued at £2000 and silver at £1000.[247] The wealth of the trade is illustrated by a catalogue published in 1831 by Thomas Cox Savory of 47 Cornhill. The firm was founded in 1751 and 80 years later their stock filled 24 pages and included silver cutlery sets priced from £55 to £90 and silver tea sets from £34 to £63.[248]

Pigot also listed 109 toymen. These dealers in small trinkets often overlapped with jewellers and both Henry Shephard and Bird and Branston called themselves 'toymen' as well as jewellers and gold-smiths. One firm of toymen, Child and Co of 123–4 Upper Thames Street, traded throughout the period 1775–1825, insuring for £1650 in 1771 and for £9000 in 1821.[249] Profits could be very high. Leonard Hill in Fleet Street averaged £1140 a year over the decade prior to his bankruptcy in 1826,[250] and John Harker £909 in the 19 years before ceasing to trade in 1825.[251]

Pawnbrokers Not included in the retail sector as such, but closely linked with both the retail jewellery trade and the trade in used clothes, were London's pawnbrokers. The century from 1750 to 1850 has been described as the period of fastest growth for the trade. In 1796 Patrick Colquhoun had estimated 240 in London and 30 years later Pigot listed 245. Undoubtedly these were understatements. In 1830 there were 380 licensed pawnbrokers in London, a quarter of

TABLE 6.24 Pawnbrokers

Capital insured (£)	No. of firms 1770s	Percentage of total	No. of firms 1820s	Percentage of total
100 and under	17	6.0	1	1.3
101–500	131	46.0	7	9.1
501–1000	54	18.9	13	16.9
1001–2999	58	20.4	19	24.7
3000 and over	25	8.8	37	48.1
Total	285	100.0	77	100.0

Source: Sun and other London fire office registers

all those in Britain, but there were also many unlicensed and illegal businesses charging more than the rates of interest laid down in the succession of Acts from 1756 to 1800.[252] Many jewellers and gold-smiths were also involved in pawnbroking. By the 1820s pawnbrokers insured capital valued at over £760,000. Generally speaking they insured three distinct categories of risk: plate and watches; 'stock as a salesman', that is mainly used clothes; and general 'pledges'. The trade card of John Flude of 3 Gracechurch Street stated in 1780 that he 'Lends Money on Plate, Watches, Jewells, Wearing Apparel, House-hold Goods, & Stock in Trade'.[253] In 1836 a Glasgow pawnbroker, whose stock of pledges would have been little different to those of any substantial London firm over the previous 60 or 70 years, listed no less than 4725 items of clothing (including 539 men's coats, 1980 women's gowns and 540 petticoats), 860 pieces of bedding (including 108 pillows and 300 pairs of sheets), 102 Bibles, 216 rings, 36 table-cloths, 48 umbrellas and the same number of Waterloo medals.[254]

Pawnbrokers were an essential part of London life. In the same year, 1747, as Hogarth prominently displayed the pawnbroker's sign in both his 'Beer Street' and 'Gin Lane' engravings, Campbell had an unusually good word for them when he described them as 'a Kind of broker for the Poor ... so necessary to the poor labouring Tradesmen in this Metropolis'.[255] Two years earlier it had been noted that annual rates of interest on small pledges were 50 per cent, when the legal maximum was supposed to be five.[256] In the 1770s, well over half insured capital valued at £500 or less, although 29 per cent insured for over £1000. Fifty years later these proportions were 10 per cent and 73 per cent. The average value of capital insured rose from £1021 to £3117 and the number of 'large' firms insuring for £3000 or more from under 9 per cent to over 48 per cent. Table 6.24 shows the full breakdown by value of capital insured.

In 1775 Timothy and Nathaniel Parker of Prince's Street, Leicester Fields, insured pledges valued at £7000.[257] However, this was over-shadowed by the pledges insured for £14,000 by Filmer and Sons in Kent Road in 1823.[258] Profits could be very substantial: Thomas Stafford in St John Street averaged £4400 a year over a four-year period prior to his bankruptcy in 1827.[259] A typical smaller pawnbroker was William Matthews at 36 Stanhope Street who insured pledges for £300, plate and watches for £180 and general stock and utensils for £50 in 1825.[260]

Apothecaries, Chemists and Druggists Pigot listed no fewer than 929 London apothecaries, chemists and druggists in 1826–27. Perhaps one reason was that London, like all upwardly mobile and increasingly wealthy societies, was preoccupied with its health. Another may be explained by Campbell's famous description of the trade of apothe-cary in 1747: 'There is no Branch of Business, in which a Man requires less Money to set him up, than this very profitable Trade ... His profits are unconceivable; Five Hundred per Cent is the least he receives.'[261] By the 1820s the trade as a whole insured capital valued at nearly half a million pounds.

Although it was in the latter part of the eighteenth century, and particularly after the Apothecaries Act of 1815, that clearer distinc-tions began to emerge between the practice of medicine, the retailing of drugs and medicines and their manufacture, these distinctions had long been recognised. Seventy years earlier Campbell had noted that the apothecary 'is only employed in composing of Medicines, by the Doctor's Prescriptions'.[262] The 1815 Act was the first to require licensing by examination for the medical profession. However, it did not apply to the 'lowly chemist and druggist' with a shop and it is interesting to note that in the first four years after the Act only 59 people qualified in London, at a time when the number of retailers of medicines and drugs was little short of a thousand.[263] For the purposes of this book, the dispenser of medicines, whatever he called himself, is dealt with as a retailer. A recent study of the English apothecary stresses that by 1760:

The difference between the practice of a dispensing chemist and of an apothecary was not necessarily great ... Both operated a shop where drugs, compound preparations and household commodities were sold, both dispensed prescriptions ... both carried out in their shops minor surgical operations such as drawing teeth, lancing boils, or bandaging wounds. The major difference was that the apothecary travelled to the patient's house ... the dispensing chemist seems not to have left his shop.[264]

Even this may go too far. The medical profession proper appears to have looked down on the apothecary as a mere tradesman and certainly Lichtenberg in 1775 took it for granted that they were shopkeepers when he described how 'the apothecaries and druggists in Cheapside and Fleet Street display glasses filled with gay-coloured spirits'.[265] As late as 1841 the *Pharmaceutical Journal* was still complaining that:

In the same street may be seen two shops, fitted up exactly alike. The windows of each are adorned with coloured show bottles, cut smelling bottles, medicine chests, tooth-brushes, and perchance a few proprietary medicines. One of these shops belongs to a member of the College of Surgeons, and a licentiate of the Apothecaries Company; the other is the establishment of a Chemist and Druggist who is probably a member of no society, and who is not obliged by law to know the difference between jolap and rhubarb, much less to distinguish fungus haematodes from a cancer, or peripneumonia from pleurisy.[266]

The other side of the coin is stressed by Roy Porter in his study of 'quackery'. Indeed, he regards 'quack' as a neutral term for anyone, formally qualified or not, 'who drummed up custom largely through self-orchestrated publicity: who operated as individual entrepreneur ... and who depended heavily upon vending secret nostrums'.[267]

Contemporary trade descriptions also stress the retailing aspect. In 1819 the bankruptcy file of James Hyde, an apothecary in Union Place, New Road, described his trade as 'making and compounding medicines, and vending the same when made, and also ... vending and selling drugs'.[268] Long before this, in 1776, Samuel Parkes, who described himself as a chemist and druggist and kept a shop at 68 Chiswell Street, circulated a handbill listing over 60 drugs, oils and herbs for sale.[269] The trade was still as profitable in 1829 as Campbell claimed in 1747. Godfrey Cooke, a chemist with branches in Southampton Street and Conduit Street, invoiced in 1829 for 'Two

TABLE 6.25 Apothecaries, chemists and druggists

Capital insured (£)	No. of firms 1770s	Percentage of total	No. of firms 1820s	Percentage of total
100 and under	100	39.7	52	28.3
101–500	118	46.8	89	48.4
501–1000	14	5.6	21	11.4
1001–2999	14	5.6	16	8.7
3000 and over	6 ·	2.4	6	3.3
Total	252	100.0	184	100.0

Source: Sun and other London fire office registers

Pint Bottles of the finest Cold Drawn Castor Oil' at a cost of one guinea,[270] while nine years earlier Shephard's camphor lozenges were priced at between 2s 6d and 10s a bottle.[271] Medical expenses could be a considerable proportion of a family's outgoings. A bankruptcy file from 1828 showed that nearly 15 per cent of household expenditure went on 'medicines and medical attention', £159 6s 3d out of £1084 6s 3d over an 11-year period.[272]

Perfumers were already linked with retailers of drugs and medicines. In the 1820s Thomas Blofield described his business at 6 Middle Row, Holborn, as perfumer and dealer in patent medicines.[273] In 1807 Patey, Butts and Co stocked soaps, tooth powders, razors, razor strops, perfumes, creams, lavender water and pomatum in their Lombard Street shop.[274]

All the eighteenth-century career guides suggest as little as £50 or £100 was required to set up in business as an apothecary, although up to £500 might be required for a chemist and druggist. The average capital insured was £379 in the 1770s and no more than £513 fifty years later. In both the 1770s and 1820s, nearly half of all businesses insured capital valued at between £100 and £500, with a substantial proportion insuring for £100 or less, 40 per cent and 28 per cent respectively. Only 8 per cent insured for over £1000 in the earlier period and this rose very little to 12 per cent in the later. Table 6.25 shows the full breakdown by value of capital insured.

There were a small number of larger firms, invariably describing themselves as 'druggists' or 'chemists and druggists'. In 1772 William Sheppard of 103 Newgate Street insured stock and utensils valued at

£6000,[275] and exactly 50 years later Thomas Wilson and Co insured their warehouse at 86 Snow Hill for £700, and stock, utensils and goods for £4500.[276] A herbalist, Peter Bailey of Bow Street, insured his shop for £60, and stock and utensils for £1040.[277] Typical of the businesses describing themselves as 'apothecaries' was John Powell, who in 1819 insured his shop at 62 Newman Street for £60 and stock and utensils for £80.[278] Of this order of magnitude too was the tiny druggist's shop at 94 St John's Street, measuring only 6 feet by 26 feet and insured for just £30 by James Remant in 1819.[279] Perfumery could be a very fashionable and highly capitalised trade. In 1825 Thomas and William Ross insured the glass display cases in their shop at 119–20 Bishopsgate Street for £350, looking-glasses and chandeliers for £200 and stock and utensils for £4150.[280]

Other retailers There were, of course, innumerable other retail trades in London. The fire office registers contain, for example, policies issued to dealers in firearms, minerals and shells, toothpicks and mathematical instruments, as well as florists and dealers in flowers, plants, seeds, pets and animal feedstuffs. Seedsmen often traded on a very large scale indeed. Thomas Gibbs and Co had their premises in Piccadilly and in 1822 promised 'the best selected Grass & other Agricultural Seeds, Kitchen Garden & Flower Seeds, Fruit and Forest Trees, Shrubs, Greenhouse & Hothouse Plants, Dutch Bulbs, etc., etc'.[281] Another firm of seedsmen, Minier, Nash and Adams, insured their Strand 'warehouse' for £2000 in 1819, and stock, utensils and goods for £5000 the following year.[282] How large the trade could be in the 1820s is shown by the bankruptcy file of Archibald Thompson of New Grove, Mile End Road. He was described as a 'nursery and seedsman' and achieved an average annual profit of £2300 in the seven years prior to cessation of trading in 1826.[283]

Employment in Retailing

A very large proportion of London's labour force was employed in wholesale, and more particularly retail, distribution. The 1831 Census identified 79,000 men aged 20 or over. This suggests about 129,000 in total, based on the proportion that men aged 20 or over represented in 1841. By 1841 the number employed was over 188,000, nearly 38 per cent of London's total labour force, rather more than

TABLE 6.26 Numbers of employers and employees in selected trades, 1841

Trade	Employers	Employees	Average number
Warehousemen	250	3834	15.3
Nurserymen and florists	113	492	4.4
Cheesemongers	638	1737	2.7
Grocers	1422	4986	3.5
Ironmongers	374	1173	3.1
Chemists and druggists	507	1806	3.6
Linen drapers	598	1939	3.2
Silk mercers	87	470	5.4
Stationers	430	1705	4.0
Booksellers	718	5499	7.7
Perfumers	70	337	4.8
Oil- and colourmen	510	1344	2.6

Source: 1841 Census; and *Post Office London Directory*

were employed in manufacturing (170,000). Well over half were employed in the retail and bespoke clothing, footwear and textiles sector (107,000). However, the large majority were tailors (23,500), dressmakers (30,000) or shoemakers (28,600), most of whom would have been either self-employed or outworkers. Another 21 per cent were employed in food and drink (39,000), books and stationery employed over 8000 and hardware and ironmongery nearly 6000. A further 16,000 people were employed in the wholesale sector. Table 6.26 lists a few selected examples.

A few examples have survived of employment in individual firms. It has already been noted that claims were made for employment of 20 or 30 staff by the fashionable West End linen draper of the 1820s. This would have been very exceptional. The only distributive sector where hard evidence bears out employment on this scale is the City warehouseman. The Centre for Metropolitan History database for the City of London Textile Marketing Area in 1841 identifies 35 firms with 267 employees, 199 of whom were warehousemen, 26 clerks, 19 porters, 9 shopmen and 6 apprentices. Some were much larger than the average. Thomas Hyatt employed 29 people at 7 Love Lane, Eden and Wyeth employed 24 at 17 Aldermanbury and Robert Glazier, also of Love Lane, employed 21. Few other firms were of this size although John Chalmers, a boot- and shoemaker, employed 12 staff at his premises in High Holborn,[284] and a fashionable ladies' shoe-maker, George Taylor, had seven employees in his Old Bond Street shop in the 1820s.[285] Moser's, ironmongers in Borough High Street, employed eight adults in 1823.[286]

Data survives in the bankruptcy files for a small number of firms for which employee details were recorded. Of a sample of 48 businesses in the retail sector in the 1820s, 13 employed only one person and 14 only two. Only four employed five or more staff. Some examples are George Henley, a cheesemonger at 299 Strand, who employed 'two men and a boy' in 1825,[287] William Smith, a hatter and hosier, who employed two men, one porter and a woman at his shop in Lombard Street in 1826,[288] Francis Robine, a jeweller in Regent Street, who employed two porters, a clerk, a shopman and a woman in 1825,[289] John Wood, a grocer, who employed a shopman and a porter in his Bishopsgate shop in 1822[290] and Samuel Robinson, a Fenchurch Street stationer, who employed two porters, a warehouse-man and a shopman in 1825.[291]

. . . .
London: Prototype Service Economy

The point has already been made that service industries made no less contribution to the British economy during the Industrial Revolution than manufacturing, and that nowhere was this more true than in London. Its service economy was on a very large scale, serving the nation as a whole as well as the capital. Quite apart from the financial and professional services not dealt with in this book, and the wholesale and retail distribution sectors already described above, London had long been the focal point for a highly complex and rapidly growing transport infrastructure and also possessed a large catering and personal services sector. Pigot listed 6252 businesses, nearly 13 per cent of all London businesses, and they insured capital valued at £5.5 million in the 1820s, over 7.5 per cent of the total. London's service industries underpinned both its own and the national manufacturing and commercial infrastructure and at the same time contributed to the new 'commercialisation of leisure'. No industry better exemplified this duality than transport.

Transport

An efficient transport system for moving both passengers and freight is an essential part of the economic infrastructure for any industrial economy. With regard to passenger transport, its expansion was as much part of the consumer revolution as the increase in the consumption of tea or the demand for the latest fashion in dress. In the words of two recent historians of Britain's roads, J. A. Chartres and G. L. Turnbull, 'as incomes in general rose between 1750 and 1850, and as those of middle-income groups in particular rose substantially in real terms, so too expenditure on the luxury of travel increased at least proportionately'.[1] Good roads have been described as both the cause and the result of eighteenth-century prosperity,[2] and by the 1830s there were 20,000 miles of turnpiked road.[3] More important, perhaps, than the statistics was the growing perception that travel was at last safe. In mid-century, it was said:

> In the twenty years of peace, from 1815 to 1835, the horse locomotives – mails and stages – rapidly attained their epoch; nor were the highways behind; turnpike roads had been extended and improved … coach building and all the incipient trade branches connected with this business was in a flourishing state; and confidence having been acquired in the safety of the internal transit, travellers had ceased to call in the lawyer to make their wills, before they left their homes for a 50-mile journey.[4]

Journey times were slashed. In 1772 the London to Manchester service took two days in the summer and three in the winter; by 1824 it took 22 hours all the year round. Similarly, the service to Leeds took two and a half days in 1769 but only 26 hours in 1821.[5] By the 1770s every provincial centre of any significance had a direct scheduled service to London; even as relatively insignificant a town as Salisbury had 32 scheduled regular coach and carrier departures a week in 1769.[6]

Chartres and Turnbull estimate that road passenger mileage from London to a number of particular provincial destinations rose eleven-fold between 1773 and 1816, from 183,000 to 2,043,000.[7] As will be seen below, their estimates for freight traffic have been questioned and it may be that they are too high for passenger traffic too. What is certain is that London had been the centre of a stagecoach system linking it with every major provincial city or town since the middle of the seventeenth century and that it continued to grow considerably throughout the eighteenth century and up to the onset of the railway age. As early as 1764 a syndicate of five London and Essex coach-masters advertised in an Ipswich newspaper that,

> The London and Ipswich Post Coaches set out … at seven o'clock in the morning from the Black Bull Inn, in Bishopsgate, London, and at the same time from the Great White Horse Inn, in Ipswich, and continue every day (Sunday excepted) to be at the above places the same evening at five o'clock; each passenger to pay three-pence per mile, and to be allowed eighteen pounds luggage … The coaches, hung upon steel springs

TABLE 7.1 Coaches from London to 12 provincial destinations

Destination	No. of coaches
Brighton	40
Birmingham	84
Chester	19
Manchester	70
Liverpool	20
Preston	12
York	18
Hull	12
Newcastle	6
Glasgow	13
Edinburgh	39
Inverness	3

... carry six inside but no outside passengers whatsoever; but have great conveniences for parcels or game ... which will be delivered at London or Ipswich the same night.[8]

By 1827 Pigot and Co's *Metropolitan New Alphabetical Directory* identified 974 passenger services out of London, including scheduled services to Calais, Paris and Brussels. Five years later the *Huntingdon Gazette* listed 336 coaches serving twelve major provincial destinations (see Table 7.1).[9]

Of even greater significance to London was its regular local services. London's population explosion from the latter part of the eighteenth century onwards was served by building outwards rather than upwards. Unlike Paris, it was not constrained by city walls and so it required regular transport services to and from the centre to the new suburbs like Pentonville (begun in 1780), Somers Town (1786), and Camden Town (1791). Although Shillibeer's first omnibus did not come into service from Paddington to the Bank until 4 July 1829, there were numerous regular services before that. Four years earlier the City Police Committee took a record of 418 vehicles making 1190 short-stage journeys from the City to 68 termini. For example, 54 coaches made 158 return journeys a day to Paddington, 23 made 104 journeys to Camberwell and 21 made 57 journeys to Clapham. Closer to the City, 29 coaches made 72 return journeys a day to

Blackwall and 11 made 53 journeys to Islington. All these short-stage services also called at numerous stops along the way. In addition to the services from the City it is estimated that another 200 coaches made 600 daily return journeys from the West End.[10] All these services were widely advertised. Most are, for example, listed in Pigot and Co's *Metropolitan New Alphabetical Directory for 1827*.

Some idea of passenger numbers per coach is conveyed by a census of traffic through the Shenfield turnpike gate carried out in February and March 1838.[11] The coaches surveyed could hold up to 17 passengers inside and out although in fact 15 travelling to London carried only 134 passengers and 15 out of London carried 126. This was an average of nearly nine per coach at a relatively quiet time of year. These vehicles were not untypical and, if an average of nearer ten to twelve is assumed over the year as a whole, it suggests that London's local services carried not less than 35,000 passengers a day. If only half of London's longer distance services ran on any given day, it suggests that not less than 5000 passengers were served.

Another measure of the scale of the passenger transport sector is that in 1836 the third largest coach proprietor in London, Benjamin Horne, paid £26,717 'for licences and duties on the travelling of his coaches'. This was over 5 per cent of the entire national tax yield (£498,500 in 1836) which had itself doubled since 1815 (when it was £217,700).[12] Benjamin's father William Horne had kept the Golden Cross in Charing Cross which he insured for £2500 in 1825, having insured the stock, utensils and goods therein for £1000 six years previously.[13] Benjamin kept 700 horses as did Edward Sherman of the Bull and Mouth Inn, later the Queen's Hotel, in St Martin's le Grand. Horne ran 92 services from the Golden Cross, the Cross Keys in Wood Street and the George and Blue Boar, the Bull and the Old Bell in Holborn while Sherman ran 77.[14] Neither of these firms was half the size of William Chaplin, who eventually merged with Horne and who is discussed in more detail below, although Sherman offered so many services to Scotland and the north-west of England that the Bull and Mouth has been called 'the Euston of the Era of Road Travel'.[15] He also operated the *Thames*, the first steamboat to ply between London and Margate. The other major London coach proprietor was Robert Nelson at the Belle Sauvage in Ludgate Hill. He kept 400 horses and ran services to Cheltenham, Bath, Brighton, Cambridge and Manchester. His father John had kept the Bull Inn in

TABLE 7.2 Coachmasters and stablekeepers

Capital insured (£)	No. of firms 1770s	Percentage of total	No. of firms 1820s	Percentage of total
100 and under	37	15.9	15	11.5
101–500	142	61.2	39	29.8
501–1000	36	15.5	34	26.0
1001–2999	17	7.3	34	26.0
3000 and over	0	0	9	6.9
Total	232	100.0	131	100.0

Source: Sun and other London fire office registers

Aldgate. On his death John's widow Ann ran the business, operating coaches to all parts of Essex and East Anglia, as well as to Exeter. She also offered travellers 200 beds at the inn where she employed 30 to 40 staff.[16]

The contemporary term for the proprietors of passenger transport services was coachmaster. This was used interchangeably with the term stablekeeper, especially in the 1770s. Thus, George Williamson of Swan Yard, Westminster, described himself as a coachmaster in a policy taken out in 1769, but as a stablekeeper in another taken out the following year.[17] Pigot listed 307 firms in 1826–27. Their size increased considerably between the 1770s and the 1820s, the average value of capital insured more than doubling from £411 to £1045. In the earlier period, 77 per cent of businesses insured for £500 or less, 61 per cent for between £100 and £500; 50 years later these proportions had fallen to 41 per cent and 30 per cent. Conversely, whereas only 7 per cent insured for more than £1000 in the 1770s, by the 1820s this had risen to 33 per cent and 7 per cent were 'large' firms insuring £3000 or more. Table 7.2 shows the full breakdown by value of capital insured.

The size of the individual firm can be somewhat misleading since stagecoach services were often run by syndicates. William Chaplin, who was also proprietor of the Caledonian Hotel in Robert Street, Adelphi, insuring there for £5150 in 1823,[18] had an interest in no fewer than 68 coaching syndicates. He also owned 1800 horses and supplied them to 14 of the 27 mail coach services out of London. Although he started as a mere coachman, his annual turnover was estimated to be half a million pounds by the 1830s when he operated 106 services from the Swan with Two Necks in Lad Lane, the Spread Eagle in Gracechurch Street and the White Horse in Fetter Lane.[19] More than half a century earlier in 1774, Thomas Field insured his stables and coach houses at the Talbot Livery Stables in Grays Inn Lane for £1700, and stock and utensils for £260.[20] A number of firms operated on a much larger scale in the 1820s. Joseph Aldridge insured stables alone in Newport Street valued at £5150 in 1825.[21] Five years earlier Richard Dixon insured stables, lofts and carriages at the City Depository in Barbican for £2500, and other property, stock, utensils and goods for £3950.[22]

Even more fundamental to London's economic infrastructure was an efficient system for carrying goods and freight. Improved roads reduced the numbers of horses required, lowering costs and making road haulage more competitive with water transport. Considerable controversy has developed in recent years over the size of the increase in freight traffic to and from London in the latter part of the eighteenth century and the early nineteenth. Chartres and Turnbull computed an increase of 243 per cent in weekly ton miles between London and selected provincial centres between 1765 and 1816, from 80,000 to 275,000.[23] Dorian Gerhold has estimated a considerably lower increase of 40 per cent in ton miles per week between 1765 and 1818 and 52 per cent between 1765 and 1826.[24] It has to be concluded that the increase in London's population and the growth of its manufacturing and distributive sectors suggest that it is most unlikely that the increase in so vital a service as freight transport could have grown as little as computed by Gerhold, especially as he tabulates a 108 per cent increase in the *number* of carrying services per week from London between 1765 and 1826.[25] The Shenfield gate survey recorded 13 wagons on their way to London on 26 February 1838 and 22 from there on 4 March. The latter carried 94 tons of freight.[26]

Over the period 1775–1825 the largest carriers ceased to operate from inn yards, a characteristic they had shared with the coach-masters, and began to acquire their own yards. Nevertheless, wagons for 16 destinations as geographically dispersed as Manchester, Bristol, Yarmouth and Southampton left Nelson's General Coach and Waggon Office in the Bull Inn Yard in Aldgate in 1822.[27] A quarter of a century earlier in 1797 one Morphew had advertised services from the Queen's

Head Inn in Borough High Street: 'Stage Waggons Which load Tuesdays and Fridays, at Noon, for Tonbridge, Tunbridge Wells and Places adjacent.'[28] A trade card circulated by the London Carrier Company stated: 'The Public are respectfully informed, that this Company is Established to Facilitate the Conveyance of Goods and Parcels of any description, not exceeding two cwt to every part of the Metropolis and its Vicinity ... Numerous receiving houses are appointed in various parts of London ... at which, directions for Carts to call at any House, will be received.'[29] Interestingly, the firm operated out of the same yard at 69 Great Queen Street as had been used by a prominent coachmaster, John Sargeaunt, in the 1770s. Carmen operating within the City were subject to stringent regulations on loads, methods of loading and unloading, speed, age and experience of drivers and, above all, rates. Thus, for example, a load was limited to four packs of Irish cloth, ten barrels of oil, three hogsheads of tobacco or 50 firkins of butter. With regard to prices, the price for a full load carried from the quays below London Bridge to Lower Thames Street was 2s 9d, but 3s 6d if it was wine or spirits.[30] It is unsurprising that only 270 of the 410 licences available by law were taken up in 1829, and these by only 118 operators.[31]

Pigot listed 2445 places served by scheduled 'van, waggon and cart conveyance' and 878 carriers in 1827. Some of these would have been the London yards of provincial carriers although it was the London carriers who were described as 'blue ribband operators'.[32] Thomas Russell and Co of Exeter, established in 1676 and still operating in the 1820s, ran daily services to and from London with horses and wagons kept at yards all along the route and in London itself. They used 200 horses, employed between 60 and 70 staff and at any one time had nine wagons en route to London.[33] In the 1820s London's carriers insured capital valued at over a million pounds.

Unfortunately, the surviving fire office registers contain policies for very few of London's carriers. The average value of capital insured rose sharply between the 1770s and the 1820s, from £354 to £1148. In the earlier period over 80 per cent insured capital valued at £500 or less and it was still two-thirds 50 years later. However, by the 1820s nearly a quarter insured for over £1000 compared with 5 per cent in the 1770s. Table 7.3 shows the breakdown by value of capital insured for those firms for which fire insurance details have survived.

An example of a relatively large firm in the 1770s was Thomas

TABLE 7.3 Carriers and carmen

Capital insured (£)	No. of firms 1770s	Percentage of total	No. of firms 1820s	Percentage of total
100 and under	8	21.1	8	22.2
101–500	23	60.5	16	44.4
501–1000	5	13.2	4	11.1
1001–2999	2	5.3	4	11.1
3000 and over	0	0	4	11.1
Total	38	100.0	36	100.0

Source: Sun and other London fire office registers

Griffin of Hoxton who insured for £1700 in 1775.[34] Operating on a quite different scale in the 1820s was Daniel Deacon. He operated out of the White Horse in Cripplegate and in 1822, 1823 and 1825 he insured for £16,550.[35]

Inland water transport, with its far lower costs for bulk or low-value freight, was highly important to London too; in the eighteenth century the greater part of freight traffic into London was by sea or river. A vital element in its transport infrastructure was servicing ships loading and unloading on the river and in the docks, both the wharfingers who operated the wharves and the lightermen who serviced the ships at anchor and moved cargo in dock. The first quarter of the nineteenth century saw a huge expansion of London's docks to cope with the enormous increase in trade. In 1827 there were 2190 places served from London by canal or coastal shipping. Services were advertised at 65 wharves, 47 on the river, 10 in City Road and 8 at Paddington. Pigot listed 144 lightermen, 74 wharfingers and 18 granary keepers in 1826–27. Many firms, such as James Smith at 1 Bennet's Hill, Upper Thames Street, described themselves as all three.[36]

Most firms were quite small; 57 per cent of lightermen and wharfingers insured for under £500 in the 1770s and 45 per cent in the 1820s. However, there were also some very large firms, especially in the 1820s when 21 per cent insured capital valued at over £5000. For lightermen and wharfingers the average value of capital insured was £1392 in the 1770s and this nearly doubled to £2547 fifty years later. As early as 1772 Griffin, Liscoe and Cox insured for £10,500 at

Hayes Wharf in Southwark.[37] Nearly 50 years later in 1820, Pomeroy and Brander of Shad Thames insured for £15,000.[38] Even this paled beside the risks insured by London's granary keepers. They were among the largest businesses in the capital, averaging over £26,000 in the 1820s. Almost all were to be found in Horsleydown, like William Landell and Son at 40 Thomas Street who insured for £102,650 in 1820. This included seven barges valued at £2050, a granary insured for £2000, warehouses for £3300 and a cooperage for £600. The firm's stock, utensils and goods were held in three locations besides Thomas Street: at Crown Wharf on Bankside, King's Mills in Rotherhithe and at Cole's Wharf in Shad Thames.[39] Two other very large granary keepers, both in Gainsford Street, were William and George Jones at number 24 and Joseph Blackstone and Son at number 20. The former insured for £93,000 in 1821,[40] and the latter for £75,600 in 1820.[41]

Mention must also be made of London's shipowners in this context. In practice many also described themselves as merchants and very few were specialist owners. Ownership was usually divided into shares of eighths, sixteenths, thirty-seconds and so on, often held by ten or twenty individuals who spread their investment among a number of vessels to minimise the risk.[42] Of the 55 owners to be found in the fire office registers, 80 per cent insured for over £1000, 40 per cent for over £5000 and a quarter for over £10,000. One ship could be insured for as much as £35,000,[43] although John Chapman and Co of 2 Leadenhall Street insured 20 for £37,000 in 1822.[44] Some policies provide full details of the ships insured. Isbister and Horley of 11 Leadenhall Street insured four for £30,000 in 1825: the *Ganges* of 672 tons valued at £10,000; the *Columbus* of 350 tons insured for £6000; the *Georgina Ford* insured for £9000; and another vessel of 467 tons insured for £5000.[45]

Catering

Long before the last quarter of the eighteenth century, taverns, inns, coffee houses, eating houses and rooming houses had abounded in London. The 1826–27 edition of Pigot listed 3863 'public houses, hotels, inns, taverns and coffee houses', nearly 8 per cent of all businesses in London. They insured capital valued at over £1.7 million in the 1820s, 2.3 per cent of all commercial capital insured. Fifty years earlier in the 1770s, the Sun insured 2864. Since this cannot possibly be a full count, it suggests that at least one in ten businesses in London was devoted to provision of food, drink and accommodation. There is a clear impression that Londoners in this period lived a large portion of their lives in public. Certainly, the ill reputation of English cuisine in the twentieth century does not seem to have been the case in the late eighteenth and early nineteenth. The composer Weber described to his wife a dinner he had enjoyed on 12 March 1826 in glowing terms,

> The food's marvellous here. Of such oysters we who live deep inland can have no conception. Then a few slices of mutton and a draught of porter – delicious! I like English cooking very much for its honest simplicity. The excellence of the meat and poultry is indescribable ... the meat is tender and juicy, and it is nothing unusual to have three or four courses of meat together. That is apart from soup, a great joint of beef or mutton, fish, capons, with lots of vegetables. Then come different kinds of pudding ... ham, cooked pork, pies and more of the kind. Then a colossal cheese [and] fruit of all kinds.[46]

Although alehouses had to be licensed by JPs, it is difficult in practice to distinguish between public houses or licensed premises, inns or hotels and coffee or eating houses. Much the most frequent term used in fire insurance policies was victualler. This could mean a coffee or eating house, or even a retailer of food and drink, but in the overwhelming majority of cases (around 85 per cent in both the 1770s and 1820s) it clearly meant licensed premises; the bankruptcy file of William Farrer, proprietor of a very large City inn, the White Horse in Friday Street, described him as a victualler.[47] There was also an overlap between inns, taverns and hotels. By 1826–27 Pigot's list of 3545 public houses compared with a far smaller list (318) of hotels, inns, taverns and coffee houses. Coffee houses had clearly lost their early eighteenth-century role as centres of London literary and commercial life since at that time it was estimated that there were 2000.[48] However, these distinctions in terminology were not always very important to contemporaries. In 1830 Nathaniel Hartley described the Axe Inn in Aldermanbury, which he owned, as a 'Tavern, Hotel and Coffee House'.[49]* An invoice from the Ship Tavern in Water Lane

---

* The most recent historian of the English alehouse, Peter Clark, categorises establishments as follows: 'we can distinguish with reasonable confidence between inns, usually large, fashionable establishments offering wine, ale and beer, to-

described its proprietor, William Rusby, as an 'Importer of Foreign Wines & Spirits' and offered 'Fine Ales, Bottled Stout & Porter. Beds &c. Excellent Accommodation for Passengers arriving from or passing to the Continent'.[50]

What is very clear is that such establishments played as major a role in the economy of London as they did in its social life. The prolonged development of London's inns began with the rapid expansion of passenger coach and freight carrier services from the middle of the seventeenth century which has already been noted above. There was a close association between particular groups of London inns and specific parts of the country which lasted until the onset of the railway age in the 1840s. Thus, for example, the west Midlands was served by inns in Friday Street, Bread Street and Wood Street.[51] In the 1770s nearly a third of London coachmasters also described themselves in their fire policies as 'victuallers' or 'innkeepers'; 50 years later it was still a quarter.

In the eighteenth century, inns also played an important role as employment agencies. Dorothy George described how 'for a large number of trades, the public house was the recognised employment agency. There were houses of call for hatters, smiths, carpenters, weavers, boot- and shoemakers, metal workers, bakers, tailors, plumbers, painters and glaziers, and bookbinders, and others.'[52] The fire office registers show that in the 1770s, 123 victuallers described themselves as having 57 other trades, with carpenters, turners, coopers, smiths, cabinet makers, builders and shipbuilders being the most common. By the 1820s this role seems to have declined; there are only 21 examples in the fire office registers.

By the 1820s, recognisably modern hotels had emerged in London, some of them very large. Bond Street became particularly famous for its hotels and as early as 1814, war notwithstanding, the Clarendon at number 169 was charging three or four pounds for dinner and a guinea for a bottle of champagne.[53] John Bailey insured the building of the Thomas Hotel in Berkeley Square for £5500 and fittings for

---

gether with quite elaborate food and lodging to well-heeled travellers; taverns, selling wine to the more prosperous, but without the extensive accommodation of inns; and alehouses, normally smaller premises serving ale and beer (and later spirits) and providing rather basic food and accommodation for the lower orders.' However, he also admits to much confusion in the contemporary use of the terminology. Peter Clark, *The English Alehouse: A Social History 1200–1830* (1983), 5.

£2200,[54] and David Hickinbotham, proprietor of the St Petersburg Hotel in Dover Street, insured for £7000,[55] both in 1825.

Another interesting group of businesses described themselves as cooks or pastry cooks, a term usually understood by contemporaries to denote a supplier of outside catering. Two receipts from 1769 and 1788 describe the business of Samuel Cannadine of 76 Cheapside, who called himself a 'cook', as 'Dinners dressed at Home & Abroad on the shortest Notice. Turtles dress'd, French Pyes, & all Kinds of made Dishes in the most elegant Taste. Deserts for Publick or Private Entertainments.'[56] The day book of Lucas Birch of 15 Cornhill, who described himself as a 'pastry cook', described 74 dinners catered in 1776, mostly for livery companies. He employed 15 people, had a turnover of £2154 and made a profit of £420. On 7 August 1776 he catered a dinner for the Merchant Tailors for which he charged them £72 15s 0d and showed a profit of £7 1s 8d. By far the most expensive item was nine haunches of venison which cost £22 10s 0d; by contrast, the wages of seven labourers came only to £1 1s 4d.[57] The firm described itself as 'cooks and venison dealers' in 1839 and was still trading from the same address in 1846.

Pigot also listed 230 confectioners. The large majority were quite small although a few were to be found at the most fashionable addresses and achieved considerable size. In 1771 William Smith of New Bond Street circulated a trade card stating that he 'Makes and Sells all sorts of fine Sweetmeats, Jellys, Creames, Sorbetts, Lemond Ice, Ice'd Fruits and Waters. Also Furnisheth Entertainments after the Neatest Taste.'[58] Nearly 50 years later in 1822, James Hoffman insured utensils and goods valued at £5200 at his much less fashionably located business premises in Houndsditch.[59] However, it was Negri and Gunter of Berkeley Square who became known as 'the most celebrated confectioners in London'. They had started off as Negri and Wetter and in 1771 insured for £2000.[60] By 1786 they were Negri and Gunter and the firm was still trading as Gunter's in the twentieth century. They catered parties, balls and weddings for the very wealthiest in society and were acknowledged by Thackeray as the ultimate caterers for 'first-rate' dinners. One dinner catered for Mrs Fitzherbert included two pineapples priced at £3 18s and cherries at 9s a pound.[61]

However, most businesses were very small. Contemporary sources suggested that an initial capital of £50 to £300 was all that was

TABLE 7.4 Victuallers, hotels, inns and coffee and eating houses

Capital insured (£)	No. of firms 1770s	Percentage of total	No. of firms 1820s	Percentage of total
100 and under	798	27.9	199	11.5
101–500	1876	65.5	1179	68.3
501–1000	168	5.9	241	14.0
1001–2999	20	0.7	89	5.1
3000 and over	2	0.1	17	1.0
Total	2864	100.0	1725	100.0

Source: Sun and other London fire office registers

required to set up in business. The average value of capital insured was £234 in the 1770s; it had nearly doubled by the 1820s but was still only £441. In the earlier period over a quarter insured for £100 or less and another two-thirds for between £100 and £500. Less than 1 per cent insured for over £1000. By the 1820s the proportion insuring for £100 or less had fallen to under 12 per cent, but over two-thirds insured for between £100 and £500. Just over 6 per cent insured for over £1000 and 1 per cent came into the category of 'large' businesses insuring for £3000 or more. In the 1770s nearly 78 per cent of all capital in the sector was accounted for by firms insuring £500 or less; it was still 47 per cent 50 years later. Table 7.4 shows the full breakdown by value of capital insured.

An example of a substantial City inn in the 1770s is the Castle in Wood Street which was insured for £3020 by John Handforth in 1775.[62] The previous year Thomas Griffith insured the Cocoa Tree Coffee House in Pall Mall for £1350.[63] Fifty years later there were far more large establishments. Sarah Ann Mountain insured the Saracen's Head in Snow Hill for £1600 in 1822, and stock, utensils and goods for £6080.[64] She had taken over the business four years earlier when her husband died. He had inherited it from his father. She was also a coachmistress, keeping 200 horses and operating 21 services a day from the inn in 1836. She ran the Louth and Boston Mail service, a night service to Bristol and day services to Leeds and Birmingham, the latter the famous 'Mountain's Tally Ho'. She also ran a coach-building business in the extensive inn yard and reckoned to build a coach for between 110 and 120 guineas. These she let at the rate of

3½d a mile to her partners in the stagecoach business.[65] It was at the Saracen's Head that Mr Squeers attended when in town in *Nicholas Nickleby*.[66] Another large proprietor was Joseph Hearn who insured the King's Head in Holborn for £7900 in 1820.[67] There were still some large coffee houses too. In 1823 Robert Chatham, proprietor of the Furnivale Inn Coffee House in Holborn Hill, insured stock, utensils and goods for £2000.[68] Martha Wood, a cook at 54–6 Great Tower Street, insured for the same sum in 1819.[69] However, much more typical of the thousands of small victuallers in London was John Fell at the George and Vulture in Ratcliffe Highway who insured for £280 in 1819.[70]

The value of the licensed premises itself could vary widely. In 1769 John Lee insured the tap house of the King's Head in the Borough for £400 and the other inn buildings for £450.[71] Eight years later Richard Nickson insured the building of the Three Compasses in New Street, Shadwell, for £500.[72] In 1825 the Boot at 94 Grub Street was insured for £800 by its proprietor, William Avis.[73] Five years earlier 'An old-established, roomy, respectable Tavern and Hotel, with a lucrative Liquor Shop and Tap [in] one of the principal streets in the city of London' was advertised for sale in *The Times* for £1400.[74] Purpose-built public houses started to appear in London from about 1810, and in 1814 it was estimated that the average cost would be between £1000 and £2000 pounds.[75] A number of victuallers were proprietors of more than one licensed house, often spread right across London. The fire office registers record 13 in the 1770s and 15 in the 1820s. In the earlier period Thomas Webb kept the Three Compasses in Little Wild Street, The Edinburgh Castle in Lower East Smithfield and the Red Lion in Redcross Street, Southwark.[76] Fifty years later John Simpson insured five public houses for a total of £1500. They were the Seymour Arms in Seymour Place, the Dolphin in Tonbridge Street, Somers Town, the Star and Garter in Upper Street, Islington, the Champion in Goswell Road and the Three Tons at Billingsgate.[77] Large numbers of premises were already owned by brewers in the 1790s; the security for a mortgage of £18,000 taken out with Smith's Bank in March 1792 by Cox, King, Curtis and Payne, brewers in City Road, was a number of named taverns,[78] and it was estimated that by 1800 Barclay Perkins owned 88 leases and that in 1805 over 80 per cent of the houses supplied by Whitbread's were 'tied' either through leases or loans.[79] At the upper end of the market, William Chaplin not only owned two hotels but also five major London coaching inns; the Spread Eagle and the Cross Keys in Gracechurch Street, the Swan with Two Necks in Lad Lane, the White Horse in Fetter Lane and the Angel in the Strand.[80]

Throughout the period 1775–1825 the lowest sums insured were south of the river; £176 compared with an average of £234 in the 1770s and £341 compared with £441 fifty years later. In the earlier period the highest valuations were to be found in the City (£268) and in the later in the West End (£573).

Bankruptcy files for 12 inns in the 1820s show average annual profits of £595. However, this small sample contains wide variations. John Miles, proprietor of the Feathers Tavern in Hand Court, High Holborn, averaged £1410 in the five years prior to his bankruptcy in 1826; at the other end of the scale, William Croft at the Greyhound in West Smithfield showed a profit of only £100 in the year before he ceased trading in 1823.[81]

Personal and Other Services

Apart from domestic service – the 1841 Census enumerated 169,000 domestic servants – there were a number of service industries which were of considerable importance to the life of the metropolis. Pigot listed 735 businesses in a wide variety of trades, and almost certainly this figure is understated. Although Pigot had no listing for hairdressers, the 1841 *Post Office London Directory* contains 341. Most described themselves as 'hairdressers and perfumers' and were to be found in the more fashionable districts. For example, J. Dickenson of 3 Tavistock Row, Covent Garden, circulated a trade card in 1820 which promised 'Hair cut in the most fashionable style. Gentlemen's Perukes, Ladies' Head Dresses, Dealer in all kinds of Perfumery'.[82] In 1822 Peter Truefitt at 20–1 Burlington Arcade insured for £500.[83] In less fashionable areas they called themselves 'barbers', as did John Dore of Lower Queen Street, Rotherhithe, who insured stock, utensils and goods for just £100 in 1769.[84] However, in all districts businesses were generally very small. In the 1770s, 80 per cent insured for £100 or less and 50 years later it was still 64 per cent. The average value of capital insured was only £124 in the 1770s and £140 fifty years later.

London also had a number of public baths which catered for the wealthy and were capitalised on a substantial scale. John Farnell, proprietor of the Royal Bagnio in Long Acre, insured the baths themselves for £1000 in 1777.[85]

The 1841 Census counted no fewer than 16,363 'launderers, washers, manglers and lace cleaners'. Most would have been self-employed. However, the fire office registers show that there were a number who operated as formal businesses, albeit usually on a very small scale. Thus, in the first quarter of the nineteenth century, E. Dench, a clear starcher of 30 New Street Square, circulated a trade card which stated 'Gauze, Crepe, Tiffanys, and Muslins, also Point, Brussels, Blond, and all Kinds of Lace, cleaned and mended'.[86] Mrs Baker, a laundress at 24 Wellington Street, Pentonville, advertised 'Mangling, by Baker's Patent, 1½d per Dozen. Excellent Drying Ground'.[87] Another 'respectable' laundress was specialised enough in her trade to aim her advertisement in The Times at hotel and tavern keepers.[88] Policies survive for 107 businesses in the 1770s and 88 in the 1820s. The average value of capital insured was £74 and £54 respectively. None insured capital valued at over £500 and 90 per cent insured for £100 or less. A very few businesses were larger than the average, for example Mary Crowther of 15 Tinker Row, City Road, who insured stock, utensils and goods for £450 in 1825.[89]

Yet another essential service, and one much more highly capitalised in an age of low life expectancy and high infant mortality, was provided by London's numerous undertakers. Pigot listed 200 but many other trades offered an undertaking service as well. Sometimes these were carpenters or cabinet makers who also made coffins, but there were also appraisers, brokers of household goods, hosiers and glovers, watchmakers, carvers, victuallers and painters. Joseph Hubbard described himself as 'Undertaker, Broker, Appraiser and Auctioneer' in his 1769 trade card and promised 'Coffins and Shrouds ready made, and Funerals Perform'd ... Funeral Furniture let at Hire'.[90] In fact, undertaking services were offered by twice as many firms describing their main trade as something other than undertaker as by firms who did describe themselves as undertakers in the 1770s, and by nearly the same number in the 1820s. Most specialist undertakers were small, 80 per cent insuring for £500 or less in both the 1770s and 1820s. The average values of capital insured were £376 and £557 respectively. However, some were much larger. In 1777 Thomas Jarvis insured his workshop at Duke's Court, St Martin's Lane, for £150, and stock, utensils and goods for £1900.[91]

Of some interest are two firms which traded right through the period 1775–1825. William Crasswell insured for £400 at premises at 75 Whitechapel Road. By 1821 the business had moved to number 5 and the proprietor, John, now spelled his surname Cressall. By that time the business had grown substantially and he insured a coffin manufactory for £700, and stock and utensils for £1200.[92] The firm was still trading as Cressall's in 1846. The Ayscough family were similar. In 1771 William Ayscough and Son insured their workshop at 1 Fore Street for £125, and stock and utensils for £575. By 1819 the firm had become Ayscough and Sadler and insured for £3800.[93]

Much more basic services had also to be provided and the fire office registers and other contemporary sources provide a glimpse of how this was organised. These were such trades as scavengers, nightmen, lamp lighters and chimney sweeps. Scavenging could be a profitable business. For the Calthorpe estate in Somers Town the contract was let out to competitive tender. John Burge of Mount Pleasant paid £15 for the privilege in 1820 and £20 in 1821, the desirable commodity being ashes and breeze.[94] In 1825 William Cooper insured warehouses and sheds at 26 St Ann Street, Westminster, for £1200, a counting house and smith's shop for £200, a wheeler's shop for £100, and stock, utensils and goods for £1100.[95] This implies a whole fleet of vehicles to carry away the materials scavenged. Edward Kelly, a scavenger with premises in North Wharf Road, Paddington, showed average annual profits of £1450 over an eight-year period prior to his bankruptcy in 1829.[96] As unlikely a source as the composer Joseph Haydn noted with awe in June 1792: 'The City of London keeps 4000 carts for cleaning the streets, and 2000 of these work every day.' Fifty years later, in March and April 1842, it was estimated that 550 cartloads of manure alone were removed from the streets of the City every week.[97]

Some firms combined several of these trades, such as H. Kermot of 4 New Rents, St Martin's le Grand. He described himself as a chimney sweep and nightman in a trade card sent out in 1816 and promised 'Privies, Drains and Cesspools emptied ... Smoak Jacks Cleaned, Oiled and Repaired, Chimnies swept by the Year'.[98] Another nightman, Samuel Foulger of 5 Denmark Street, Ratcliffe Highway, described how the trade operated in his handbill of 1783: 'Gentlemen &c. may depend on having their Business decently performed, being at the Work himself, and having the New Invented Machine for the Quick dispatch of Business. NB to be heard of every day at the 3

Pigeon's, Butcherhall Lane, Newgate Street & Black Moor's Head, Cartwright Street, Rosemary Lane.'[99] A few years later the trade card of Henry Hastings of Ewers Street, Southwark, who described himself as 'Nightman for the City and Suburbs', was even more specific. He 'Empties Vaults & Cesspools, unstops Tunnels & cleans Drains'.[100] These were firms operating on a substantial scale. In 1823 John Gore, a chimney sweep and nightman, insured his warehouses at 17–18 Harrow Road, Paddington, for £1000, and valued stock, utensils and livestock at £2000 the following year. He also dealt in hay, straw and manure.[101] Lamp lighting contractors were also firms of some size. In 1772 Balchen, Search, Spencer and Lucas in Rupert Street insured their stock and utensils for £1570.[102]

Finally, a glimpse can be provided of the firms offering such diverse services as circulating libraries, tennis courts, billiard halls and lottery offices. Pigot listed 140, half of them being circulating libraries. One aspect of the commercialisation of leisure in the eighteenth century had been the growth of circulating libraries, many involving their proprietors in an investment in thousands of volumes like the 8000 estimated to be on offer to subscribers to John Bell's circulating library at 132 Strand in the 1770s.[103] Three smaller libraries were advertised for sale in 1820 with respectively 800, 700 and 500 volumes.[104] Alexander Smith at 12 Orange Street insured his stock for £300 in 1823,[105] and this may be compared with the £84, £95 and £43 asked for the three libraries mentioned above. Bond Street was particularly noted for them and at number 157 was to be found Tabart and Co's specialised 'Juvenile Library'.[106] From a very different location in 1800, Dockhead in Bermondsey, Bowen's Circulating Library circulated a trade card which advertised: 'Books are lent to read at Ten Shillings and Sixpence per Year, Three Shillings per Quarter, One Shilling and Three Pence per Month, Or by the Single Book ... Likewise, Magazines and Weekly Publications, as soon as published.'[107] Some of these trades required very little investment; thus, both Thomas Langford, a tennis court keeper in St Martin's Lane,[108] and William Smith, a lottery office keeper at 152 Drury Lane,[109] insured for just £50 in 1775 and 1774 respectively. However, by 1824 William Lees, a billiard table keeper at 27 Little Moorfields, was insuring his billiard tables alone for £400,[110] and the following year William Stuckey, who described himself as a 'clubhouse keeper', insured for £1050.[111]

Employment in Services

Excluding domestic service, London's service industries employed at least 53,000 people in 1841, well over 10 per cent of the total labour force. Road freight services employed 4000 and road passenger services over 6600, with William Chaplin alone claiming to employ 2000.[112] Inland water transport and the docks employed over 7000. All these figures exclude casual labourers. The catering trades employed nearly 12,000 people and undoubtedly many of London's 169,000 domestic servants were actually employed in the catering sector. Various other services employed 24,000. It has already been noted that there were over 16,000 launderers, washers and manglers and there were also 2200 hairdressers and over 1000 chimney sweeps.

CHAPTER 8

Commercial London

A number of recent studies have done belated justice to London's pre-eminence as a centre of merchant enterprise in the late eighteenth and early nineteenth centuries, most notably in the 1990s Stanley Chapman's *Merchant Enterprise in Britain* and volume I of David Kynaston's *The City of London, A World of its Own 1815–1890*. These are definitive accounts making it unnecessary for this book to do more than place London's innumerable merchants, factors, brokers and agents within the overall statistical framework of its economy as a whole. What is undoubtedly the case is that they accounted for an enormous proportion of London's commercial capital, as represented by the risks insured with the London fire offices. The fire office registers show that London's merchants alone insured capital valued at nearly £16.5 million in the 1820s. Factors, brokers and agents insured a further £6.25 million. Together these represented nearly a third of all capital employed by businesses in London.

Merchants

Merchants form possibly the single most important group of businesses in London in this period. The ledgers of imports and exports compiled by the Inspector General of Imports and Exports show that over the first three-quarters of the eighteenth century London's imports increased by 94 per cent and exports by 145 per cent, so that by 1772–74 its share of British trade was 72 per cent and 66 per cent respectively.[1] Thereafter war provided the opportunity for Britain to increase its share of world trade to replace Amsterdam, languishing under French control, as the leading financial centre. The banker Henry Thornton observed as early as 1803 that 'London is become, especially of late, the trading metropolis of Europe, and indeed, of the whole world'.[2] London stood at the centre of an international web of connections. In 1774 Postlethwayt's *Universal Dictionary of Trade and Commerce* judged:

> The most capital houses of the mercantile trade throughout Europe being generally composed of several partners, it is customary for one or the other to travel into foreign countries to make better judgement of the credit and fortune of their correspondents, cement ties of commercial friendship, and extend their traffic in general. As foreign merchants resort to England with this intent, so the English frequently take the tour into foreign countries.[3]

Stanley Chapman calls the foreign merchant families who migrated to London and played such a vital role in British mercantile development in the eighteenth and nineteenth centuries 'international houses'.[4] Railli Brothers, who traded in London from 1818 at 5 Finsbury Chambers, City Road, and 25 Finsbury Circus, had their origins in Greece and family connections in Odessa and Marseilles. Later in the nineteenth century their family network extended to New York, New Orleans, Rostov, St Petersburg, Taganrog, Constantinople, Tabriz, Calcutta, Bombay and Karachi, as well as to Manchester and Liverpool.[5] Thus, for the largest merchant houses the capital insured in London, however considerable, represented only a part of that invested by the house as a whole.

There are accurate counts of London merchants from the second half of the eighteenth century. Mortimer's *The Universal Director*, published in 1763, listed 1365 and the 1774 edition of Kent's *Directory* contained 1220. Mortimer included firms like wine and timber merchants who are classified in the retail and wholesale trades for the purposes of this book, so his count of merchants proper is actually very close to Kent's. Half a century later in 1826–27, Pigot listed 1370.

In both the 1770s and 1820s considerable numbers of merchants insured for very large sums indeed. The average values of capital insured were £4059 and £11,882 respectively. Even the median values were £1790 and £3600. It should be remembered that the latter probably represents a million pounds at 1990s money values. Campbell suggested in 1745 that the start-up capital required by a merchant was 'unlimited' and in 1786 Kearsley suggested that it might be up to £30,000. By 1819 it was estimated that the minimum lay between £2000 and £10,000. In the 1770s nearly 60 per cent of merchants

TABLE 8.1 Merchants

Capital insured (£)	No. of firms 1770s	Percentage of total	No. of firms 1820s	Percentage of total
100 and under	18	4.0	13	3.7
101–500	75	16.7	33	9.3
501–1000	89	19.8	49	13.8
1001–2999	99	22.0	60	16.9
3000 and over	169	37.6	201	56.5
Total	450	100.0	356	100.0

Source: Sun and other London fire office registers

insured capital valued at over £1000 and 38 per cent were 'large' firms insuring for £3000 or more. By the 1820s these proportions had risen to 73 per cent and 57 per cent. Indeed, in the earlier period 11 per cent insured for over £10,000 and 50 years later the figure was 26 per cent. By the latter period nearly 5 per cent insured for over £50,000, representing an eight-figure sum at 1990s values. Table 8.1 shows the full breakdown by value of capital insured.

As early as 1772, Godfrey Thornton of 19 Aldermanbury insured capital valued at £47,500.[6] Two years earlier a policy taken out by Gibson and Wellbank of 1 Crown Court, Threadneedle Street, specified their stock as hemp and flax valued at the immense sum of £37,300.[7] Mortimer often specified the area with which the merchant traded. For example, Andrew Thompson of 32 Old Bedlam was identified as a Russia merchant who insured for £36,000 in 1772.[8] Bosanquet and Fatio were Hamburg merchants. In 1769 they insured stock and utensils in their warehouse at 31 Mincing Lane for £20,800 and the warehouse itself for £800.[9] Two years later Benjamin Kidney insured warehouses in Lawrence Poutney Lane for the much larger figure still of £4000.[10] It is interesting to note in the light of the events of the 1990s that the three original Baring brothers, John, Francis and Charles, described themselves in 1769 as merchants and insured stock, utensils and goods at 6 Mincing Lane for £27,000.[11]

By the 1820s the amounts of capital insured by individual houses had increased enormously. Smith, Inglis and Co in George Street insured for no less than £167,000 in 1820,[12] and five other firms insured for over £100,000 with the Sun Fire Office. Corrie and Co insured for

TABLE 8.2 Agents, factors and brokers

Capital insured (£)	No. of firms 1770s	Percentage of total	No. of firms 1820s	Percentage of total
100 and under	4	2.2	4	2.4
101–500	35	18.8	22	13.4
501–1000	57	30.6	23	14.0
1001–2999	48	25.8	28	17.1
3000 and over	42	22.6	87	53.0
Total	186	100.0	164	100.0

Source: Sun and other London fire office registers

£154,750 in 1821 at their premises at 24 Mincing Lane, this quite apart from capital in Liverpool.[13] Abel Gower, Nephews and Co at 28 Coleman Street insured capital valued at £143,840 in 1825,[14] and Bazett and Co of 71 Broad Street for £120,000 in 1822.[15] In the latter year Pearsons and Price insured three warehouses in Seething Lane for the immense sum of £8000.[16] Many more types of stock were identified in the 1820s policies. Tallow was a commodity involving a particularly large degree of speculation because of the combination of high demand and uncertainty of supply from Russia. David Carruthers of 9 Copthall Street insured tallow for £10,000 in 1820.[17] McTavish, Fraser and Co at 2 Suffolk Lane insured furs,[18] and Charles Le Jeune in Moorfields wool,[19] for the same sum the following year. A stock of butter was also insured for £10,000 in 1819, by King and Co at 15 Great Elbow Lane.[20]

Agents, Factors and Brokers

Overlapping with merchants on the one hand and wholesalers on the other were London's numerous and highly important agents, factors and brokers. Pigot listed 1254. The average value of capital insured by them more than doubled between the 1770s and the 1820s, from £2541 to £6779. Nearly half insured capital was valued at over £1000 in the 1770s; 50 years later it was over 70 per cent. Large firms insuring for £3000 or more were nearly a quarter of the total in the earlier period and over half in the later. Table 8.2 shows the full breakdown by value of capital insured.

TABLE 8.3 Factors

	1770s (£)	1820s (£)
Corn factors	3406	12916
Hop factors	1694	9100
Blackwell Hall factors	3979	5813

The most highly capitalised firms were corn and hop factors and Blackwell Hall factors.* Table 8.3 shows the average value of capital insured by them.

Pigot listed 158 corn factors, 96 hop factors and 174 Blackwell Hall factors. Most corn factors were to be found either in the City or in the area around Horsleydown; most hop factors located their premises in and around Borough High Street. Blackwell Hall factors were to be found in and around Basinghall Street. There were a number of very large firms indeed in all these trades throughout this period. As early as 1775 one firm of corn factors, Nelson, Trotman and Worlidge, insured several warehouses in New Bridge Street for £1000 and corn and other stock, utensils and goods for £26,200.[21] Two years later Rondeau and Breese at 5 Savage Gardens insured for £30,700.[22] By 1820 Robert and John Wilson at 3 The Crescent, Minories were insuring for the huge sum of £104,500.[23] The following year Scott, Garnett and Palmer of 12 Aldermanbury insured their granary in Rotherhithe alone for £13,000 as well as stock, utensils and goods valued at £33,000.[24] Hop factors rarely achieved such levels of capitalisation though Baldwin and Bayly in George Inn Yard, off Borough High Street, insured for £6900 in 1770,[25] and just a few yards away but 54 years later Thomas Nash and Co in Nags Head Yard insured for £28,000.[26] There were also a substantial number of very large Blackwell Hall factors. In 1825 Thomas Sheppard at 84 Basinghall Street insured for £26,000.[27]

There were, of course, many other factors, brokers and agents, often insuring capital of a very high value. In the textile trades, Adair, Jackson and Wagner of 5 Fountain Court, Aldermanbury, who des-

---

* Dealers in wool. Until it was demolished in 1820, they traded from Blackwell Hall in Basinghall Street.

cribed themselves as Irish factors, insured for £30,000 in 1775,[28] and James Truchard, a silk broker in Spital Square, insured for £10,000 two years later.[29] Half a century later in 1823, Robert Lawson, a muslin factor at 78 Watling Street, insured for £17,000.[30] The fire office registers also contain policies taken out by factors and brokers of such diverse commodities as beer, wine and spirits, tea, fish, flour, fruit, bacon, cheese, skins, drugs, boots and shoes, looms, tallow, ironmongery and leather. In the 1770s Layton and Samdell, tea brokers at 41 Lime Street, insured for £10,000,[31] and Edward Walker, a drug broker at 12 Billiter Square, for £3300.[32] In the 1820s John King, a leather broker in Philpot Lane, insured for £15,500,[33] and George Millward, a bacon broker at 120 Goswell Street, for £5000.[34]

The 1841 Census showed that 7000 people were employed by merchants, factors, agents and brokers. It also counted separately over 20,000 clerks, a large proportion of whom would have been employed in London's many commercial houses.

. . . .
The London Businesswoman

However disadvantaged in law women continued to be throughout the period 1775–1825, and despite the overwhelming presumption that their place was in the home, the fire office registers show that they owned and ran a small but significant number of businesses in London. This went much further than simply daughters inheriting a concern from their fathers or widows keeping the business going after their husbands' death. Peter Earle found that 6.4 per cent of bankruptcies in the years 1711–15 and 9 per cent of fire insurance policies for 1726–29 were for businesses owned by women.[1] The rather larger samples for the 1770s and 1820s show that the proportions of London businesses of which the proprietors were one or more women were 7.8 and 7.1 per cent respectively. In addition, women were co-proprietors of about another 1 per cent throughout the period. This means that there were probably some 2300 businesses in London owned by women in the 1770s and 3500 in the 1820s, with up to about another 300 in the earlier period and 500 in the later of which they were co-proprietors.

However, if numbers of female-owned businesses increased between the 1770s and 1820s, there can be little doubt that their relative size declined. In the 1770s they accounted for just over 3 per cent of all capital insured; by the 1820s the proportion had declined to under 1.4 per cent. The average size of firms owned by women measured in terms of capital insured was substantially smaller than for all firms in London. In the 1770s the average was £291, only 43 per cent of the average for all businesses (£672). Over the next 50 years the average size of female-owned businesses increased very little to £291. This represented a decline to just 19 per cent of the average for all firms of £1510. However, these crude comparisons across the whole spectrum

TABLE 9.1 Firms in London with female proprietors

Capital insured (£)	No. of firms 1770s	Percentage of total	No. of firms 1820s	Percentage of total
100 and under	672	51.7	481	48.0
101–500	505	38.8	399	39.8
501–1000	70	5.4	72	7.2
1001–2999	46	3.5	39	3.9
3000 and over	8	0.6	11	1.1
Total	1301	100.0	1002	100.0

Source: Sun and other London fire office registers

of London trades over-state the position. Much the highest capitalised firms in London were merchants, factors, brokers and wholesalers. These were also the firms which exhibited the largest increases in value of capital insured over the period 1775–1825. Very few were owned by women. If these are excluded, the average value of capital insured by female-owned businesses as a proportion of all London firms rises to exactly half in the 1770s and to 32 per cent in the 1820s. Nevertheless, this still represents a considerable relative decline in the position of female-owned businesses. It will also be seen below that comparisons within those trades where female-owned businesses were most common show an even greater decline in their size relative to all firms in those trades. Table 9.1 shows the full breakdown by value of capital insured for all businesses of which women were proprietors.

Small firms were overwhelmingly predominant. In the 1770s nearly 90 per cent of all businesses owned by women insured capital valued at £500 or less, with well over half insuring for £100 or less. This was rather more extreme than the breakdown for all London firms, but not drastically so; for all firms the proportions were 75 per cent and 32 per cent. Half a century later the comparison was rather more extreme. In the 1820s it was still the case that 88 per cent of female-owned businesses insured capital valued at £500 or less, 48 per cent insuring for £100 or less; the comparative figures for all businesses were 63 per cent and 21 per cent. Conversely, only 4 per cent of female-owned businesses insured capital valued at over £1000 in the 1770s compared with 13 per cent for all firms; by the 1820s the comparative figures were 5 per cent and 23 per cent. In neither period

TABLE 9.2 Number of female-owned firms by industrial sector

Sector	Number	Percentage of all firms in the sector	Number	Percentage of all firms in the sector
Retailing	831	12.4	619	9.7
Services	295	8.0	191	8.2
Manufacturing	145	3.3	157	4.4

Source: Sun and other London fire office registers

did the number of 'large' businesses insuring for £3000 or more rise to more than 1 per cent, compared to 4.5 per cent for all businesses in the 1770s and 11 per cent in the 1820s. The fire office registers show that only eight out of 759 businesses insuring capital valued at £3000 or more in the 1770s were female-owned and that in the 1820s it was still just 11 out of 1534.

The large majority of London's female-owned firms were in three sectors of the economy (see Table 9.2); retailing, the service industries and manufacturing. These accounted for over 97 per cent of all firms owned by women throughout the period 1775–1825.

The highest proportions of female-owned businesses were to be found in the retail sector. The average capital insured by them was £240 in the 1770s. This compares with £462 for all retailers. In other words, female-owned businesses insured capital valued at 52 per cent of that for all businesses. This declined further to only 33 per cent by the 1820s. While the average capital insured by all retailers rose to £804, that for female-owned businesses increased only to £268. Within the retail sector the large majority of female-owned businesses were either in clothing and textiles or food and drink. These accounted for 65 per cent and 22 per cent respectively in the 1770s and 50 per cent and 28 per cent in the 1820s.

In clothing and textiles 22 per cent of all businesses were female-owned in the 1770s and 15 per cent in the 1820s. Much the largest number – 45 per cent of all female-owned retail businesses in the 1770s and 27 per cent in the 1820s – were dressmakers (usually described as mantua makers in the 1770s) and/or milliners. There were also significant numbers in most of the other trades. Thus, 16 per cent of haberdashers, hosiers, glovers, hatters and drapers were female-owned in the 1770s and 23 per cent of dealers in ready-made clothing; in the 1820s the proportions were 11 per cent and 15.5 per cent. Despite their small and relatively declining size, there were some quite substantial female-owned retail firms. It has already been noted that one dressmaker, Ann Smith, who was very fashionably located at 9 Waterloo Place off Regent Street, insured for £2500 in 1821.[2] Over 50 years earlier in 1769, Sarah Hyde, a milliner in Parliament Street, insured stock and utensils for double that figure,[3] and in 1774 Mary Driffield, a hatter in Worcester Street, Southwark, insured stock valued at £1800.[4] The following year Mary Smith, a haberdasher at 107 Cheapside, insured for £3000.[5] The largest surviving policy in this period was taken out by Elizabeth Saunders, a haberdasher and hosier in Upper Shadwell. She insured stock and goods valued at £5600 in 1777.[6] Returning to the 1820s, Elizabeth Poland, a furrier at 90 Oxford Street, insured for £4000,[7] and Elizabeth Austin, a linen draper at 22 Rathbone Place for £2800, both in 1825.[8]

In the food and drink trades about 8 per cent of retailers were women in both the 1770s and the 1820s. Although there were small numbers of female butchers, bakers, poulterers, greengrocers and fishmongers, the large majority were in the grocery and provisions trades. In fact, nearly one-fifth of London's innumerable chandlers were women. These were usually very small-scale businesses indeed; the average value of capital insured by female chandlers was only £69 in the 1770s and £100 in the 1820s. Even for the more fashionable grocers and cheesemongers, the average value of capital insured by female-owned businesses was only £250 in the 1770s and £270 in the 1820s. This compared with £471 and £557 for all retail grocers and cheesemongers, so here too the relative size of female-owned businesses declined over the period 1775–1825. Nevertheless, policies survive for some larger female-owned businesses. Much the largest, in the most highly capitalised of the retail food and drink trades, was that of Bridget Allan. She was a wine merchant at 67 Mark Lane and she insured stock and utensils for £5000 in 1773.[9] It is significant that this was in the 1770s rather than the 1820s. Two years earlier in 1771, Sarah Hill of 82 West Smithfield, described in an age before political correctness as an 'oilman', insured stock and goods valued at £1200.[10] In the same year Margaret Fitchcomb in Upper Thames Street, describing herself as a fruiterer, insured stock and utensils for £800.[11] On a lesser scale, Mary Haberjam, a butcher at 279 Gun Dock, Wapping, insured her slaughterhouse for £200, and stock and utensils for the same sum in 1775.[12] A rare example of a larger female-owned business in the 1820s was the bakery of Catherine Stewart at 17 King Street, Golden Square. She insured stock, utensils and her oven for £500 in 1821.[13] One other retail trade in which significant numbers of women were to be found was tobacco and snuff. Over 6 per cent of tobacconists were female in the 1770s and by the 1820s this had risen to 17 per cent. Most were small, but Dorothy Schoen of 75 Newgate Street insured stock and utensils valued at £600 in 1771.[14]

Although fewer in number, there were female-owned businesses in several other retail trades. There were, for example, women perfumers, dealers in patent medicines, hardware, china, glass and earthenware and mats, shoemakers, proprietors of carpet and blanket warehouses, ironmongers, toywomen, oil- and colourwomen, tallow chandlers, cutlers, pewterers, printsellers, music sellers, brokers of household goods, booksellers, stationers, goldsmiths, silversmiths and jewellers. Here too a few were of a substantial size. Mary Collingwood, a bookseller, insured her shop premises at 138 Strand for £1000 in 1821, and goods for £2500 four years later.[15] In a very different trade was Ann Barber, an ironmonger at 19 Rotherhithe. In 1821, she insured for the very substantial sum of £3200.[16] The following year stock, utensils and goods at the Minton showroom in Regent Street valued at £2500 were insured in the name of Susannah Minton.[17] Esther West, a silversmith and jeweller at 3 Ludgate Street, insured her stock and utensils for £3000 in 1825.[18] In the 1770s there had been nothing on quite this scale. Letitia Clark, a dealer in mats at 29 Bishopsgate Street, insured stock and utensils for £1600 in 1772,[19] and three years earlier Elizabeth Tunecliffe, describing herself as a carpet and blanket warehousewoman in Piccadilly, insured for £1500.[20] In 1770 Elizabeth Blackburn, a dealer in oils in the Strand, insured for £1300.[21]

The large majority of businesses owned by women in the services sector were to be found either in catering or personal services. In the former, 5 per cent were female-owned in the 1770s and 6 per cent in the 1820s. Though these are modest percentages, the numbers were very considerable, probably of the order of 200 in the 1770s and 250 in the 1820s. Interestingly, there was very little difference in average size of capital insured in the 1770s, £195 for female-owned businesses compared with £234 overall, and in the 1820s the average size of female-owned businesses was actually considerably larger, £528 compared with £441. Women were to be found described in the fire office registers as eating house keepers, coffee house keepers, innkeepers, cooks and most frequently as victuallers. Some were in business on a considerable scale. As early as 1769 Jane Goodchild, proprietress of the Tumbledown Dick in Borough High Street, insured for £1050,[22] and it has already been noted that Sarah Ann Mountain of the Saracen's Head in Snow Hill insured for £7680 in 1822.[23] Three years earlier Martha Wood, who described herself as a cook, insured stock and utensils at 54–6 Great Tower Street for £2000.[24] Very different was the business of Ann Little at King John's Court, Holywell Lane. She was a scavenger and insured stock, utensils and livestock for £800 in 1819.[25]

The overwhelming majority of the 16,220 laundresses counted in the 1841 Census could scarcely be described as businesswomen. However, a significant number (88 in the 1770s and 74 in the 1820s) were in business on a sufficient scale to take out fire insurance. In 1825 Mary Crowther of 15 Tinker Row, City Road, insured stock, utensils and goods for £450.[26] Forty-eight years earlier in 1777, Ann Holmes of Richardson Gardens, Kensington, insured utensils and goods for £400.[27] Women were to be found in many other service industries; for example as pawnbrokers, carriers, stablekeepers, coachmistresses, hairdressers, undertakers and even scavengers. Once again a small number traded on a considerable scale, such as Esther Wallace, a pawnbroker at 119 Bishopsgate Street who insured pledges and plate valued at £2300 in 1771,[28] and Ann Reid, an undertaker and coffin maker at 53 Goodge Street who insured for £1400 in 1825.[29] Two years before that Eliza Nichol kept a livery stable at the Adam and Eve in Kensington where she insured for £900.[30]

Although in total there was a significant number of female-owned manufacturing firms in London, in no individual trade were they very numerous. In the 1770s the average value of capital insured by firms owned by women was £374 compared with £712 for all firms; 50 years later the average for female-owned firms had actually fallen to £313 while the figure for all firms rose to £1412, a further indication of the relative decline in the position of women in business. Most female-owned firms were to be found in clothing and textiles, 7 per cent in the 1770s and 9 per cent in the 1820s. Yet again a few firms stood out, mostly in the textile finishing trades. Jane Thompson, a callenderer, insured her warehouse in London Wall for £300 in 1769, as well as stock and utensils valued at £2200,[31] and two years later Mary Aungier, a dyer in Bromley by Bow, insured stock, utensils and goods for £2000.[32] Fifty years later Anna Phelp, a silk and satin dresser in Osborn Place, Spitalfields, insured for £1800.[33] Interestingly, two of the largest dyers in London in the 1820s were Elizabeth Whitehead and Co in Bankside and Ann Kirk and Son in Osborn Place. They insured their firms for £7000 in 1822[34] and £5800 in 1824[35] respectively. An example of a smaller but still substantial female-owned firm was that of the straw hat manufactory of Letitia Fitzpatrick insured for £770 in 1823.[36]

There were a few female-owned businesses to be found in most other manufacturing trades. These included many not usually thought of as likely avenues for female enterprise. There were, for example, women soap, metal household goods, paper goods and jewellery manufacturers, beer engine makers, gunmakers, boat and barge builders, brass and ironfounders, nail makers, braziers, coachmakers, distillers, brewers, mathematical instrument makers, watchmakers, tanners, curriers, saddlers, bellows makers, trunk makers, coopers, carpenters, turners, joiners, cabinet makers, mattress makers, printers, musical instrument makers and tobacco pipe makers. The most famous was perhaps Eleanor Coade,[37] but there were several other larger female-owned firms. Ann Varnham has already been mentioned as the owner of one of the largest fellmongering firms in London in the 1770s,[38] indeed one of the most highly capitalised of all London's manufacturing firms in that period. There were several other large female-owned firms in the leather trades. Already mentioned has been Mary Townsend, a trunk maker in Leadenhall Street who insured stock and utensils for £1850 in 1769,[39] while Elizabeth Crowley at 35 Camomile Street, a currier, japanner and leather hat manufacturer, insured for £1350 in 1819.[40] Even larger were Susannah Ash, a tanner who insured her industrial buildings in Russell Street, Bermondsey, for £950, and stock, utensils, goods and livestock for £1400,[41] and Sarah Margetson, a leather dresser at 214 Bermondsey Street, who insured for £3500,[42] both in 1825.

An example from another trade was Mary Say, a printer at 10 Ave Maria Lane who insured stock and utensils valued at £4900 in 1772.[43] She had taken over the firm from her late husband and traded under her own name until 1809 even though she remarried in 1787. She published several newspapers and journals, including *The Craftsman, or Say's Weekly Journal*, which ran from 1775 to 1810. In the 1780s she achieved great notoriety by being three times prosecuted for libel, once by a House of Commons vote, and on one occasion being sentenced to six months in prison as well as being fined.[44] From other manufacturing trades were Ann Spencer, a cooper who insured her cooperage in Mitchell Street for £550 in 1777, a warehouse for £200, and stock and utensils for £1500,[45] and Rebecca Winter, a boatbuilder in Rotherhithe who insured for £800 in 1770.[46] Catherine Naish was sufficiently distinguished in the trade to become cradle maker to George III in the late 1760s.[47] Half a century later in 1819 Mary James, an upholsterer at 30 Old Compton Street, insured stock and utensils valued at £1800,[48] and in 1822 Ann Freeman, a cork cutter, insured her warehouse at 72 Watling Street for £200, and stock and utensils for £1700.[49] Elizabeth Oliver was an anchorsmith at 56 Wapping Wall. She insured a workshop for the very large sum of £1500 in 1824, and stock and utensils valued at £1000 the next year.[50]

There were very few female-owned merchant or wholesale houses, virtually none at all in the 1820s. However, half a century earlier there had been one or two to be found in the fire office registers, such as Elizabeth Ure, a hair merchant in Duck Lane, West Smithfield, who insured stock and goods valued at £4000 in 1772,[51] Elizabeth Wilson, a Manchester warehousewoman in Holliwell Street, who insured for £1900 in 1769,[52] and Leah Salomons in Little Carter Lane, who described herself as a merchant when she insured stock valued at £1750 three years later.[53]

The fire office registers provide only a tantalising glimpse of the status of the women shown as the owners of businesses in London in the period 1775–1825. In the 1820s the designation 'wife of' was used to identify a married woman engaged in a trade different to that of her husband and just over 9 per cent of female-owned businesses were described in this way. Interestingly, these businesses were almost invariably very small. The average capital insured by them in the 1820s was only £88 compared with £291 for all female-owned businesses and £1510 for all businesses. One of the largest was the dressmaking business of Mrs Thomas Willoughby at 34 Honey Lane Market. She insured stock, utensils and goods for £250 in 1819.[54] The only other evidence provided by the registers relates to those firms where the owners were two or more women bearing the same name, sisters perhaps, or mother and daughter. Forty-one per cent of firms where the owners are shown as one or more women appear to be family concerns in the 1770s and this increased to 56 per cent in the 1820s. One policy where a definite mother/daughter relationship is stated was that of the Pughs, both named Rachel, who were milliners in Russell Street in 1772 when they insured for £30.[55] Examples of many firms almost certainly owned by sisters were Ann and Mary Dorsett, who were haberdashers in King Street, Covent Garden, and insured for £220 in 1769,[56] and Mary, Sarah and Ann Conoway, hosiers in Queen Street, Soho, who insured for £200 two years later.[57] On a much larger scale in the 1820s was the retail china, glass and earthenware business of Margaret, Sarah and Charlotte Bevan at 34 Great Portland Street. They insured stock and utensils for £1500 in 1825.[58] Already noted above are two sisters in the bookselling trade, Priscilla and Agnes Nicol of 3 Great Newport Street.[59] However, the large majority of firms owned by several women relatives in the 1820s were milliners like Elizabeth, Rose and Eliza Jaques of 12 Great Russell Street who insured for £700 in 1821.[60]

Other evidence is provided by the trade card collections. One trade card from the 1760s specifies the owners of a millinery business in Marylebone Street as Ann Lisett and Sisters.[61] In the case of a trade card referred to above, in 1820 Elizabeth Procter, a plumber, painter and glazier at 59 Shoe Lane, describes herself as 'widow of Thomas Procter'.[62] This is also implied by an invoice sent out in 1772 by Hannah Jones, a wax chandler at 35 Poultry.[63] Another widow who definitely carried on her late husband's business was Elizabeth Randall. The firm was established as music sellers, printers and publishers in Catherine Street in 1766 but Elizabeth ran it alone from 1776 to 1783.[64] In the upholstery trade, Mrs Powle took over the business of her late husband William in Lombard Street in the late 1760s,[65] as did Elizabeth Swain at 8–10 Brokers Row, Moorfields, in the 1790s.[66] A rather more complicated family arrangement occurred in the case of Richard Tonkins, who took over the turnery business of his late uncle Thomas Newton in Clifford Street, Savile Row, in about 1783 and was succeeded by his own widow Esther who ran it until about 1805.[67] Other firms are shown only as run by a married woman, who might or might not be a widow taking over from her late husband. Thus, the trade card of a late eighteenth-century corset, stay and habit maker at 33 Tavistock Street was circulated by Mrs Frieake[68] and one from the 1820s describes a laundress in a clearly substantial way of business in Pentonville as Mrs Hazell.[69] At the end of the period Mrs Janet Taylor was making nautical instruments at 1 Fen Court. She was probably the widow of Edmund Taylor, an optical instrument maker who worked at 15 White Horse Yard in the early 1820s. Subsequently in 1833 she produced a new set of lunar tables under the patronage of Queen Charlotte and established what was known as the nautical warehouse at 103–4 Minories, where she was the sole agent for Dent's chronometers. She also took over the Nautical Academy under the patronage of the Admiralty, Trinity House and the West India Company. As Janet Taylor and Co the business prospered until 1875.[70]

There are also small numbers of multi-proprietor firms to be found in the fire office registers where both men and women were named as owners. In many cases these were clearly family businesses, brothers and sisters, fathers and daughters and even mothers and sons like Ann Kirk and Son of Bankside.[71] Sixty years earlier in the late 1760s, Elizabeth Bell and Son had been an important firm of cabinet makers in St Paul's Churchyard.[72] A number of other mother and son partnerships were recorded in the fire office registers, such as Elizabeth Cox and Son, medical booksellers in St Thomas's Street near the hospital, who insured for £1500 in 1819,[73] Sarah Woolley and Sons, fender and fire iron manufacturers at 34 Duke Street, West Smithfield, who insured for £400 in 1824,[74] and it has been noted that Mary Phillips and Son, beaver cutters, hatters and furriers at 5 Middlesex Street insured for £3200 the previous year.[75]

It is not possible to know whether, for example, a firm described as Mary and Thomas Haines is husband and wife, father and daughter, mother and son or brother and sister, with numbers of other theoretical possibilities too. However, it was probably husband and wife in this case since they were proprietors of Tom's Coffee House in Russell Street in 1771 when they insured stock and utensils valued at £175.[76] All that can be said is that dozens of policies throughout the period are designated in this way and most likely indicate husband and wife partnerships. In the 1770s a few actually state that the proprietors are husband and wife, for example Mr and Mrs Thomas Hedges of Piccadilly, described as salesmen (sic) and mantua makers in 1775 when they insured stock, utensils and goods for £400,[77] or Mr and Mrs Nicholas Cole, hairdressers and milliners also in Piccadilly, who insured for £330 in 1777.[78] In the case of Mr and Mrs Hale Miller of 1 Charles Street, Long Acre, their 1777 fire insurance policy describes him as a dealer in glass and her as a mantua maker, with a joint capital of just £50.[79] Sometimes a number of brothers and sisters are suggested as with Mary, James and Henry Mist of Long Acre. They were founders and ironmongers and insured for £4050, again in 1777.[80] Nearly 50 years later in 1825, John, Elizabeth and Sophia Exeter, twine spinners at 20 Whitechapel Road, insured for £1850.[81]

Family connections were to be found in 32 per cent of firms with both male and female proprietors in the 1770s; 50 years later this had risen to 56 per cent. This still leaves two-thirds in the 1770s and nearly half in the 1820s which were jointly owned by men and women with no apparent family relationship. Either way, a significant number of women were partners in some very substantial firms. For example, in 1777 Mary Brittnor was in partnership with John and Daniel Cholmley, Peter Champion, Charles Spence and John Harrison in a brewery in Morgan's Lane, Southwark, which was insured for £16,500 with the Sun, Royal Exchange and Union fire offices.[82] Other examples were Frances Pulteney, William Pulteney and William Southall of 17 Newman Street, who described themselves as carpenters and in 1772 took out a policy covering 18 houses under construction and valued at £9000,[83] and Dorothy and Matthew Whiting, sugar refiners in Broad Street, Ratcliffe, who insured for £7000 in 1769.[84] In the retail sector Ann Cremer was in partnership with William Boak as hosiers in High Holborn, insuring stock and utensils for £2400 in 1775.[85] Forty-six years later in 1821, Margaret, John and Matthew Craven insured their sugar refinery in Red Lion Street, Whitechapel, for £15,500,[86] and Sarah Watkins of 18 Pinners Hall, Broad Street, was in partnership with John Idle and James Brougham as shipowners who insured 17 ships for £8000 in 1820.[87] Mary Priestley and John Neale, booksellers at 5 St Giles High Street, insured for £3500 in 1821.[88]

The role of women in business in London does seem to have declined in the period 1775–1825. Nevertheless, even at the later date they were to be found in virtually every trade of any significance and a small number were proprietors, either alone or in partnership, of a number of firms of very considerable size.

CHAPTER 10

Conclusion: London, the World's First Modern City

As if seen from above by a high-flying aircraft – or perhaps a time-machine might be a more appropriate metaphor – an overview of the structure of industry in London in the last quarter of the eighteenth century and the first quarter of the nineteenth does show it as the hub of the Industrial Revolution. The preceding chapters present statistical data and/or examples of individual firms for over a thousand different London trades which provide answers to the five sets of questions posed in Chapter 3, and in doing so provide convincing evidence that London was indeed such a hub in those years. It must be recalled again that in comparison Dorothy George described just 25 trades and only a handful of individual firms in her classic study of London in the eighteenth century.

Taken one by one, answers to the five sets of questions place the structure of London's economy in the period 1775–1825 firmly into context within the British Industrial Revolution as a whole.

With regard to manufacturing, there can be no doubt that London was a major manufacturing centre and that it was still growing throughout the period 1775–1825. This can be seen from every point of view: the number of different trades to be found was increasing, as was their specialisation; the number and size of firms was also increasing, and so was the capital employed by them and their numbers of employees. What can also be concluded from the comprehensive overview of London's innumerable manufacturing trades is that they were characterised by no single or over-riding phenomenon. Some were labour intensive, such as shipbuilding or, on a very different scale, brushmaking, and some capital intensive, such as soap, while others were characterised by both (sugar), or neither (furniture). Some were dominated by very large-scale enterprises, such as brewing or glassmaking, others by a multitude of small firms, such as clothing. Most had a mix of both large and small firms. There were luxury trades, such as coachmaking or gunmaking, industries aimed at the widest possible market, such as manufacture of metal household goods, and those satisfying wider trade needs, such as shipbuilding or those of other industries such as industrial chemicals. Other trades can undoubtedly be described as finishing trades, especially in the textiles sector, but others in the clothing trades, such as hatmaking, were involved at every stage of the production process. While most firms in every trade employed very few people, in some a few employed very large numbers, such as hatmaking or wallpaper manufacture. Even in trades totally dominated by small-scale workshops, such as clockmaking, there were a few firms which operated on a sufficient scale to employ substantial numbers of people. In the application of steam power, London was in no way behind the major provincial centres in its application. Nor was it behind in the application of the emerging new technologies. At the same time, large-scale factories and heavy capital equipment existed side-by-side with small workshops, sometimes in the same trade, such as printing. Indeed, it is interesting to note that the fire office registers contain policies for 337 workshops, but also for 196 manufactories. Finally, while some trades were to be found predominantly in one or two particular districts, such as silk in Spitalfields and later Bethnal Green, tanning in Bermondsey and watches in Clerkenwell, most were spread across all areas of the metropolis, from the poorest riverside districts of the East End to the streets around Grosvenor or Berkeley Squares.

Increasing wealth and rapidly expanding population both ensured that London would experience a construction boom in these years, even despite two decades of war. It is clear that long before Victoria came to the throne what the historian of the Victorian construction boom, H. J. Dyos, called 'the irresistible growth of London' had become 'a magnet for speculative capital'. Such was its scale that it could hardly fail to impact on the economy of the metropolis as a whole and it was accompanied by, for example, a huge increase in the business of such suppliers of building materials as timber merchants, three of which insured for over £40,000 each in the early 1820s. Although brickmaking and glass manufacture were not major London industries, most of their supply to the building trade was carried out by London firms. London's housing stock increased by over 120,000 between 1750 and 1831; indeed, by twenty to thirty thousand in each decade from 1801 to 1831. Added to this was the vast expansion in the commercial and public domains – docks, bridges, roads, warehouses, factories, shops, theatres and so on. Over 14 per cent of London's working population was employed in the construction industry, about one in seven. It is no surprise to find Thomas Cubitt one of London's largest employers, possibly its very largest. The foundations for the further huge expansion in the later nineteenth century had been well and truly laid during the half century from 1775 to 1825.

That there was a consumer revolution during this period, and that London was at its heart in every sense, can scarcely be doubted. Not only did London exhibit all the characteristics to be expected from an economy in the throes of the consumer revolution described by McKendrick, but it was one of the major driving forces behind it. In his words: 'England possessed another prime advantage for the creation of a consumer society in the size and character of its capital city.'[1] Difficulties in defining the precise boundaries of retailing and its inevitable overlap with wholesaling on the one hand and small-scale manufacturing on the other, should not detract from the main thrust of the argument. Data derived from the fire office registers and trade directories clearly demonstrate that by the 1770s London had a network of retail businesses which both specialised to a bewildering degree and reached down to every class of society. The registers show that in the 1770s there were businesses describing themselves as involved in 164 separate retail trades; by the 1820s this had increased to 245. For retailers of clothing and textiles the increase was only from 55 to 61, demonstrating how far the consumer revolution had advanced by the 1770s. However, for household goods the increase was from 26 separate trades to 59, and for food from 33 to 49. Even in those trades at the upper end of the market, retailers were to be found in large numbers in the poorest neighbourhoods. Thus, for example, while 43 per cent of linen drapers and mercers were to be found in the City and 41 per cent in the West End and west central districts in the 1770s, there were still 12 per cent to be found in the poorer areas of the East End and south of the river. Fifty years later, 73 per cent were still to be found in the City, West End and west central area, but the proportion in the East End and south-east London had increased to 20 per cent. By the 1820s half the 20 linen drapers to be found in Wapping, Shadwell, Whitechapel, Rotherhithe and Bermondsey insured capital valued at £2000 or more.

At the other end of the scale, used clothes salesmen and pawn-brokers reached a long way down the social scale in response to new and expanding consumer demand for the newly fashionable in clothing, or as nearly new as could be afforded. Pigot listed 336 such businesses in London in 1826–27 and another 448 responding to the same demands for cheap new and used household goods. The fire office registers show that the number catering for the demand for cheap ready-made and used clothes increased by 21 per cent between the 1770s and 1820s, and the number dealing in cheap household goods by 16 per cent.

Such an enormous and diverse retail sector could hardly have functioned without an equally well developed wholesale sector. This too London possessed. In one sense the traditional dual role of many of its major retail houses in serving both the London public and the provincial shopkeeper, especially in the clothing and textiles sector, made it easier for specialist wholesale houses to emerge in the latter part of the period. Nevertheless, it has been amply demonstrated that they already existed by the last quarter of the eighteenth century. What is not in doubt is the increase in their size and number. By the 1820s there were at least a dozen wholesale houses insuring for more than £30,000 and the sector as a whole accounted for 13 per cent of all capital insured by London businesses.

The consumer revolution also had a profound impact on London's manufacturing infrastructure. The 'orgy of spending' described by McKendrick and the 'commercialization of leisure' described by his collaborator J. H .Plumb meant both demands for new products by consumers at the luxury end of the market and for a much wider range of old, and formerly luxury, products from new consumers lower down the social scale. The important point about this is that to a very large extent it was London firms which manufactured as well as distributed the products to satisfy many of the new demands. What most distinguished London at this time was not that in very many cases it kept up with the newly emergent manufacturing dis-tricts of the Midlands and north, though it did, but that it was overwhelmingly predominant in a large number of luxury manufac-turing trades as diverse as clocks and watches, coaches and carriages, furniture, wallpaper, jewellery and silks. The book trades demonstrate one example of the impact of the commercialisation of leisure. Pigot in 1826–27 listed 5669 firms in these seven trades alone, nearly one in eight of all London businesses. The total capital insured by them rose from a little over £900,000 in the 1770s to £2.25 million in the 1820s, an increase of 155 per cent. By the 1820s this represented over 11 per cent of all commercial capital insured.

Again, the data set out in this book demonstrate conclusively the existence of a full-scale service economy in London by the end of the first quarter of the nineteenth century. It had become the focal point of a fully developed passenger transport network, many of the proprietors of which were also involved in inns and hotels and coach-building. Coachbuilding itself had reached the highest peak of its development as one of London's luxury trades *par excellence*. The range of London's inns, taverns, eating houses and outside caterers had never been greater and, if the coffee house was disappearing, the modern hotel was beginning to makes its appearance. This was a period when the commercialisation of leisure and its conspicuous enjoyment reached further down into society than ever before. All of this existed long before the last quarter of the nineteenth century, but by 1825 the scale and diversity of the various service sectors were far greater, as were the size and number of the firms involved. Underpinning London's manufacturing and distribution sectors, too, was an ever more sophisticated road freight transport system, itself focused on London, and the new docks added to the importance of the waterborne transport industry. Finally, personal services of all sorts proliferated, none of them new, but all evolving to satisfy increasing demand.

There is little need to demonstrate the importance of the role of commercial London. For centuries London's merchants, agents, factors and brokers had underpinned the economy of the metropolis and provided the services without which it could neither have evolved nor functioned. They inter-related with every other sector of the economy, be it manufacturing, construction, wholesale and retail distribution or transport. By the early 1820s they accounted for over 31 per cent of all capital insured in London and it is a measure of the importance of the sector that no other had firms insuring individually for over £100,000, the equivalent of at least £25 or £30 million pounds in the 1990s.

In summary, London evolved into a city unique in time and place during the latter part of the eighteenth century and the first 30 years or so of the nineteenth. Not only did it acquire the largest urban population the world had ever seen but it became the model for the modern city of the later years of the nineteenth century in the western world and for the entire globe in the twentieth. It was still a major manufacturing centre with an absolute predominance in certain trades and industries. At the same time it was the prime mover in the world's first consumer revolution and, even before the onset of the railway age, it was the focal point for a complex national and local transport infrastructure for both passengers and freight. In addition it had a sophisticated network of service industries. Most important of all, this revolutionary complex of urban services, in which the metropolitan population was both provider and consumer, reached down to serve every class in society.

Of course, London was also evolving the financial infrastructure which was to make it the wonder of the Victorian age. One of the more important reasons why London was able to capitalise an empire and a large part of the rest of the world in the later Victorian era was the wealth created by tens of thousands of small businesses, thousands of medium-sized firms and hundreds of enormously large undertakings in the period 1775–1825. It is argued in this book that the flexibility provided by London's bewildering diversity of trades and industries on the one hand, and size of firm on the other, enabled it to function as the hub of the Industrial Revolution while also enabling it to withstand the inevitable fluctuations in the trade cycle with minimum disruption to the build-up of its wealth. London was little more than just another large European capital in 1700, overwhelmingly pre-eminent within the national economy but of no particular world significance. Within a century or so it had evolved into a phenomenon entirely new to the world, the very prototype for the later twentieth-century city and its role in the predominant world economies of the 1990s. In a very real sense to walk the streets of New York or Tokyo in the 1990s is to observe the direct result of that revolution in the potential for urban economic development, urban standards of living and the evolution of urban society and the institutions which serve it which began in London more than two hundred years earlier.

Standard Industrial Classification

SIC and Class	SIC and Group	SIC and Activity
01 Agriculture & horticulture	010 Agriculture & horticulture	
17 Water supply	170 Water supply	
22 Metals	223 Ferrous metals	
	224 Non-ferrous metals	
24 Non-metallic mineral products	241 Clay products	
	242 Cement, lime & plaster	
	245 Stone working	
	246 Abrasive products	
	247 Glass & glassware	2471 Glass
		2472 Glassware
25 Chemicals	248 Ceramics	
	251 Industrial chemicals	2511 Dyes
		2512 Other
	255 Paints, varnishes & inks	2551 Paints & varnishes
		2552 Inks
	256 Specialised chemical products	
	257 Pharmaceutical products	
	258 Soaps & toiletries	2581 Soap
		2582 Perfume
	259 Chemical products for household use	2591 Wax & tallow
		2592 Cleaning materials
31 Metal goods	311 Foundries	
	313 Nails & metals treatment	3131 Metals treatment
		3132 Nails etc.
	316 Finished metal goods	3161 Implements & tools

3162 Household goods
3163 Other

32 Mechanical engineering

323 Textile machinery
324 Food machinery
325 Mechanical handling equipment
328 Other machinery
    3281 Engines
    3282 Other
329 Small arms & ammunition
    3291 Guns
    3292 Ammunition

36 Ship & vehicle building

361 Shipbuilding
365 Other vehicles
    3651 Coachbuilding
    3653 Wheelwrights

37 Precision instruments

371 Measuring apparatus
    3711 Mathematical instruments
    3712 Other
372 Medical equipment
373 Optical instruments
374 Clocks & watches

41/2 Food, drink & tobacco

411 Organic oils
412 Meat products
414 Fruit & vegetables
416 Milling
418 Starch
419 Bread & biscuits
420 Sugar
421 Chocolate & confectionery
423 Miscellaneous foods
424 Distilling
426 Wines, cider & perry

SIC and Class	SIC and Group	SIC and Activity
43 Textiles	427 Brewing	
	428 Soft drinks	
	429 Tobacco	
	431 Woollens & worsteds	
	432 Silk & cotton	
	434 Flax & hemp	
	435 Jute	
	436 Hosiery	
	437 Textile finishing	4371 Dyeing & bleaching
		4372 Callendering & hot pressing
		4373 Dressing
		4374 Other
	438 Carpets	
	439 Miscellaneous textiles	4391 Hair
		4392 Ribbon, lace & trimmings
		4393 Other
44 Leather & leather goods	441 Tanning & dressing	
	442 Leather goods	4421 Saddles & harnesses
		4422 Luggage
		4423 Other
45 Footwear & clothing	451 Footwear	
	453 Clothing, hats & gloves	4531 Clothing
		4532 Hats
		4533 Other
	455 Household & other made-up textiles	

46 Furniture & timber

- 456 Fur goods
- 461 Sawmilling & planing
- 463 Builders' carpentry
- 464 Wooden containers
- 465 General carpentry
- 466 Cork, baskets & brushes
  - 4661 Cork
  - 4662 Basketware
  - 4663 Brushes & brooms
- 467 Furniture

47 Paper, printing & publishing

- 471 Paper & board
- 472 Paper & board products
- 475 Printing & publishing
  - 4751 Printing
  - 4752 Publishing

49 Other manufacturing

- 491 Jewellery
- 492 Musical instruments
- 494 Toys & sports goods
- 495 Miscellaneous
  - 4951 Pens, pencils & quills
  - 4952 Other

50 Construction

- 500 General construction
- 501 Construction & repair of buildings
- 503 Installation of fixtures & fittings
- 504 Building completion work
  - 5042 Painters & glaziers
  - 5043 Paperhanging & plastering
  - 5044 Other

61 Wholesale distribution

- 611 Agricultural raw materials
  - 6111 Hops
  - 6112 Corn
  - 6113 Other cereals
  - 6114 Livestock

SIC and Class	SIC and Group	SIC and Activity
	612 Fuels, ores, metals & industrial materials	6115 Leather & skins
		6116 Textile raw materials
		6117 Other
		6121 Coal
		6123 Metals
		6124 Other
	613 Timber & building materials	
	615 Household goods	6151 Glass & ceramics
		6153 Ironmongery & hardware
		6154 Oils & paints
	616 Textiles & clothing	6161 Clothes
		6162 Textiles
		6163 Footwear
		6164 Other
	617 Food, drink & tobacco	6171 Meat, fish & poultry
		6172 Grocery & provisions
		6173 Beer, wine & spirits
		6174 Fruit & vegetables
		6175 Tobacco
		6176 Other
	618 Medical & chemists' goods	
	619 Other & general wholesale distribution	6191 Merchants
		6192 Stationery & books
		6193 Other
62 Dealing in waste materials	622 Dealing in scrap materials	

63 Commission agents

630 Commission agents

- 6301 Agricultural raw materials
- 6302 Textiles & textile raw materials
- 6303 Food & drink
- 6304 Household goods
- 6305 General
- 6306 Other

64/5 Retail distribution

641 Food

- 6411 Meat & poultry
- 6412 Bakery
- 6413 Fruit & vegetables
- 6414 Fish
- 6415 Drink
- 6416 Grocers & cheesemongers
- 6417 Chandlers
- 6418 Dairy & other

642 Confectionery, tobacco, wine, beer & spirits

- 6421 Beer & cider
- 6422 Wine & spirits
- 6423 Confectionery
- 6424 Tobacco
- 6425 Newspapers

643 Chemists

645 Clothing

- 6451 Tailors & dressmakers
- 6452 Slopsellers
- 6453 Corsets & stays
- 6454 Hats, hosiery & gloves
- 6455 Haberdashery
- 6456 Fabrics & fur
- 6457 Multiple specialism clothing & textile retailers

SIC and Class	SIC and Group	SIC and Activity
	646 Footwear & leather goods	6458 Umbrellas & sticks
		6459 Other new & ready made clothing retailers
		6461 Footwear
		6462 Leather goods
	647 Household textiles	
	648 Household goods	6481 Hardware & ironmongery
		6482 Oils, candles & paints
		6483 Cutlery
		6484 Furniture
		6485 Ceramics & glass
		6486 Pictures & prints
		6487 Music & musical instruments
		6488 Other
		6489 Brokers of household goods
	653 Books & stationery	6531 Books
		6532 Stationery
	654 Other specialised retailing	6541 Coal & fuel
		6544 Jewellery
		6545 Flowers, plants & seeds
		6546 Pets & feedstuffs
		6547 Other
	656 Mixed retail businesses	
	661 Eating places	
	662 Public houses	
66 Hotels & catering		

	665 Hotels	
72 Inland transport	722 Road passenger	7221 Stablekeepers
		7222 Coachmasters
	723 Road freight	
	726 Inland water	
74 Sea transport	740 Sea transport	7401 Shipowners
77 Storage	770 Storage & warehousing	7701 Warehousing
		7702 Granaries
81 Financial services	815 Credit institutions	8151 Pawnbrokers
83 Professional & technical services	831 Activities ancillary to banking & finance	
	834 House & estate agents	8341 Surveyors
	839 Professional services	8391 Appraisers
		8392 Auctioneers
92 Sanitary services	921 Refuse disposal	
	923 Cleaning services	
96 Public services	969 Public services	9691 Lighting
97 Artistic & recreational services	976 Artistic services	
	977 Libraries & museums	
	979 Sport & recreation	
98 Personal services	981 Laundries & dyers	
	982 Hairdressing, beauty treatment & public baths	
	989 Other personal services	9891 Funeral services

Notes

Abbreviations

B3   Bankruptcy Commission files, Series B3, Public Record Office.
GL   Guildhall Library trade card collection.
Globe   Globe Fire Office registers, Guildhall Library, Ms 11679.
HC   Heal collection of trade cards and shopbills, British Library.
HH   Hand in Hand Fire Office registers, Guildhall Library, Ms 8674.
Lond   London Assurance Fire Office registers, Guildhall Library, Ms 8747.
ML   Museum of London Printed Ephemera Collection, trade cards, invoices
        etc.
RE   Royal Exchange Fire Office registers, Guildhall Library, Ms 7253.
Sun   Sun Fire Office registers, Guildhall Library, Ms 11936.

1. Introduction

1. Quoted in Roy Porter, *London: A Social History* (1994), 165.
2. Ibid., 1.
3. Quoted in ibid., 187.
4. Quoted in Paul Johnson, 'Economic Development and Industrial Dynamism in Victorian London', *London Journal*, 21, 1 (1996), 27.
5. Dorothy George, *London Life in the Eighteenth Century* (1987 edn), 15.
6. I. J. Prothero, *Artisans and Politics in Early Nineteenth Century London* (1979), 2.
7. G. Stedman Jones, *Outcast London* (1971), 19–21.
8. George Rudé, *Hanoverian London 1714–1808* (1971), 28.
9. Leonard Schwartz, *London in the Age of Industrialisation* (1992), 2–3.
10. Martin Daunton, *Progress and Poverty* (1995), 138.
11. Porter, *London*, 187.
12. Pat Hudson (ed.), *Regions and Industries* (1989), 3.
13. E. A. Wrigley, 'A Simple Model of London's Importance in Changing English Society and Economy, 1650–1759', *Past and Present*, XXXVII (1967).
14. Clive Lee, 'Regional Growth and Structural Change in Victorian Britain', *Economic History Review*, 2nd Series, XXXIII (1981), 438–52.
15. Johnson, 'Economic Development', 27–36.
16. David Green, 'The Nineteenth-Century Metropolitan Economy: A Revisionist Interpretation', *London Journal*, 21, 1 (1996), 9–24.
17. T. S. Ashton, *The Industrial Revolution 1760–1830*, (1968 edn), 40.

18. W. D. Rubinstein, *Men of Property* (1981).

19. Quoted in Porter, *London*, 165.

20. Quoted in Paul Bailey, *The Oxford Book of London* (1995), 119.

21. Peter Earle, *A City Full of People* (1994).

22. George Dodd, *Days at the Factories, Series I – London* (1843), 15.

23. H. A. L. Cockerell and Edwin Green, *The British Insurance Business 1547– 1970* (1976), 18–33.

24. Clive Trebilcock, *Phoenix Insurance and the Development of British Insurance, I, 1782–1879* (1985), 1–11.

25. David T. Jenkins, *Indexes of the Fire Insurance Policies of the Sun Fire Office and the Royal Exchange Assurance 1775–1787* (typescript, University of York, 1986), 131.

26. See P. G. M. Dickson, *The Sun Insurance Office 1710–1960*, (1960); Barry Supple, *The Royal Exchange Assurance, A History of British Insurance 1720–1970* (1970); and Bernard Drew, *The London Assurance: A Second Chronicle* (1949).

27. Jenkins, *Indexes*, 23. See also the study of Sun policies for 1780, Leonard Schwartz and L. J. Jones, 'Wealth, Occupations and Insurance in the Late Eighteenth Century: The Policy Registers of the Sun Fire Office', *Economic History Review*, XXXVI, 3 (1983), passim; and Stanley Chapman, 'Business History from Insurance Policy Registers', *Business Archives*, 32 (1970), 10–16. For a full evaluation of the registers as a data source, and of the other sources used in this book, see D. C. Barnett, *The Structure of Industry in London*, PhD thesis (1996), 5– 23.

28. Jenkins, *Indexes*, 25.

29. Trebilcock, *Phoenix Insurance*, 367–80.

30. Cockerell and Green, *British Insurance*, 30–3; and Dickson, *Sun Insurance*, 78–9 .

31. Trebilcock, *Phoenix Insurance* , 370.

32. Jenkins, *Indexes*, 30.

33. Cockerell and Green, *British Insurance*, 21.

34. Jenkins, *Indexes*, 31.

35. Robin Pearson, 'Fire Insurance and the British Textile Industries during the Industrial Revolution', *Business History*, 34, 4 (1992), 1–19.

36. Jenkins, *Indexes*, 29.

37. Dickson, *Sun Insurance*, 79.

38. Jenkins, *Indexes*, 25.

39. GL.

40. Dickson, *Sun Insurance*, 79.

41. All these indexes are set out in full in Daunton, *Progress and Poverty*, 577– 80.

2. The Metropolis Defined

1. Horwood's map is published in full in Paul Laxton (ed.), *The A to Z of Regency London* (1985).

2. George, *London Life*, 15.

3. See the 1821 Census, *Abstract of Answers and Returns, Parish Register, Abstract Appendix B*, 159; and *Parliamentary Accounts and Papers, Population (Great Britain)*, LXXXV, 1852–3.

4. Hugh Clout (ed.), *London History Atlas* (1991), 72–3.

5. Ibid., 74.

6. Quoted in Hermione Hobhouse, *A History of Regent Street* (1975), 14.

7. J. D. Burn, *Commercial Enterprise and Social Progress* (1858), 12.

8. Quoted in Porter, *London*, 199–200.

9. Unless otherwise stated, the detailed street analyses which follow rely on *Johnstone's London Commercial Guide and Street Directory* (1817).

10. Quoted in Andrew Saint and Gillian Darley, *The Chronicles of London* (1994), 151.

3. Industrial London

1. Central Statistical Office (CSO), *Standard Industrial Classification, Revised 1980* (1984), 2.

2. R. Campbell, *The London Tradesman* (1747), v–xii.

3. Sun, 1775, 242, 359757.

4. Sun, 1777, 255, 381405.

5. Porter, *London*, 187.

6. CSO, *Standard Industrial Classification*, 2.

7. Sun, 1769, 191, 273190.

8. Sun, 1820, 483, 972677.

9. Sun, 1819, 479, 958932.

10. Sun, 1819, 480, 952441.

11. Sun, 1819, 479, 953429; 1820, 481, 966585; 1822, 490, 997222; 1823, 494, 1010988; 1824, 497, 1014533; 1825, 503, 1031886.

12. P. J. Atkins, *The Directories of London 1677–1977* (1990), table 2.

4. The London Manufacturing Trades

1. Based on the comprehensive lists contained in Sir Ambrose Heal, *London Furniture Makers 1660–1840* (1988 edn); and Ian Maxted, *The London Book Trades 1775–1800* (1977).

2. David Green, *From Artisans to Paupers, 1790–1870*, DPhil thesis, (1996), 30.

3. See Stanley Chapman, *The Cotton Industry in the Industrial Revolution*, (1987), 27–8; 'Fixed Capital Formation in the British Cotton Industry, 1770–1815', *Economic History Review*, XXIII, 2 (1970), 239 and 260–6; and 'The Transition to the Factory System in the Midlands Cotton-Spinning Industry', *Economic History Review*, XVIII, 3 (1965), 540.

4. Dodd, *Days at the Factories*, passim.

5. Jones, *Outcast London*, 19–21.

6. Prothero, *Artisans and Politics*, 2.

7. John Lord, *Capital and Steam Power 1750–1800* (1966), 48.

8. John Kanefsky and John Robey, 'Steam Engines in 18th-Century Britain: A Quantitative Assessment', *Technology and Culture*, 21, 2 (1980), 176.

9. John Farey, *A Treatise on the Steam Engine* (1827), 654.

10. Keith Hoggart and David Green (eds), *London, A New Metropolitan Geography* (1991), 17.

11. Eric Hobsbawm, 'The Nineteenth-century London Labour Market', in Centre for Urban Studies, *London: Aspects of Change* (1964), 3–28.

12. Dodd, *Days at the Factories*, 526.

13. Ibid., 17.

14. Ibid., 187.

15. Ibid., 2–3.

16. T. R. Gourvish and R. G. Wilson, *The British Brewing Industry 1830–1980* (1994), 9 and 34.

17. Peter Mathias, 'Industrial Revolution in Brewing, Developments in the Brewing Industry: 1770–1830', *Explorations in Entrepreneurial History*, V, 4 (1953), 208–33.

18. Dodd, *Days at the Factories*, 2.

19. Sun, 1771, 204, 295104, 205, 295100, 207, 300140, 208, 302193; 1820, 480, 966456, 481, 962354.

20. Sun, 1771, 203, 293338, 208, 302215, 209, 302768, 302072, 210, 305662; 1820, 485, 968800.

21. Sun, 1820, 478, 962423, 962426, 486, 968988.

22. Sun, 1777, 259, 386137.

23. Mathias, 'Industrial Revolution in Brewing', 209.

24. Sun, 1825, 502, 1031777.

25. Sun, 1824, 494, 1017456.

26. George, *London Life*, 52.

27. Campbell, *The London Tradesman*, 264.

28. Dodd, *Days at the Factories*, 2.

29. Seager and Evans, *Mr Seager and Mr Evans, the Story of a Great Partnership* (1963), 1.

30. Sun, 1777, 254, 380741, 256, 382262, 385118, 258, 385978, 257, 384758; 1819, 480, 953695, 481, 951570; 1821, 485, 980064, 487, 978858.

31. Sun, 1771, 204, 294424, 209, 303084, 208, 301076.

32. Sun, 1825, 500, 1029900, 505, 1039540, 507, 1039849.

33. Sun, 1824, 499, 1016933.

34. Seager and Evans, *Mr Seager and Mr Evans*, 3.

35. Sun, 1823, 497, 1005227; 1824, 496, 1017181.

36. Trebilcock, *Phoenix Insurance*, 15–23.

37. Sun, 1777, 254, 381252, 258, 385370, 259, 387519.

38. Sun, 1822, 490, 989815.

39. Sun, 1777, 259, 388087.

40. Sun, 1820, 485, 974752.

41. Sun, 1777, 255, 378058, 379076, 261, 390698; 1821, 486, 976291, 980534.

42. Sun, 1820, 485, 974733.

43. Sun, 1774, 232B, 344482.

44. Douglas A. Simmons, *Schweppes, the First 200 Years* (1983), 27.

45. Sun, 1820, 481, 966562.

46. HH, 1824, 148, 94282.

47. Sun, 1820, 485, 968820.

48. Sun, 1820, 478, 964652, 966192, 484, 970213.

49. Sun, 1777, 257, 381991.

50. Sun, 1822, 491, 995823/4.

51. Sun, 1819, 479, 951867.

52. GL.

53. Sun, 1820, 483, 968233.

54. Sun, 1769, 188, 268082.

55. George Evans, *The Old Snuff House of Fribourg and Treyer* (1921), 21.

56. John Arlott, *The Snuff Shop* (1974), 20.

57. Dodd, *Days at the Factories*, 3.

58. Sun, 1820, 478, 966729.

59. Sun, 1820, 485, 974104.

60. Dodd, *Days at the Factories*, 8.

61. Maxted, *London Book Trades*, xxx.

62. Quoted in Charles Ramsden, *London Bookbinders, 1780–1840* (1956), 3.

63. Nathaniel Whittock et al., *The Complete Book of English Trades* (1837), 38–67.

64. John Feather, *A History of British Publishing* (1988), 117.

65. Maxted, *London Book Trades*, xii.

66. Frank A. Mumby, *The Romance of Bookselling: A History from the Earliest Times to the Twentieth Century* (1910), 272–3; and Maxted, *London Book Trades*, 37.

67. Quoted in Alison Adburgham, *Shopping in Style* (1979), 52.

68. Maxted, *London Book Trades*, xxx.

69. GL.

70. GL.

71. Sun, 1773, 223, 326689/90; 1820, 484, 970229, 486, 970616.

72. Sun, 1820, 480, 964480/1; and HH, 1819, 147, 100584.

73. Sun, 1820, 479, 966391.

74. Sun, 1821, 488, 981579/80.

75. B3, 5745 and 5328.

76. Sun, 1823, 496, 1008505.

77. Sun, 1821, 488, 974847/8.

78. Lond, 1822, 3, 100157; HH, 147, 96461; Sun, 1775, 239, 354048, 240, 358574.

79. Sun, 1820, 483, 970593.

80. Sun, 1821, 487, 976150, 489, 985948.

81. Sun, 1771, 205, 294638.

82. Sun, 1822, 490, 991951.

83. Sun, 1819, 481, 954991.

84. Pigot and Co, *Directory of London and its Suburbs* (1839), 9.

85. Treve Rosoman, *London Wallpapers, Their Manufacture and Use 1690–1840* (1992), 1–2.

86. Sun, 1825, 504, 1026977.

87. Sun, 1822, 489, 999263/4, 491, 987764/5.
88. Sun, 1774, 228, 335667.
89. Sun, 1825, 504, 1026977.
90. GL.
91. Sun, 1824, 497, 1014534.
92. Sun, 1825, 509, 1039277.
93. T. Griffiths, P. Hunt and P. K. O'Brien, 'Invention in British Textiles 1700–1800', *Journal of Economic History*, LII (1992), 881–906.
94. George, *London Life*, 178–196 and J. L. and Barbara Hammond, *The Skilled Labourer 1760–1832* (1995 edn), 205–20.
95. George, *London Life*, 179.
96. Dodd, *Days at the Factories*, 4.
97. Sun, 1777, 260, 388755.
98. Sun, 1777, 257, 383547; and 1773, 228, 334575.
99. Sun, 1820, 480, 964873.
100. Sun, 1774, 232A, 342763, 235, 346492.
101. Sun, 1822, 484, 980520; 1823, 492, 1001298.
102. Sun, 1819, 479, 951400; 1821, 486, 974981; 1822, 489, 989644; 1823, 496, 1003511.
103. Perrotts, *A History of 250 Years of Clothworking in London* (1961), 37–9 .
104. Both GL.
105. Sun, 1775, 237, 348958.
106. Sun, 1819, 479, 962070.
107. Sun, 1822, 489, 999295.
108. GL.
109. Sun, 1819, 479, 960553.
110. Sun, 1775, 238, 353264; 1777, 259, 387184.
111. Sun, 1821, 488, 974897; 1822, 493, 987426.
112. Sun, 1770, 203, 292479; 1775, 242, 360215.
113. Sun, 1777, 261, 388840; 1819, 480, 951468, 479, 951887; HH, 1822, 147, 96838.
114. Stanley Chapman and S. Chassagne, *European Textile Printers in the Eighteenth Century* (1981), 3–25; and Stanley Chapman, 'David Evans and Co., The Last of the Old London Textile Printers', *Textile History*, 14, 1 (1983), 29–30.
115. Sun, 1777, 262, 392628.
116. Sun, 1777, 256, 384418.
117. Sun, 1822, 490, 987636.
118. Sun, 1819, 479, 952391.
119. Sun, 1821, 485, 978535.
120. Sun, 1825, 500, 1028641.
121. Sun, 1770, 202, 292664.
122. Sun, 1819, 480, 951429; 1820, 480, 962710; 1821, 484, 981623, 485, 978504; 1822, 490, 995140; 1823, 494, 1006638; 1824, 497, 1019432.
123. B3, 3078, 541, 3637 and 4762.
124. Quoted in Dorothy George, *England in Transition* (1953 edn), 38–40.
125. Campbell, *The London Tradesman*, 2–3.

126. *The Book of English Trades and Library of the Useful Arts* (1824), 73.

127. Thomas Martin, *The Circle of the Mechanical Arts* (1813), 211–17.

128. GL; and Heal, *London Furniture Makers*, 22.

129. Dodd, *Days at the Factories*, 7.

130. Sun, 1774, 228, 334848, 230B, 341132.

131. Sun, 1772, 218, 318699.

132. Sun, 1824, 499, 1021072, 1021388, 1023685.

133. Sun, 1821, 488, 976465, 493, 987146.

134. Sun, 1771, 207, 298022, 208, 302186; 1822, 490, 989255.

135. Quoted in Mary Cathcart Borer, *The City of London: A History* (1977), 226–7.

136. B3, 4689.

137. Sun, 1771, 208, 300987.

138. Sun, 1822, 490, 995640.

139. Sun, 1823, 499, 1010786.

140. See Susanna Goodden, *At the Sign of the Fourposter: A History of Heal's* (1984), 3; and J. L. Oliver, *The Development and Structure of the Furniture Industry* (1966), 22–57.

141. Sun, 1769, 191, 271637.

142. Sun, 1771, 210, 304454.

143. Sun, 1777, 257, 384352; 1821, 485, 976966/7.

144. Sun, 1819, 480, 956975.

145. B3, 1761.

146. Sun, 1775, 238, 353230.

147. Sun, 1822, 492, 997549.

148. *Book of English Trades*, 388.

149. Dodd, *Days at the Factories*, 161.

150. B3, 1099.

151. Campbell, *The London Tradesman*, 233–4.

152. Sun, 1824, 503, 1023194/5.

153. Sun, 1820, 481, 968025, 485, 968825.

154. Sun, 1820, 480, 962720.

155. GL.

156. Sun, 1769, 193, 275652.

157. HH, 1819, 147, 43892.

158. Sun, 1820, 481, 962359.

159. Sun, 1822, 493, 991427.

160. Campbell, *The London Tradesman*, 190 passim.

161. *Public Advertiser*, 14 January 1771.

162. GL.

163. William Hull, *The History of the Glove Trade* (1834), 50.

164. David Corner, 'The Tyranny of Fashion: The Case of the Felt-Hatting Trade in the late 17th and 18th Centuries', *Textile History*, 22, 2 (1991), 157.

165. Ibid., 164, but see a submission to the Treasury entitled *The Case of Thomas Chapman of Crossby Row, Long Lane, Southwark*, Guildhall Library, PAM 7927.

166. *Book of English Trades*, 202–3.

167. Dodd, *Days at the Factories*, 5.

168. For a full history of these two houses, see Arthur Sadler, *One Hundred and Seventy Five Years of the House of Christy* (1951); and H. L. Morgan, *The History of James Lock and Co, Hatters* (1948).

169. Sun, 1775, 237, 351229.

170. Sun, 1820, 484, 974534/5.

171. Dodd, *Days at the Factories*, 138.

172. Sun, 1822, 492, 993205, 995981.

173. B3, 4987.

174. Sun, 1824, 501, 1023412, 1023465.

175. Sun, 1819, 953057; 1823, 498, 999967, 496, 1005659.

176. Sun, 1820, 479, 962494/5.

177. D. J. Smith, 'Army Clothing Contractors and the Textile Industries in the 18th Century', *Textile History*, 14, 2 (1983), 153–62.

178. Sun, 1777, 254, 381635.

179. Sun, 1775, 238, 355110.

180. Sun, 1819, 479, 954056.

181. Sun, 1820, 484, 968765.

182. Sun, 1824, 501, 1019733.

183. Sun, 1769, 193, 275770.

184. Sun, 1825, 500, 1033814.

185. Sun, 1821, 487, 976631/2.

186. Sun, 1777, 260, 389702 .

187. B3, 1570.

188. Sun, 1822, 491, 993665.

189. Martin, *Mechanical Arts*, 546–8.

190. H. Hamilton, *The English Brass and Copper Industries to 1800* (1926), 242–3.

191. Dodd, *Days at the Factories*, 14.

192. GL.

193. HC.

194. GL.

195. Pigot and Co, *Metropolitan New Alphabetical Directory for 1827* (1827), advertising section.

196. GL.

197. Victoria and Albert Museum Trade Catalogue Collection.

198. Hamilton, *Brass and Copper Industries*, 271.

199. Pigot and Co, *Metropolitan New Alphabetical Directory*.

200. Sun, 1824, 496, 1017172, 503, 1023877, 1021526.

201. Sun, 1825, 503, 1029683, 1037577/8.

202. Sun, 1819, 478, 953383.

203. B3, 4099 and 2348.

204. Sun, 1775, 243, 359236.

205. Sun, 1772, 217, 314529.

206. Sun, 1771, 209, 303167.

207. Sun, 1821, 488, 978715.

208. Sun, 1769, 193, 275278; 1777, 257, 384387, 256, 384043, 388497.

209. RE, 1825, 90, 352348/9.

210. Sun, 1822, 490, 995172.

211. Sun, 1777, 260, 388968.

212. Heal, *London Furniture Makers*, 5.

213. GL.

214. Dodd, *Days at the Factories*, 68.

215. Gourvish and Wilson, *British Brewing Industry*, 93.

216. Pat Hudson and Lynette Hunter (eds), 'The Autobiography of William Hart, Cooper, 1776–1857; A Respectable Artisan in the Industrial Revolution', *London Journal*, 7, 2 (1981), 157.

217. Sun, 1769, 187, 266020; 1774, 230B, 341182; 1775, 239, 354849.

218. B3, 1384.

219. Sun, 1824, 497, 1012428.

220. HH, 1819, 147, 93247.

221. GL.

222. Sun, 1821, 484, 978325–7.

223. Sun, 1819, 479, 964011.

224. William Kiddier, *The Brushmaker* (1923), 134.

225. HC.

226. G. A. Thrupp, *The History of Coaches* (1877), 95–6.

227. Campbell, *The London Tradesman*, 229–33.

228. Dodd, *Days at the Factories*, 12.

229. James W. Burgess, *A Practical Treatise on Coach-Building* (1881), 148.

230. Many detailed examples survive of prices quoted or charged for coaches of all descriptions. The best source is William Felton, *A Treatise on Carriages* (1794–6); but see also John Bennett, *The Artificer's Complete Lexicon for Terms and Prices* (1833), 34 and 107.

231. John Copeland, *Roads and Their Traffic* (1968), 134–5.

232. B3, 3055. The firm had been in existence since at least 1755 (Sun, 109, 145367) and at Wells Street since 1786 (Sun, 334, 514180).

233. William Bridges Adams, *English Pleasure Carriages* (1837), 174.

234. Sun, 1772, 218, 317530/1.

235. Sun, 1823, 492, 1001211.

236. Sun, 1825, 504, 1026509/10.

237. HH, 1819, 147, 93636.

238. Sun, 1821, 488, 980145.

239. Quoted in Paul Gillingham, 'The Macartney Embassy to China, 1792–94', *History Today*, 43 (November 1993), 28.

240. Susan Fairlie, 'Dyestuffs in the Eighteenth Century', *Economic History Review*, XVII, 3 (1965), 488–97.

241. GL.

242. Sun, 1774, 235, 346532.

243. Sun, 1769, 192, 273900.

244. Sun, 1774, 231, 340411.

245. Sun, 1820, 483, 967000.

246. Sun, 1824, 502, 1021495/6.

247. Sun, 1821, 485, 980058.
248. Campbell, *The London Tradesman*, 106–7.
249. Sun, 1824, 497, 1012442.
250. B3, 692.
251. Sun, 1819, 478, 953316.
252. *Book of English Trades*, 96–8.
253. Geoffrey Tweedale, *At the Sign of the Plough, 275 Years of Allen and Hanbury's and the British Pharmaceutical Industry 1715–1990* (1990), 14–86.
254. Sun, 1821, 486, 985056 .
255. Sun, 1821, 487, 980986.
256. E. Wynne Thomas, *The House of Yardley 1770–1953* (1953) 41.
257. A. E. Musson, *Enterprise in Soap and Chemicals, Joseph Crosfield and Sons Ltd, 1815–1965* (1965), 22.
258. Ibid., 22.
259. Ibid., 24–6.
260. Sun, 1771, 209, 303091, 1819, 478, 960469.
261. Sun, 1820, 484, 972422, 972446.
262. Musson, *Enterprise in Soap and Chemicals*, 26.
263. Price's Patent Candle Co Ltd, *Still the Candle Burns* (1947), 16–17.
264. Sun, 1821, 485, 978513–5.
265. Sun, 1825, 501, 1033297, 1033495, 1033497.
266. Sun, 1825, 509, 1039165.
267. Where not based on the fire office registers and trade directories, these sections derive from David S. Landes, *Revolution in Time* (1983), 138 and 223–31; George, *London Life in the Eighteenth Century*, 175–8; and *Book of English Trades*, 418–22.
268. Sun, 1769, 194, 278627.
269. Sun, 1820, 480, 964458, 485, 972583; 1821, 486, 980858.
270. Sun, 1825, 500, 1037637.
271. Sun, 1820, 487, 972873.
272. S. Pollard, 'The Decline of Shipbuilding on the Thames', *Economic History Review*, III, 1 (1950), 72.
273. GL.
274. ML.
275. Sun, 1775, 240, 356241.
276. Sun, 1775, 243, 359865/6.
277. Lond, 1821, 3, 69853.
278. Sun, 1821, 485, 981752/3.
279. Sun, 1824, 494, 1016240, 495, 1016407, 1014881.
280. Sun, 1825, 502, 1037912, 503, 1029196, 1031956.
281. Anita McConnell, 'From Craft Workshop to Big Business: The London Scientific Instrument Trade's Response to Increasing Demand 1750–1820', *London Journal*, 19, 1 (1994) 36.
282. Charles Dickens, *Dombey and Son* (1963 edn), 64.
283. Edwin Banfield, *Barometer Makers and Retailers 1660–1900*, (1991) 155.
284. Sun, 1769, 190, 271065.

285. Sun, 1820, 485, 970423.

286. Sun, 1774, 231, 339593; 1821, 484, 985350.

287. David Wright, *An Index of London Surgical Instrument Makers 1822–65* (1989).

288. Pigot and Co, *Metropolitan New Alphabetical Directory*.

289. ML.

290. Sun, 1824, 1016787/8; 1825, 503, 1031286.

291. Campbell, *The London Tradesman*, 241–2.

292. GL.

293. Sun, 1771, 210, 304895; 1773, 223, 326807.

294. Sun, 1825, 504, 1031037, 509, 1039643.

295. Sun, 1825, 501, 1031112.

296. Sun, 1820, 483, 962817/8, B3, 3516.

297. Sun, 1825, 501, 1029417.

298. GL.

299. GL.

300. GL.

301. Sun, 1775, 243, 360182; 1777, 260, 391446.

302. GL and Sun, 1775, 243, 360182; 1777, 260, 391446.

303. Francis Sheppard, *London 1808–1870: The Infernal Wen* (1971), 175–6.

304. Sun, 1825, 504, 1031343/4.

305. GL.

306. Sun, 1820, 480, 962764.

307. Francis Buckley, *Old London Glasshouses* (1915), 6–34.

308. Sun, 1821, 487, 976682, 981470, 489, 985918/9.

309. Sun, 1772, 214, 311617; 1774, 231, 338830.

310. Sun, 1777, 256, 382041, 259, 386842.

311. Elizabeth Adams, 'The Bow Insurances and Related Matters', *English Ceramic Circle Transactions*, 9, 1 (1973), 73–9.

312. Sun, 1825, 504, 1035498.

313. Alison Kelly, *Mrs Coade's Stone* (1990), passim.

314. Sun, 1769, 192, 274233; 1771, 206, 299458.

315. Sun, 1769, 187, 266243.

316. Sun, 1819, 481, 954325.

317. Sun, 1819, 479, 951873.

318. Sun, 1819, 479, 960524; 1821, 492, 987382.

319. Sun, 1771, 204, 296686.

320. Brian W. Harvey, *The Violin Family and its Makers in the British Isles* (1995), 113–29.

321. Ibid., 313–401.

322. Laurence Elvin, *Bishop and Son, Organ Builders* (1984), 45.

323. Ibid., 46–52.

324. *Book of English Trades*, 267; and see *The Times*, 11 September 1820.

325. Sun, 1769, 191, 273496.

326. Sun, 1819, 480, 954883.

327. Sun, 1825, 504, 1028246.

328. B3, 5294.

329. Sun, 1824, 503, 1023186.
330. GL.
331. Hamilton, *Brass and Copper Industries*, 242–3.
332. Sun, 1771, 206, 297714.
333. Sun, 1777, 258, 388501.
334. Sun, 1824, 497, 1017821; 1825, 501, 1037927, 503, 1029140, 1029146.
335. Sun, 1822, 492, 989511; 1825, 503, 1029137.
336. ML.
337. Dodd, *Days at the Factories*, 10.
338. GL.
339. Sun, 1824, 492, 987932.
340. Sun, 1824, 497, 1016197, 1016791, 501, 1026082.
341. Sun, 1775, 240, 355523.
342. Sun, 1777, 257, 383901.
343. Sun, 1775, 240, 356271.
344. Sun, 1773, 223, 326555.
345. Sun, 1823, 494, 1006064, 1006067.
346. Sun, 1824, 502, 1021973.
347. Sun, 1823, 494, 1006052/3.
348. Hoggart and Green (eds), *London*, 15.
349. Parliamentary Papers, XXVII, 1844; 1841 Census, *Reports from Commissioners, vol 13, Population: Occupation Abstract*, 9.
350. B3, 5016, 5048, 3637, 4713.
351. Elvin, *Bishop and Son*, 51.
352. Dodd, *Days at the Factories*, 138.
353. Pollard, 'Decline of Shipbuilding', 88.
354. Rosoman, *London Wallpapers*, 14.
355. N. McKendrick, J. Brewer and J. H. Plumb, *The Birth of a Consumer Society* (1982), 28.
356. A. L. Humphreys, 'Long Acre and the Coach Builders', *Notes and Queries*, 181 (1941), 228.
357. Sheppard, *London 1808–1870*, 176.
358. Guildhall Library, Ms 6796.
359. Hudson and Hunter, 'Autobiography of William Hart', 147.

5. The Construction Trades in London

1. John Summerson, *Georgian London* (1978 edn), 38.
2. Ibid.
3. Sun, 1771, 203, 293326/7; 1772, 212, 306866.
4. Sun, 1774, 230A, 338248.
5. Thomas Mortimer, *The Universal Director* (1763), 15–17.
6. Sun, 1771, 206, 287329, 298234, 210, 305226.
7. Summerson, *Georgian London*, 98.
8. Sheppard, *London 1808–1870*, 96.
9. C. G. Powell, *An Economic History of the British Building Industry 1815–1979*, (1982), 9.

10. Ibid., 12.

11. Sun, 1775, 236, 350701/2, 237, 349290-2; 1777, 254, 379794/5.

12. Sun, 1825, 500, 1035348-53, 509, 1037457-66.

13. Sun, 1823, 497, 1008680.

14. Powell, *British Building Industry*, 30-1.

15. Ibid., 31.

16. Sun, 1775, 239, 353406/7, 353587-94, 242, 361994-362000.

17. Sun, 1774, 230B, 346086-91; 1777, 254, 379520, 379599, 257, 384267, 261, 391838.

18. Sun, 1819, 482, 953218; 953857; 1820, 483, 968234, 970563.

19. Sun, 1770, 202, 290933; 1772, 214, 313204; 1774, 229, 336711; 1819, 478, 956096, 480, 960608; 1821, 485, 981776; 1824, 502, 1019882.

20. This is the subject of Linda Clarke, *Building Capitalism, Historical Change and the Labour Force in the Production of the Built Environment* (1992).

21. Sun, 1819, 482, 956830/1, 958727-9; 1820, 483, 964346, 970554, 972357-9; 1821, 488, 978457/8, 981815-8, 985113-8; 1822, 493, 999011-4; 1823, 498, 1008145-8; 1824, 499, 1014612/3, 1016933, 1019615-8; 1825, 504, 1028732.

22. Sun, 1821, 488, 981535-8; 1822, 493, 995094/5, 999045-9; 1823, 498, 1001622-4, 499, 1010701-8; 1824, 499, 1023932-7, 501, 1019740/1; 1825, 504, 1035255, 509, 1035814.

23. Natwest Group Archives, Smiths/10/Lombard Street, 4662.

24. H. J. Dyos, 'The Speculative Builders and Developers of Victorian London', *Victorian Studies*, XI (1968), 645-8.

25. Sheppard, *London 1808-1870*, 96-7.

26. Both GL.

27. Sun, 1775, 236, 348497, 350695.

28. Sun, 1819, 482, 956266; 1823, 498, 1005939.

29. Lond, 1823, 3, 100802-4.

30. Sun, 1819, 482, 954120.

31. B3, 123, 1158, 1803 and 3018.

32. Powell, *British Building Industry*, 31-2.

6. London and the Consumer Revolution

1. McKendrick et al., *The Birth of a Consumer Society*, 9.

2. Ibid., 31.

3. Hoh-Cheung and Linda H. Mui, *Shops and Shopkeeping in Eighteenth-Century England* (1989), 3 and 200.

4. David Alexander, *Retailing in England During the Industrial Revolution* (1970), 5-6 and 24.

5. Adburgham, *Shopping in Style*, 98.

6. Porter, *London*, 143-5.

7. Dorothy Davis, *A History of Shopping* (1966), 182.

8. Quoted in Hugh and Pauline Massingham, *The London Anthology* (n.d.), 439-40.

9. Christopher Hibbert, *London, the Biography of a City* (1969), 148.

10. Davis, *Shopping*, 189.

11. Walter M. Stern, 'Where, Oh Where, are the Cheesemongers of London?', *London Journal*, 5, 2 (1979), 236–44.

12. Sun, 1772, 214, 312757.

13. J. A. Rees, *The Grocery Trade, Its History and Romance*, vol 2 (1932), 99.

14. Sun, 1820, 478, 966168, 479, 952616; and see Joseph Travers and Sons, *A Few Records of an Old Firm* (1970), 9–10; and David W. Thoms, 'Joseph Travers and Sons and the London Wholesale Grocery Market, 1824–1861', *Guildhall Miscellany*, III, 2 (1970), 141 .

15. Sun, 1823, 495, 1005586.

16. Sun, 1823, 492, 1003163, 494, 1006025, 1008828, 495, 1008393.

17. Sun, 1824, 494, 1017496, 495, 1017565, 1019124.

18. Sun, 1820, 478, 966148, 484, 968174, 487, 968642; 1821, 492, 987385/6.

19. B3, 1454.

20. Charles Godwin, *Hanson's of Eastcheap* (1947), 3.

21. Cook's, *Cook's of St Pauls, 150 Years 1807–1957* (1957), 4–5.

22. RE, 1823, 83, 340870; Sun, 1823, 496, 1005603.

23. Leslie Hayman, *An Account of W Williams and Son (Bread Street) Ltd 1819–1975* (1976), 5–9.

24. Stanley Chapman, *Merchant Enterprise in Britain* (1992), 167.

25. Ibid., 168. See also David Kynaston, *The City of London. I, A World of Its Own* (1994), 57–8.

26. B3, 1033.

27. Sun, 1771, 208, 302590, 1823, 489, 999806.

28. Sun, 1777, 261, 388870.

29. Lond, 1822, 3, 100554.

30. Sun, 1822, 491, 9894634, 492, 995385/6.

31. Kynaston, *City of London*, 58; and see Richard Gatty, *Portrait of a Merchant Prince, James Morrison 1789–1857* (1977), 17–19.

32. Sun, 1825, 501, 1033285 and 7.

33. Anon., *A Short History of Bradbury Greatorex and Co Ltd* (1967), 1; and Sun, 1824, 495, 1014363, 497, 1016800.

34. Sun, 1824, 495, 1017063; HH, 1825, 148, 95654.

35. B3, 1379.

36. C. G. Dobson, *A Century and a Quarter, the history of Hall and Co, Croydon* (1951), 34–5.

37. Sun, 1774, 231, 340348, 235, 347251.

38. Sun, 1819, 478, 953946, 956074, 479, 951304, 956714, 480, 958511, 481, 951014.

39. Sun, 1820, 481, 962986, 966550, 485, 968376, 970451, 972053, 486, 974215.

40. Sun, 1819, 478, 960985/6, 479, 958912, 480, 960164–6, 960607, 960680.

41. Sun, 1822, 491, 995887.

42. B3, 2726.

43. Sun, 1771, 209, 301243.

44. Sun, 1777, 254, 380337.

45. Sun, 1823, 496, 1010623; 1824, 497, 1017855.

46. Sun, 1820, 479, 966857, 485, 972524.

47. Sun, 1823, 498, 999619.

48. Sun, 1819, 478, 960937.

49. M. W. Flinn, *The History of the British Coal Industry, II, 1700–1830: The Industrial Revolution* (1984), 274–8.

50. Sun, 1820, 483, 962577.

51. Raymond Smith, *Sea-Coal for London* (1961), 147–53.

52. GL.

53. HH, 1820, 147, 100785.

54. B3, 1033 and 2490.

55. Sun, 1775, 236, 348499.

56. Sun, 1823, 497, 1005825/6.

57. Charles Dickens, *Dombey and Son* (1963 edn), 65.

58. Sun, 1769, 193, 274038.

59. ML.

60. Sun, 1822, 491, 995228.

61. Sun, 1820, 481, 968042, 485, 968393.

62. Sun, 1819, 481, 954334.

63. Sun, 1821, 485, 980052, 487, 980302.

64. Mui, *Shops and Shopkeeping*, 36 and 106.

65. Richard Perren, *The Meat Trade in Britain 1840–1914* (1978), 3.

66. Sun, 1775, 240, 356655, 243, 359300.

67. Sun, 1823, 494, 1010495, 495, 1008347.

68. Sun, 1820, 484, 970800.

69. Sun, 1771, 209, 303543.

70. Sun, 1822, 490, 993472, 995143; 1825, 500, 1026624, 501, 1028484, 503, 1028511.

71. *Book of English Trades*, 164.

72. Sun, 1821, 488, 974807/8.

73. Sun, 1825, 503, 1029698–700.

74. J. Collyer, *The Parents and Guardians Directory* (1761).

75. HC.

76. Godwin, *Hanson's*, 1; and Sun, 1770, 195, 280013.

77. GL.

78. Sun, 1821, 485, 983355.

79. Sun, 1824, 494, 1012575.

80. Sun, 1821, 484, 985353.

81. Campbell, *The London Tradesman*, 280.

82. Ibid., 281.

83. GL.

84. GL.

85. *Lawes and Co's List of Teas, Grocery, Foreign Fruits, Honey, and other Domestic Articles* (1825), Guildhall Library, PAM 2735.

86. *The Times*, 12 July 1820.

87. McKendrick et al., *Birth of a Consumer Society*, 29.

88. *An Inventory of the Fixtures and Fittings in a Grocers Shop* (1826), Guildhall Library, PAM 1289.

89. *The Times*, 25 August 1825.
90. Sun, 1770, 195, 279211.
91. Sun, 172, 212, 307801, 214, 310310.
92. Sun, 1824, 495, 1017576 and 8.
93. Sun, 1824, 499, 1013330.
94. Fortnam and Mason, *The Delectable History of Fortnam and Mason* (n.d.).
95. Ambrose Keevil, *The Story of Fitch Lovell 1784–1970* (1972), 2–13.
96. P. J. Atkins, 'The Retail Milk Trade in London c1790–1814', *Economic History Review*, XXXIII, 4 (1980), 522–9.
97. GL.
98. GL.
99. Sun, 1775, 237, 350572.
100. Sun, 1825, 502, 1033407.
101. Sun, 1825, 502, 1039472.
102. A. D. Francis, *The Wine Trade* (1972), 296.
103. GL.
104. GL.
105. Joseph Hartley, *The Wine and Spirit Merchant's Companion* (3rd edn, 1850).
106. Charles James Wild, *John Wild, 1729–1801* (1914).
107. Sun, 1774, 235, 348043.
108. Sun, 1772, 217, 317361.
109. Sun, 1772, 216, 316522, 218, 319981.
110. Sun, 1819, 480, 954879/80.
111. RE, 1825, 87, 350805.
112. Sun, 1820, 484, 968194.
113. B3, 1402.
114. B3, 1768.
115. B3, 976.
116. B3, 1423.
117. B3, 1032.
118. Robert C. Nash, 'The English and Scottish Tobacco Trades in the Seventeenth and Eighteenth Centuries: Legal and Illegal Trade', *Economic History Review*, XXXV, 3 (1982), 356.
119. Sun, 1777, 256, 382245.
120. Sun, 1825, 495, 1019151.
121. RE, 1822, 83, 334487.
122. McKendrick, et al., *Birth of a Consumer Society*, 21.
123. Alison Adburgham, *Shops and Shopping 1800–1914* (1964), 14.
124. Richard Walker, *The Savile Row Story* (1988), 21.
125. Dodd, *Days at the Factories*, 5.
126. GL.
127. *The Times*, 14 December 1820.
128. GL.
129. Sun, 1769, 187, 266270.
130. Sun, 1769, 190, 272853.
131. Sun, 1820, 479, 956152.

132. Sun, 1823, 497, 1008697.

133. Sun, 1821, 486, 978768.

134. Sun, 1777, 258, 388138.

135. Sun, 1771, 202, 293745.

136. ML.

137. *Book of English Trades*, 226–30.

138. GL.

139. Sun, 1777, 263, 392640.

140. Sun, 1770, 202, 291397.

141. Sun, 1772, 216, 315316.

142. Sun, 1820, 483, 972970.

143. RE, 1823, 82, 336187/8, 84, 339388; Sun, 494, 1008207.

144. Sun, 1823, 497, 1005892.

145. Sun, 1825, 509, 1037438.

146. Sun, 1822, 490, 997268.

147. Sun, 1819, 482, 954795.

148. RE, 1819, 76, 313875.

149. GL.

150. Maurice Corina, *Fine Silks and Oak Counters: Debenham's 1778–1978* (1978), 21–9 .

151. Sun 1770, 195, 280201.

152. Sun, 1771, 208, 301785.

153. RE, 1819, 76, 311993; Sun, 480, 954812.

154. Sun, 1820, 486, 968946.

155. Hobhouse, *Regent Street*, 48.

156. GL.

157. *Catalogue of a Hatter's Stock, to be sold by auction on 19th September 1834 at 36 Lombard Street*, Guildhall Library, PAM 6739.

158. *The Times*, 11 September 1820.

159. Sun, 1769, 188, 266979, 267359, 190, 273233.

160. Sun, 1773, 223, 326144.

161. Sun, 1823, 498, 999670.

162. Lond, 1821, 3, 70046.

163. Sun, 1825, 504, 1029711.

164. Beverley Lemire, 'Developing Consumerism and the Ready-Made Clothing Trade in Britain, 1750–1800', *Textile History*, 15, 1, 1984, 21–44.

165. Beverley Lemire, 'Peddling Fashion: Salesmen, Pawnbrokers, Taylors, Thieves and the Second-hand Clothes Trade in England, 1700–1800', *Textile History*, 22, 1 (1991), 67.

166. Campbell, *The London Tradesman*, 338.

167. Beverley Lemire, *Fashion's Favourite: The Cotton Trade and the Consumer in Britain, 1660–1800* (1991), 178.

168. GL.

169. *Public Advertiser*, 14 January 1771 .

170. ML.

171. *The Times*, 18 November 1820.

172. Sun, 1819, 481, 956495; 1824, 499, 1017137, 494, 1014776, 495, 1014332.
173. GL.
174. Thomas Mortimer, *General Commercial Dictionary* (2nd edn, 1819), 980.
175. Sun, 1770, 195, 280591.
176. Sun, 1821, 487, 983128.
177. Sun, 1824, 495, 1019144.
178. Sun, 1821, 485, 981763.
179. George, *London Life in the Eighteenth Century*, 196–7.
180. GL.
181. GL.
182. Quoted in George, *London Life in the Eighteenth Century*, 197.
183. Sun, 1770, 202, 292651.
184. Sun, 1769, 192, 274324.
185. Sun, 1823, 494, 1010465.
186. Sun, 1819, 482, 960068.
187. B3, 2430.
188. B3, 1433.
189. B3, 3471, 1749 and 1797.
190. B3, 5286.
191. GL.
192. GL.
193. Sun, 1770, 194, 279651.
194. Sun, 1819, 480, 948971.
195. *Mosers of the Borough* (1936), 10–14.
196. Ann Eatwell and Alex Werner, 'A London Staffordshire Warehouse, 1794–1825', *Journal of the Northern Ceramics Society*, 8 (1991), 91–2.
197. ML.
198. Sun, 1770, 194, 279742 & 4, 202, 290979.
199. Sun, 1769, 191, 272726; 1772, 216, 317104.
200. Sun, 1824, 494, 1016249, 10017943/4, 496, 1016515.
201. Sun, 1771, 210, 304306; 1824, 499, 1016614; and see Neil McKendrick, 'Josiah Wedgwood: an Eighteenth-century Entrepreneur', *Economic History Review*, XII (1960), 418–19.
202. Adams, 'The Bow Insurances', 80.
203. William Thackeray, *The Newcomes* (1995 edn), 824.
204. GL.
205. GL.
206. Sun, 1819, 481, 958121.
207. Sun, 1823, 498, 1003790.
208. Sun, 1819, 478, 953978.
209. Both GL.
210. Sun, 1775, 237, 349695, 242, 359531, 361855.
211. Sun, 1820, 481, 962959/60.
212. Sun, 1771, 208, 301434/5.
213. Campbell, *The London Tradesman*, 239.
214. ML.

215. Dodd, *Days at the Factories*, 14–15.
216. GL.
217. Sun, 1820, 480, 962756, 484, 968188.
218. Sun, 1819, 481, 951525.
219. Sun, 1820, 483, 966528, 485, 972503.
220. Sun, 1773, 223, 324561.
221. Sun, 1821, 488, 980764.
222. B3, 1409.
223. B3, 4012.
224. B3, 4324.
225. B3, 3028 .
226. Sun, 1777, 257, 382900.
227. Fritz Redlich, 'Some English Stationers of the Seventeenth and Eighteenth Centuries: In the Light of their Autobiographies', *Business History*, 8 (1966), 91–8.
228. Sun, 1769, 193, 275208.
229. Sun, 1825, 500, 1028178.
230. Sun, 1820, 483, 966621.
231. B3, 581.
232. B3, 121.
233. Sun, 1777, 255, 381073, 258, 387021; Lond, 1825, 4, 102580.
234. *The Times*, 1 July 1820.
235. Sun, 1820, 483, 966601.
236. Sun, 1825, 501, 1029500, 502, 1029501.
237. B3, 125.
238. Sir Ambrose Heal, *The London Goldsmiths 1200–1800* (1972 edn), 91–276.
239. Ibid., 157.
240. GL.
241. Sun, 1825, 502, 1028465.
242. Sun, 1772, 214, 313403.
243. Sun, 1774, 230B, 340089.
244. Sun, 1825, 499, 1026164.
245. Sun, 1822, 491, 987736.
246. Bevis Hillier, *Asprey of Bond Street 1781–1981* (1981), 19–20.
247. Sun, 1819, 482, 954141.
248. *Catalogue of Thomas Cox Savory, Goldsmiths and Jewellers, 47 Cornhill* (1831), Guildhall Library, PAM 1928.
249. Sun, 1771, 205, 295487; 1821, 487, 976686.
250. B3, 2439.
251. B3, 2382.
252. Kenneth Hudson, *Pawnbroking* (1982), 35–7.
253. GL.
254. Hudson, *Pawnbroking*, 44.
255. Campbell, *The London Tradesman*, 296–7.
256. Quoted in Peter Earle, *The Making of the English Middle Class* (1989), 50.
257. Sun, 1775, 240, 355582.
258. Sun, 1823, 491, 999800, 495, 101527, 497, 1008052.

259. B3, 4712.

260. Sun, 1825, 509, 1037435.

261. Campbell, *The London Tradesman*, 64–5.

262. Ibid., 62.

263. Roger French and Andrew Wear (eds), *British Medicine in the Age of Reform* (1991), 54.

264. Juanita Burnby, 'A Study of the English Apothecary from 1660 to 1760', *Medical History*, Supplement no. 3 (1983), 53–4.

265. Massingham, *London Anthology*, 440.

266. Tweedale, *At the Sign of the Plough*, 6.

267. Roy Porter, *Health for Sale, Quackery in England, 1660–1850* (1989), 4–44.

268. B3, 2281.

269. GL.

270. HC.

271. *The Times*, 25 August 1820.

272. B3, 123.

273. Sun, 1821, 491, 987224.

274. GL.

275. Sun, 1772, 214, 311976.

276. Sun, 1822, 492, 993224; HH, 147, 61516.

277. Sun, 1819, 482, 956846/7.

278. Sun, 1819, 482, 954131.

279. HH, 1819, 147, 93812.

280. Sun, 1825, 502, 1026838.

281. HC.

282. Sun, 1819, 482, 956541; 1820, 483, 968580.

283. B3, 5009.

284. B3, 965.

285. B3, 5052.

286. *Mosers*, 12.

287. B3, 2373.

288. B3, 4670.

289. B3, 4302.

290. B3, 5256.

291. B3, 4298.

7. London: Prototype Service Economy

1. J. A. Chartres and G. L. Turnbull, 'Road Transport', in D. H. Aldcroft and M. J. Freeman (eds), *Transport in the Industrial Revolution* (1983), 65–6.

2. W. T. Jackman, *The Development of Transportation in Modern England* (1916), I, 235.

3. T. C. Barker and C. I. Savage, *An Economic History of Transport in Great Britain* (1974), 45.

4. J. E. Bradfield, *The Public Carriages of Great Britain* (1855), 18.

5. Jackman, *Development of Transportation*, II, 687–98.

6. Paul Langford, *A Polite and Commercial People, England 1727–1783* (1992), 398–401.

7. Chartres and Turnbull, 'Road Transport', 69.

8. Stanley Harris, *The Coaching Age* (1885), 152.

9. Quoted in *Roads and Their Traffic*, Copeland, 101.

10. T. C. Barker and Michael Robbins, *A History of London Transport* (1963), 4 and 391–2.

11. John Copeland, 'An Essex Turnpike Gate', *Journal of Transport History*, VI, 1963–64, passim.

12. Bradfield, *Public Carriages*, 19.

13. Sun, 1819, 482, 956841–5; 1825, 503, 1033509.

14. See Bradfield, *Public Carriages*, 19; also Borer, *The City of London*, 246–8; Harris, *The Coaching Age*, 100–62; Edward Corbett, *An Old Coachman's Chatter* (1890), 287–93; Alex Bates, *Directory of Stage Coach Services*, 1836 (1969), passim; and Harold W. Hart, 'Sherman and the Bull and Mouth', *Journal of Transport History*, V, 1 (1961), 12–21.

15. Hart, 'Sherman', 15.

16. Borer, *The City of London*, 248.

17. Sun, 1769, 189, 267098; 1770, 202, 291006.

18. Sun, 1823, 498, 1006373.

19. Barker and Savage, *An Economic History of Transport*, 50–1; Copeland, *Roads and Their Traffic*, 86; Harris, *The Coaching Age*, 107–9; and Bates, *Directory*.

20. Sun, 1774, 228, 335792, 229, 336705.

21. Sun, 1825, 504, 1029773.

22. Sun, 1820, 478, 962457/8.

23. Chartres and Turnbull, 'Road Transport', 85.

24. Dorian Gerhold, 'The Growth of the London Carrying Trade, 1681–1838', *Economic History Review*, XLI, 3 (1988), 400.

25. Ibid., 408.

26. Copeland, 'An Essex Turnpike Gate', 89–90.

27. Copeland, *Roads and Their Traffic*, 100–1.

28. HC.

29. GL.

30. *Regulations for Carmen, with Rates of Carriage* (1799), Guildhall Library, PAM 4906, 23–42.

31. *To the Right Honourable the Lord Mayor ... Petition of Jeremiah Shoobert*, Guildhall Library, PAM 233.

32. Chartres and Turnbull, 'Road Transport', 83.

33. Dorian Gerhold, *Road Transport Before the Railways* (1992), 1–4.

34. Sun, 1775, 239, 353585.

35. Sun, 1822, 490, 993427, 497, 991586; 1823, 489, 999893, 490, 999989; 1825, 503, 1035132.

36. Sun, 1820, 479, 964231, 485, 970411.

37. Sun, 1772, 212, 306709, 308612.

38. Sun, 1820, 479, 966867, 484, 968785.

39. Sun, 1820, 479, 964287, 966332, 966855, 966887, 480, 964855 & 9, 481,

966583, 484, 968751, 968763 & 6, 968770, 968779–84, 970801, 970833, 972430, 974086/7, 485, 970464, 972597, 486, 968906, 968962, 970623, 972706, 974224, 487, 968638–40, 968658, 970183/4, 970715–7, 972204, 972210, 972290/1, 974463/4.

40. Sun, 1821, 484, 983290/1, 485, 978579, 486, 981986/7, 983496, 487, 980303–5, 980935/6, 98322–4, 490, 987023/4, 492, 987362.

41. Sun, 1820, 485, 972010/1, 479, 964422–4, 484, 968169/70, 968773–5, 972486, 486, 972119, 487, 970787, 974418/9.

42. Daunton, *Progress and Poverty*, 294–6.

43. Lond, 1825, 4, 102493.

44. Lond, 1822, 3, 70148, 100008, 100013, 100020, 100022–7, 100151, 100167, 100169–71, 100271/2, 100315, 100402, 100448.

45. Sun, 1825, 500, 1028629, 501, 1033203, 1037288, 503, 1033519.

46. Hermione Hobhouse, *Weber in London 1826* (1976), 14.

47. B3, 1732.

48. Anon., *Old English Coffee Houses* (1954), 29.

49. GL.

50. GL.

51. J. A. Chartres, 'The Capital's Provincial Eyes: London's Inns in the Early 18th Century', *London Journal*, III, 2 (1977), 24–30. See also Peter Clark, *The English Alehouse: A Social History, 1200–1830* (1983), 9.

52. George, *London Life in the Eighteenth Century*, 284.

53. Jean Desebrock, *The Book of Bond Street Old and New* (1978), 80.

54. Sun, 1825, 506, 1039749.

55. Sun, 1825, 504, 1026397, 509, 1039688.

56. GL.

57. Guildhall Library, Ms 458.

58. ML.

59. Lond, 1822, 3, 100234.

60. Sun, 1771, 209, 303505.

61. Gunter, *The House of Gunter 1786–1907* (1907), 3–15.

62. Sun, 1775, 239, 352197.

63. Sun, 1774, 231, 338449.

64. Sun, 1822, 491, 995205/6.

65. Harris, *The Coaching Age*, 156–7; and see Humphreys, 'Long Acre and the Coach Builders', 214 and 228–9.

66. Charles Dickens, *Nicholas Nickleby* (1988 edn), 86.

67. Sun, 1820, 485, 968316.

68. Sun, 1823, 494, 1003225.

69. Sun, 1819, 481, 954909/10.

70. Sun, 1819, 481, 960289.

71. Sun, 1769, 191, 273504.

72. Sun, 1777, 257, 382332.

73. Globe, 1825, 87121, 88049.

74. *The Times*, 13 July 1820.

75. Clark, *The English Alehouse*, 273.

76. Sun, 1772, 217, 314710; 1775, 242, 359157; 1777, 256, 382453.

77. Sun, 1821, 488, 985419; 1823, 498, 999451; 1824, 501, 1026055; RE, 1824, 86, 345991; Lond, 1825, 4, 102340.

78. Natwest Group Archives, Smiths/10/Lombard Street, 4640.

79. Clark, *The English Alehouse*, 264.

80. Borer, *The City of London*, 246–7; and Harris, *The Coaching Age*, 100–25.

81. B3, 3507 and 978.

82. GL.

83. Sun, 1822, 493, 989333.

84. Sun, 1769, 194, 278145.

85. Sun, 1777, 257, 383893.

86. GL.

87. GL.

88. *The Times*, 18 November 1820.

89. Sun, 1825, 501, 1029405, 503, 1031248.

90. GL.

91. Sun, 1777, 257, 383893.

92. Sun, 1775, 239, 354965; 1821, 485, 980658.

93. Sun, 1771, 294, 293939; 1819, 481, 956425.

94. Hermione Hobhouse, *Thomas Cubitt, Master Builder* (1971), 32.

95. Sun, 1825, 509, 1039222.

96. B3, 2870.

97. Ralph Turvey, 'Street Mud, Dust and Noise', *London Journal*, 21, 2 (1996), 131–5.

98. GL.

99. GL.

100. ML.

101. Sun, 1823, 498, 1010097; 1824, 499, 1023061.

102. Sun, 1772, 218, 319139.

103. John Brewer, *Pleasures of the Imagination* (1997), 177–8.

104. *The Times*, 14 July 1820.

105. Sun, 1823, 497, 1010879.

106. Desebrock, *Book of Bond Street*, 79.

107. HC.

108. Sun, 1775, 242, 361921.

109. Sun, 1775, 243, 361381.

110. Sun, 1824, 494, 1016256.

111. Sun, 1825, 500, 1029865.

112. Borer, *The City of London*, 247.

8. Commercial London

1. Christopher J. French, '"Crowded with traders and a great commerce": London's Domination of English Overseas Trade, 1700–1775', *London Journal*, 17, 1 (1992), 27–9.

2. Kynaston, *The City of London*, 9 and 23.

3. Quoted in Chapman, *Merchant Enterprise*, 129–30.

4. Ibid., 129.

5. Ibid., 156.

6. Sun, 1772, 216, 317171, 316277, 316300, 217, 316690, 316955.

7. Sun, 1770, 194, 280617, 202, 291709, 292220, 203, 219692, 291958.

8. Sun, 1772, 216, 314433, 317115, 218, 317816, 317931, 319884, 319979.

9. Sun, 1769, 186, 265639/40, 194, 279112.

10. Sun, 1771, 202, 293029/30.

11. Sun, 1769, 187, 265259, 191, 271338.

12. Sun, 1820, 481, 962367, 485, 970498, 487, 972226/7.

13. Sun, 1821, 484, 978997, 981670–5, 485, 983946, 985507/8, 486, 974979, 983472, 487, 980310, 980319.

14. Lond, 1825, 4, 102214, 102241/2, 102319, 102401, 102403, 102411, 102420, 102432, 102436, 102572, 102633, 102695, 102768, 102792–4, 102797, 102802, 102821, 102832, 102851.

15. Lond, 1822, 3, 100336.

16. Sun, 1822, 489, 989694.

17. Sun, 1820, 486, 972199.

18. Lond, 1821, 3, 69967.

19. Sun, 1823, 495, 1003384.

20. Sun, 1819, 480, 953628.

21. Sun, 1775, 239, 354191, 240, 355552, 242, 359138.

22. Sun, 1777, 255, 380602, 261, 390687–9, 391084–7, 262, 392201.

23. Sun, 1820, 479, 964288, 966339, 484, 974014, 485, 968859, 970497, 486, 972760.

24. Sun, 1821, 485, 976353.

25. Sun, 1770, 203, 291696.

26. Sun, 1823, 492, 1001835, 1001837, 494, 1005482, 495, 1003381, 1008385, 496, 1005133, 497, 1003667, 1003684, 1006538.

27. Sun, 1825, 501, 1028808.

28. Sun, 1775, 242, 361061.

29. Sun, 1777, 258, 386434.

30. Lond, 1823, 3, 100632.

31. Sun, 1771, 209, 300747.

32. Sun, 1769, 190, 270203, 195, 278905.

33. Sun, 1821, 487, 976132, 486, 985622/3.

34. Sun, 1820, 484, 968741.

9. The London Businesswoman

1. Earle, *English Middle Class*, 168.

2. Sun, 1821, 486, 978768.

3. Sun, 1769, 186, 265651.

4. Sun, 1774, 228, 335343, 231, 338302.

5. Sun, 1775, 238, 352242.

6. Sun, 1777, 259, 388443.

7. Sun, 1825, 509, 1035898.

8. Sun, 1825, 504, 1031359.
9. Sun, 1773, 228, 334541.
10. Sun, 1771, 208, 301353.
11. Sun, 1771, 203, 293185.
12. Sun, 1775, 240, 355564.
13. Sun, 1821, 488, 978424.
14. Sun, 1771, 209, 303031.
15. HH, 1821, 147, 90958; Lond, 1825, 4, 102561.
16. Sun, 1821, 484, 982771.
17. Sun, 1822, 493, 987498.
18. Sun, 1825, 504, 1031391.
19. Sun, 1772, 218, 317899.
20. Sun, 1769, 190, 270710.
21. Sun, 1770, 202, 291031.
22. Sun, 1769, 189. 267993.
23. Sun, 1822, 491, 995205/6.
24. Sun, 1819, 481, 954909/10.
25. Sun, 1819, 480, 956952.
26. Sun, 1825, 501, 1029405, 503, 1031248.
27. Sun, 1777, 255, 381754.
28. Sun, 1771, 207, 300132.
29. Sun, 1825, 504, 1035461.
30. Sun, 1823, 494, 1003282.
31. Sun, 1769, 190, 272113.
32. Sun, 1771, 209, 301991.
33. Sun, 1821, 486, 976551.
34. Sun, 1822, 490, 987636.
35. Sun, 1824, 497, 1016117/8.
36. Sun, 1820, 480, 966493.
37. Sun, 1769, 192, 274233; 1771, 206, 299458.
38. Sun, 1769, 191, 271637.
39. Sun, 1769, 193, 275652.
40. Sun, 1819, 478, 953947, 953978.
41. Sun, 1825, 506, 1039731–3.
42. Sun, 1825, 502, 1033412.
43. Sun, 1772, 214, 310760.
44. Maxted, *London Book Trades*, 199.
45. Sun, 1771, 207, 298701.
46. Sun, 1770, 195, 280517.
47. Heal, *London Furniture Makers*, 123.
48. Sun, 1819, 480, 960125.
49. Sun, 1822, 490, 997865.
50. Sun, 1824, 503, 1021519; 1825, 501, 1028836.
51. Sun, 1772, 214, 312480.
52. Sun, 1769, 192, 275542.
53. Sun, 1772, 212, 309908, 217, 315506.

54. Sun, 1819, 479, 954685.
55. Sun, 1772, 212, 309380, 217, 315820.
56. Sun, 1769, 189, 269114.
57. Sun, 1771, 208, 302563.
58. Globe, 1825, 85577.
59. Sun, 1820, 483, 966621.
60. Sun, 1821, 486, 980804.
61. ML.
62. GL.
63. GL.
64. Maxted, *London Book Trades*, 183.
65. Heal, *London Furniture Makers*, 142.
66. Ibid., 177.
67. Ibid., 184.
68. GL.
69. GL.
70. Banfield, *Barometer Makers*, 214.
71. Sun, 1824, 497, 1016117/8.
72. Heal, *London Furniture Makers*, 13.
73. Sun, 1819, 479, 953426.
74. Sun, 1824, 495, 1012733.
75. Sun, 1823, 490, 999967, 496, 1005659.
76. Sun, 1771, 209, 302375.
77. Sun, 1775, 239, 354433.
78. Sun, 1777, 258, 387844.
79. Sun, 1777, 258, 388119.
80. Sun, 1777, 256, 382780.
81. Sun, 1825, 500, 1037680, 501, 1037296.
82. Sun, 1777, 254, 380707, 256, 384843.
83. Sun, 1772, 217, 315067–75.
84. Sun, 1769, 191, 271339.
85. Sun, 1775, 243, 359851.
86. Sun, 1821, 485, 980072/3, 484, 981024, 489, 985910.
87. Sun, 1820, 485, 968384, 486, 974221.
88. Sun, 1821, 488, 976711.

10. Conclusion

1. McKendrick et al., *Birth of a Consumer Society*, 21.

Bibliography

Note: Unless otherwise stated, place of publication is London.

Primary sources

1. *Manuscript*

The Guildhall Library in London holds the surviving series of fire policy registers for the following London fire offices for the period covered by this book:

Globe, Ms 11679; Hand in Hand, Ms 8674; London Assurance, Ms 8747; Royal Exchange, Ms 7523; Sun, Ms 11936

In addition, Sun Fire Office Management Committee Minute Books, Ms 11932; General Committee Minute Books, Ms 11931; Accounts Committee Minute Books, Ms 11933

The Guildhall Library also holds the archives of 71 companies trading between 1760 and 1830. Details are set out alphabetically, showing the dates to which the papers refer, in Joan Bullock-Anderson, *A Handlist of Business Archives at Guildhall Library* (Corporation of London, 2nd edn, 1991).

Bankruptcy Commission Files, Public Record Office, Series B3

2. *Collections*

Guildhall Library Collection of Trade Cards and Shopbills; Heal Shopbill Collection, British Library; Museum of London, Printed Ephemera Collection, Trade Cards, Bills, Invoices and Receipts; Victoria and Albert Museum, Trade Catalogue Collection

3. *Publications*

3.1 London Trade Directories

Andrews New London Directory (1780)
Harris, W., *London Register of Merchants and Traders* (1775)
Johnstone's London Commercial Guide and Street Directory, 1817 (1817)

Kent's Directory for the Year 1774 (1774)

Kent's Original London Directory, 1818 (1818)

Mortimer, T., *The Universal Director* (1763)

Osborn, J., *Compleat Guide to all Persons Who Have Any Trade or Concern with the City of London* (1774)

Pigot and Co, *Directory of London and its Suburbs* (1839)

Pigot and Co, *London and Provincial New Commercial Directory for 1822–23* (1823)

Pigot and Co, *London and Provincial New Commercial Directory for 1826–27* (1827)

Pigot and Co, *Metropolitan New Alphabetical Directory for 1827* (1827)

Post Office London Directory, 1841 (1841)

3.2 Census

1821 Census, *Abstract of Answers and Returns, Parish Register Abstract, Appendix B*

1841 Census, *Reports from Commissioners, vol 13, Population: Occupation Abstract*

1851 Census, *England and Wales: Part I, vol LXXXV, Population Tables, 1801–1851*

3.3 Printed sources

Adams, W. B., *English Pleasure Carriages* (1837)

Bennett, John, *The Artificer's Complete Lexicon for Terms and Prices* (1833)

The Book of English Trades and Library of the Useful Arts (1824)

Bradfield, J. E., *The Public Carriages of Great Britain* (1855)

Burgess, J. W., *A Practical Treatise on Coach-Building* (1881)

Burn, J. D., *Commercial Enterprise and Social Progress* (1858)

The Cabinet of Useful Arts and Manufactures (Dublin, 1825)

Campbell, R., *The London Tradesman* (1747)

Catalogue of a Hatter's Stock, to be sold by auction on 19 February 1834 at 36 Lombard Street, Guildhall Library, PAM 6739

A Catalogue of the Elegant and Fashionable Stock in Trade ... of Mr Henry Fremont, Embroiderer ... A Bankrupt ... which will be sold by Auction ... on March 14, 1783, on the Premises, No. 1, the corner of Hay-Hill, Berkeley Square, Guildhall Library, PAM 1189

Collyer, J., *The Parents and Guardians Directory* (1761)

Dodd, George, *Days at the Factories, Series I – London* (1843)

Edgeworth, R. L., *An Essay on the Construction of Roads and Carriages* (1817)

Elmes, James, *Metropolitan Improvements; or, London in the Nineteenth Century* (1827)

Farey, John, *A Treatise on the Steam Engine* (1827)

Felkin, William, *History of the Machine-Wrought Hosiery and Lace Manufactures* (1867; centenary edn, Newton Abbot, 1967)

Felton, William, *A Treatise on Carriages* (1794–96; facsimile, New Jersey, 1995)

A General Description of all Trades (1747)

Hartley, Joseph, *The Wine and Spirit Merchant's Companion* (3rd edn, 1850)

Hull, William, *The History of the Glove Trade* (1834)

Jervis, John, *The Horse and Carriage Oracle*, revised by William Kitchener (1828)

Kearsley, G., *Kearsley's Table of Trades* (1786)

Lillie, Charles, *Lillie's British Perfumer* (1822)

Little Jack of All Trades; or, Mechanical Arts Described (1823)

Lockie, John, *Topography of London* (1813; reproduced 1994)

The London Tradesman; A Familiar Treatise on the rationale of Trade and Commerce ... by Several Tradesmen (1819)

Marshall, J., *Account of the Population, 1801, 1811 and 1821* (1831)

Martin, Thomas, *The Circle of the Mechanical Arts* (1813)

Mayhew, Henry, *The Morning Chronicle Survey of Labour and the Poor: The Metropolitan Districts* (1849–50; ed. Firle, 1980)

Middleton, J., *General View of the Agriculture of Middlesex* (2nd edn, 1807)

Mortimer, T., *General Commercial Dictionary* (2nd edn, 1819)

Pierce, Egan, *Real Life in London* (1821; 1905)

Postlethwayt, M., *Universal Dictionary of Trade and Commerce* (1774)

Quaife, James, *The Hackney Coach Directory* (2nd edn, 1824)

Regulations for Carmen (1799)

Thrupp, G. A., *The History of Coaches* (1877)

Whittock, N., et al., *The Complete Book of English Trades* (1837)

Vaux, Thomas, *Relative Taxation; or Observations on the Impolicy of Taxing Malt, Hops, Beer, Soap, Candles, and Leather* (1823)

Secondary sources

1. *General*

Ashton, T. S., *The Industrial Revolution 1760–1830* (Oxford, 1948)

— *An Economic History of England: The Eighteenth Century* (1955)

— *Economic Fluctuations in England, 1700–1800* (Oxford, 1959)

Atkins, P. J., *The Directories of London 1677–1977* (1990)

Barker, T. C., 'Business as Usual? London and the Industrial Revolution', *History Today*, 39, November 1989

Barnett, D. C., 'The Structure of Industry in London', PhD thesis, University of Nottingham (1996)

Braudel, Fernand, *Civilisation and Capitalism, 15th Century–18th Century. II, The Wheels of Commerce* (1979)

Berg, M., *The Age of Manufactures: Industry, Innovation and Work in Britain, 1700–1820* (Oxford, 1985)

Brewer, John, *Pleasures of the Imagination* (1997)

Briggs, Asa, *Victorian Things* (1988)

Central Statistical Office (CSO), *Indexes to the Standard Industrial Classification, Revised 1980* (HMSO, 2nd impression, 1982)

— *Standard Industrial Classification, Revised 1980* (HMSO, 3rd impression, 1983)

Chambers, J. D., *The Workshop of the World* (1961)

Crafts, N. F. R., *British Economic Growth during the Industrial Revolution* (Oxford, 1985)

Crossick, Geoffrey, *An Artisan Elite in Victorian Society: Kentish London 1840–80* (1978)

Daunton, M. J., *Progress and Poverty* (Oxford, 1995)

— 'Industry in London: Revisions and Reflections', *London Journal*, 21, 1, 1996

Department of Employment and Productivity, *British Labour Statistics, Historical Abstract 1886–1968* (HMSO, 1971)

Drake, Barbara, *Women in Trade Unions* (1984 edn)

Earle, Peter, *The Making of the English Middle Class* (1989)

— *A City Full of People* (1994)

Evans, Eric J., *The Forging of the Modern State, Early Industrial Britain 1783–1870* (1983)

Fisher, F. J., 'London as a Centre of Conspicuous Consumption', in Corfield, P. J. and Harte, N. B. (eds), *London and the English Economy, 1500–1700* (1990)

Floud, Roderick and Donald McCloskey (eds), *The Economic History of Britain since 1700, vol I, 1700–1860* (Cambridge, 1981)

George, M. D., *England in Transition,* (1953 edn)

— *London Life in the Eighteenth Century* (1987 edn)

Godley, Andrew, 'Immigrant Entrepreneurs and the Emergence of London's East End as an Industrial District', *London Journal*, 21, 1, 1996

Goodall, Francis, *A Bibliography of British Business Histories* (1987)

Green, David, *From Artisans to Paupers, 1790–1870*, DPhil thesis, University of Cambridge (1995)

— 'The Nineteenth-Century Metropolitan Economy: A Revisionist Interpretation', *London Journal*, 21, 1, 1996

Hammond, J. L. and Barbara, *The Skilled Labourer 1760–1832* (1995 edn)

— *The Town Labourer 1760–1832* (1995 edn)

Heal, Sir Ambrose, *London Tradesmen's Cards of the XVIII Century* (1925)

Heal, Sir Ambrose, *London Furniture Makers 1660–1840* (1988 edn)

Henderson, W. R., *J. C. Fischer and his Diary of Industrial England, 1814–1851* (1966)

Hills, Richard L., *Power from Steam* (Cambridge, 1989)

Hobsbawm, E. J., *Industry and Empire* (1990 edn)

— 'The Nineteenth Century London Labour Market', in *London: Aspects of Change*, Centre for Urban Studies (1964)

Hudson, Pat (ed.), *Regions and Industries* (Cambridge, 1989)

Johnson, Paul, 'Economic Development and Industrial Dynamism in Victorian London', *London Journal*, 21, 1, 1996

Jones, G. Stedman, *Outcast London* (Oxford, 1971)

Kanefsky, John and John Robey, 'Steam Engines in 18th-Century Britain: A Quantitative Assessment', *Technology and Culture*, 21, 2, 1980

Kynaston, David, *The City of London. I, A World of its Own 1815–1890* (1994)

Langford, Paul, *A Polite and Commercial People, England 1727–1783* (Oxford, 1992)

Lee, C H., 'Regional Growth and Structural Change in Victorian Britain', *Economic History Review*, 2nd Series, XXXIII, 1981

— *The British Economy since 1700* (Cambridge, 1986)

Lines, Clifford (ed.), *Companion to the Industrial Revolution* (1990)

Lord, John, *Capital and Steam Power 1750–1800* (2nd edn, 1966)

Lumas, Susan, *Making Use of the Census* (PRO, 1993)

Mitchell B. R. and P. Deane, *British Historical Statistics* (Cambridge, 1962)

Plumb, J. H., *England in the Eighteenth Century* (1950)

Porter, Roy, *English Society in the Eighteenth Century* (1992 edn)

Porter, Roy and John Brewer (eds), *Consumption and the World of Goods* (1994)

Prothero, I. J., *Artisans and Politics in Early Nineteenth Century London* (Folkestone, 1979)

Rubinstein, W. D., *Men of Property* (1981)

— *Capitalism, Culture and Decline in Britain* (1993)

Schwartz, L. D., *London in the Age of Industrialisation* (Cambridge, 1992)

Thompson, E. P., *The Making of the English Working Class* (1968 edn)

Tunzelman, G. N. von, *Steam Power and British Industrialization to 1860* (Oxford, 1978)

Turberville, A. S., *English Men and Manners in the 18th Century* (New York, 1957)

Wrigley, E. A., *Continuity, Chance and Change. The Character of the Industrial Revolution in England* (Cambridge, 1988)

— 'A Simple Model of London's Importance in Changing English Society and Economy, 1650–1750', *Past and Present*, XXXVII, 1967

2. London

Ash, Bernard, *The Golden City* (1964)

Atkins, P. J., 'The Spatial Configuration of Class Solidarity in London's West End 1792–1939', *Urban History Yearbook*, 17, 1990

Barker, Felix and Peter Jackson, *London: 2000 Years of a City and its People*, (1974)

Barker, T. C., *Three Hundred Years of Red Lion Square 1684–1984* (1987, Guildhall Library, PAM 3741)

Bayne-Powell, Rosamund, *Eighteenth-Century London Life* (1937)

Borer, Mary Cathcart, *The City of London: A History* (1977)

— *An Illustrated Guide to London 1800* (1988)

Broemel, P. R., *Paris and London in 1815* (1929)

Chancellor, E. Beresford, *The XVIIIth Century in London* (1920)

— *Life in Regency and Early Victorian Times* (1926)

Chartres, J. A., 'The Capital's Provincial Eyes: London's Inns in the Early 18th Century', *London Journal*, III, 2, 1977

Clarke, Linda, *Building Capitalism, Historical Change and the Labour Process in the Production of the Built Environment* (1992)

Clout, Hugh (ed.), *London History Atlas* (1991)

— and P. Woods (eds), *London: Problems of Change* (1986)

Clunn, H. P., *The Face of London* (1957 edn)

Coppock, J. T. and C. Hugh Prince (eds), *Greater London* (1964)

Dawe, Donovan, *11 Ironmonger Lane* (1952)

Desebrock, Jean, *The Book of Bond Street Old and New* (1978)

Harrison, Michael, *London Growing* (1965)

Heal, Sir Ambrose, *Sign Boards of Old London Shops* (1988 edn)

Hibbert, Christopher, *London, the Biography of a City* (1990 edn)

Hibbert, Christopher and Ben Weinreb (eds), *The London Encyclopaedia* (1983)

Hobhouse, Hermione, *The Ward of Cheap* (1963)

— *A History of Regent Street* (1975)

Hoggart, Keith and David Green (eds), *London, A New Metropolitan Geography* (1991)

Hyde, Ralph (ed.), *The A to Z of Georgian London* (1981)

Jackson, Peter, *George Scharf's London* (1987)

Laxton, Paul (ed.), *The A to Z of Regency London* (1985)

Leapman, Michael (ed.), *The Book of London* (1989)

Lewis, W. S., *Three Tours Through London in the Years 1748, 1776 and 1797* (Yale, 1941)

Mingay, G. E., *Georgian London* (1975)

Mitchell, R. J. and M. D. R. Leys, *A History of London Life* (1958)

Olsen, D. J., *Town Planning in London. The Eighteenth and Nineteenth Centuries* (Yale, 1964)

Picard, Liza, *Restoration London* (1997)

Porter, Roy, *London: A Social History* (1994)

Rasmussen, Steen Eiler, *London: The Unique City* (1960 edn)

Rudé, George, *Hanoverian London, 1714–1808* (1971)

Saint, Andrew and Gillian Darley, *The Chronicles of London* (1994)

Saunders, Ann, *Regents Park, from 1086 to the Present* (2nd edn 1981)

— *The Regent's Park Villas* (1981)

Sayle, R. T. D., *Notes on the South-East Corner of Chancery Lane – 1819–1929* (1929)

Sheppard, Francis, *London 1808–1870: The Infernal Wen* (1971)

— 'London and the Nation in the Nineteenth Century', *Transactions of the Royal Historical Society*, 5th Series, XXXV, 1985

Summerson, John, *Georgian London* (3rd edn, 1978)

Turvey, Ralph, 'Street Mud, Dust and Noise', *London Journal*, 21, 2, 1996

Weitzman, Arthur J., 'Eighteenth-Century London: Urban Paradise or Fallen City?', *Journal of the History of Ideas*, XXXVI, 1975

Winter, James, *London's Teeming Streets 1830–1914* (1993)

3. Fire Insurance

Adams, Elizabeth, 'Ceramic Insurances in the Sun Company', *English Ceramic Circle Transactions*, 10, 1, 1976

Beresford, M. W., Prometheus Insured: The Sun Fire Agency in Leeds During Urbanization, 1716–1826, *Economic History Review*, XXXV, 3, 1982

Chapman, S. D., *The Cotton Industry in the Industrial Revolution* (Basingstoke, 1987)

— 'The Transition to the Factory System in the Midlands Cotton-Spinning Industry', *Economic History Review*, XVIII, 3, 1965

— 'Fixed Capital Formation in the British Cotton Industry, 1770–1815, *Economic History Review*, XXIII, 2, 1970

— 'Business History from Insurance Policy Registers', *Business Archives*, 32, 1970

Cockerell, H. A. L. and Edwin Green, *The British Insurance Business 1547–1970* (1976)

Dickson, P. G. M., *The Sun Insurance Office 1710–1960* (1960)

Drew, Bernard, *The London Assurance: A Second Chronicle* (1949)

Jenkins, D. T., *Indexes of the Fire Insurance Policies of the Sun Fire Office and the Royal Exchange Assurance 1775–1787* (typescript, University of York, 1986)

Pearson, Robin, 'Fire Insurance and the British Textile Industries during the Industrial Revolution', *Business History*, 34, 4, 1992

Schwartz, L. D. and Jones, L. J. 'Wealth, Occupations, and Insurance in the Late Eighteenth Century: The Policy Registers of the Sun Fire Office', *Economic History Review*, XXXVI, 3, 1983

Supple, Barry, *The Royal Exchange Assurance, A History of British Insurance 1720–1970* (Cambridge, 1970)

Trebilcock, Clive, *Phoenix Insurance and the Development of British Insurance, I, 1782–1879* (Cambridge, 1985)

4. Individual Businesses, Trades and Industries

Adams, Elizabeth, 'The Bow Insurances and Related Matters', *English Ceramic Circle Transactions*, 9, 1, 1973

— 'Nicholas Sprimont's Business Premises', *English Ceramic Circle Transactions*, 13, 1, 1987

Adburgham, Alison, *Shops and Shopping 1800–1914* (1964)

— *Shopping in Style* (1979)

Alexander, David, *Retailing in England During the Industrial Revolution* (1970)

Allen, H. Warner, *Number Three Saint James's Street: A History of Berry's The Wine Merchants* (1950)

Anon., *Old English Coffee Houses* (1954)

Anon., *A Short History of Bradbury Greatorex and Co Ltd* (Nottingham, 1967)

Arlott, John, *The Snuff Shop* (1974)

Atkins, P. J., 'The Retail Milk Trade in London c1790–1814', *Economic History Review*, XXXIII, 4, 1980

Banfield, Edwin, *Barometer Makers and Retailers 1660–1900* (Trowbridge, 1991)

Barker, T. C., 'Passenger Transport in Nineteenth Century London', *Journal of Transport History*, VI, 1963/64

Barker, T. C. and Dorian Gerhold, *The Rise and Rise of Road Transport 1700–1990* (Basingstoke, 1993)

Barker, T. C. and Michael Robbins, *A History of London Transport. I, The Nineteenth Century* (1963)

Barker, T. C. and C. I. Savage, *An Economic History of Transport in Great Britain* (1974)

Barty-King, Hugh, *Maples* (1992)
— *Eyes Right, The Story of Dolland and Aitchison* (1986)
Bates, Alan, *Directory of Stage Coach Services, 1836* (Newton Abbot, 1969
Beard, Geoffrey and Christopher Gilbert, *Dictionary of English Furniture Makers 1660–1840* (1986)
Beaumont, Richard, *Purdey's: The Guns and the Family* (Newton Abbot, 1984)
Benjamin, Thelma H., *London Shops and Shopping* (1934)
Blackman, Janet, 'The Development of the Retail Grocery Trade in the Nineteenth Century', *Business History*, 9, 1967
Blackmore, Howard L., *A Dictionary of London Gunmakers 1350–1850* (Oxford, 1986)
Borer, Mary Cathcart, *The British Hotel Through the Ages* (1972)
Bowers, Ron, *Combs, Combmaking and the Combmakers' Company* (Honiton, 1987)
Brace, Harold W., *History of Seed Crushing in Great Britain* (1960)
Braithwaite, David, *Building in the Blood: The Story of Dove Brothers of Islington 1781–1981* (1981)
Briggs, Asa, *Wine for Sale* (1985)
Broadley, A. M., *The Story of Garrards 1721–1911* (1911)
Buckley, Francis, *Old London Glasshouses* (1915)
Burnby, Juanita, 'A Study of the English Apothecary from 1660 to 1760', *Medical History*, Supplement no. 3, 1983
Burnett, J., *A Social History of Housing 1815–1970* (Newton Abbot, 1980)
Chapman, S. D., *The Rise of Merchant Banking* (1988 edn)
— *Merchant Enterprise in Britain* (Cambridge, 1992)
— 'The Genesis of the British Hosiery Industry 1600–1750', *Textile History*, 3, 1972
— 'Enterprise and Innovation in the British Hosiery Industry, 1750–1850', *Textile History*, 5, 1974
— 'David Evans and Co., The Last of the Old London Textile Printers', *Textile History*, 14, 1, 1983
— 'The Innovating Entrepreneurs in the British Ready-made Clothing Industry', *Textile History*, 24, 1, 1993
Chapman, S. D. and S. Chassagne, *European Textile Printers in the Eighteenth Century* (1981)
Chartres, J. A. and G. L. Turnbull, 'Road Transport', in D. H. Aldcroft and M. J. Freeman (eds), *Transport in the Industrial Revolution* (Manchester, 1983)
Church, R. A., 'Labour Supply and Innovation 1800–1860: The Boot and Shoe Industry', *Business History*, 12, 1, 1970
Clark, Peter, *The English Alehouse: A Social History, 1200–1830* (1983)
Coleman, D. C., *The British Paper Industry 1495–1860* (Oxford, 1958)
Cook's, *Cook's of St Pauls, 150 Years 1807–1957* (1957)
Cooney, E. W., 'The Origins of the Victorian Master Builders', *Economic History Review*, VIII, 1955–56
Copeland, John, *Roads and Their Traffic* (Newton Abbot, 1968)

— 'An Essex Turnpike Gate', *Journal of Transport History*, VI, 1963–64

Corbett, Edward, *An Old Coachman's Chatter* (1890)

Corina, Maurice, *Fine Silks and Oak Counters: Debenhams 1778–1978* (1978)

Corner, David, 'The Tyranny of Fashion: The Case of the Felt-Hatting Trade in the late 17th and 18th Centuries', *Textile History*, 22, 2, 1991

Cripps, Ernest C., *Plough Court, the Story of a Notable Pharmacy 1715–1927* (1927)

Culling, Joyce, *Occupations, A Preliminary List* (Birmingham, 1994)

Cuss, T. P. Camerer, *The Story of Watches* (1952)

Davis, Dorothy, *A History of Shopping* (1966)

Dawe, Donovan, *Skilbeck's Drysalters 1650–1950* (1950)

Dobson, C. G., *A Century and a Quarter, the History of Hall and Co, Croydon* (Croydon, 1951)

Dyos, H. J., *Urbanity and Suburbanity* (Leicester, 1973)

— 'The Speculative Builders and Developers of Victorian London', *Victorian Studies*, XI, 1968

Eatwell, Ann and Alex Werner, 'A London Staffordshire Warehouse, 1794–1825', *Journal of the Northern Ceramics Society*, 8, 1991

Ellis, Joyce, 'On the Town, Women in Augustan England', *History Today*, 45, 12, 1995

Elvin, Lawrence, *Bishop and Son, Organ Builders* (Lincoln, 1984)

Evans, George, *The Old Snuff House of Fribourg and Treyer* (1921)

Fairlie, Susan, 'Dyestuffs in the Eighteenth Century', *Economic History Review*, XVII, 3, 1965

Fairrie, Geoffrey, *The Sugar Refining Families of Great Britain* (1951)

Feather, John, *A History of British Publishing* (1988)

Flinn, Michael W., *The History of the British Coal Industry, II, 1700–1830: The Industrial Revolution* (Oxford, 1984)

Fortnam and Mason, *The Delectable History of Fortnam and Mason*

Francis, A. D., *The Wine Trade* (1972)

Francis, A. J., *The Cement Industry, 1796–1914* (Newton Abbot, 1977)

Fraser-Stephen, Elspet, *Two Centuries in the London Coal Trade* (1952)

French, Christopher J., '"Crowded with traders and a great commerce": London's Domination of English Overseas Trade, 1700–1775', *London Journal*, 17, 1, 1992

French, Roger and Andrew Wear (eds), *British Medicine in the Age of Reform* (1991)

Gatty, Richard, *Portrait of a Merchant Prince, James Morrison 1789–1857* (Northallerton, 1977)

Gentle, Rupert and Rachael Field, *English Domestic Brass 1680–1810* (1975)

Gerhold, Dorian, *Road Transport Before the Railways* (Cambridge, 1992)

— 'The Growth of the London Carrying Trade, 1681–1838', *Economic History Review*, XLI, 3, 1988

Godwin, Charles, *Hanson's of Eastcheap* (1947)

Goodden, Susanna, *At the Sign of the Fourposter: A History of Heal's* (1984)

Goodman, W. L., *British Planemakers from 1700* (Needham Market, 1978)

Gourvish, T. R. and R. G. Wilson, *The British Brewing Industry 1830–1980* (Cambridge, 1994)

Green, Timothy, *Precious Heritage: Three Hundred Years of Macatta and Goldsmid* (1984)

Griffiths, T., P. Hunt and P. K. O'Brien, 'Invention in British Textiles 1700–1800', *Journal of Economic History*, LII, 1992

Grimwade, Arthur G., *London Goldsmiths 1697–1837* (3rd edn, 1990)

Gunter, *The House of Gunter 1786–1907* (1907)

Hamilton, Henry, *The English Brass and Copper Industries to 1800* (1926)

Hamlyn, Hilda, 'Eighteenth-Century Circulating Libraries in England', *Library*, 5th Series, 1, 1947

Hammond, J. L. and Barbara, *The Skilled Labourer 1760–1832* (1919)

Harris, Stanley, *The Coaching Age* (1885)

Hart, Harold W, 'Sherman and the Bull and Mouth', *Journal of Transport History*, V, 1, 1961

Harvey, Brian W., *The Violin Family and its Makers in the British Isles* (Oxford, 1995)

Hayman, Leslie, *An Account of W. Williams and Son (Bread Street) Ltd 1819–1975* (1976)

Heal, Sir Ambrose, *The London Goldsmiths 1200–1800* (Cambridge, 1935)

— *London Furniture Makers 1660–1840* (1988 edn)

Hillier, Bevis, *Asprey of Bond St 1781–1981* (1981)

Hills, Richard L., *Papermaking in Britain 1488–1988* (1988)

Hobhouse, Hermione, *Thomas Cubitt, Master Builder* (Didcot, 1995 edn)

Hudson, Kenneth, *Pawnbroking* (1982)

Hudson, Pat and Lynette Hunter (eds), 'The Autobiography of William Hart, Cooper, 1776–1857; A Respectable Artisan in the Industrial Revolution', *London Journal*, 7 , 2, 1981 and 8, 1, 1982

Humphreys, A. L., 'Long Acre and the Coachbuilders', *Notes and Queries*, 181, 15 and 17, 1941

Jackman, W. T., *The Development of Transportation in Modern England* (Cambridge, 1916)

James, Hurford, *Albion Brewery 1808–1958* (1958)

— *The Red Barrel, A History of Watney Mann* (1963)

Jeffereys, J. B., *Retail Trading in Britain, 1850–1950* (Cambridge, 1954)

Keevil, Ambrose, *The Story of Fitch Lovell 1784–1970* (1972)

Kelly, Alison, *Mrs Coade's Stone* (Upton-upon-Severn, 1990)

Kiddier, William, *The Brushmaker* (1923)

Kirkham, Pat, Rodney Mace and Julia Porter, *Furnishing the World: The East London Furniture Trade 1830–1980* (1987)

Landes, David S., *Revolution in Time* (Harvard, 1983)

Lawrence, Susan C., 'Private Enterprise and Public Interests: Medical Education and the Apothecaries Act, 1780–1825', in Roger French and Andrew Weaver (eds), *British Medicine in the Age of Reform* (1991)

Lawson, Andrew, *Handmade in London* (1978)

Lemire, Beverley, *Fashion's Favourite: The Cotton Trade and the Consumer in Britain, 1660–1800* (Oxford, 1991)

— 'Developing Consumerism and the Ready-made Clothing Trade in Britain 1750–1800', *Textile History*, 15, 1, 1984

— 'Peddling Fashion: Salesmen, Pawnbrokers, Taylors, Thieves and the Second-hand Clothes Trade in England, 1700–1800', *Textile History*, 22, 1, 1991

McCausland, Hugh, *The English Carriage* (1948)

McConnell, Anita, *Instrument Makers to the World: A History of Cooke, Troughton and Sons* (York, 1992)

— 'From Craft Workshop to Big Business: The London Scientific Instrument Trade's Response to Increasing Demand 1750–1820', *London Journal*, 19, 1, 1994

— 'Bankruptcy Proceedings Against William Harris, Optician, of Cornhill, 1830', *Annals of Science*, 51, 1994

McKendrick, Neil, 'Josiah Wedgwood: an Eighteenth-century Entrepreneur', *Economic History Review*, XII (1960)

McKendrick, Neil, John Brewer and J H. Plumb, *The Birth of a Consumer Society* (1982)

Mathias, Peter, 'Industrial Revolution in Brewing, Developments in the Brewing Industry: 1700–1830', *Explorations in Entrepreneurial History*, V, 4, 1953

Maxted, Ian, *The London Book Trades 1775–1800* (Folkestone, 1977)

Morgan, H. L., *The History of James Lock and Co, Hatters* (1948)

Mosers, *Mosers of the Borough* (1936)

Mui, Hoh-Cheung and Linda H., *Shops and Shopkeeping in Eighteenth-Century England* (1989)

Mumby, Frank A., *The Romance of Bookselling: A History from the Earliest Times to the Twentieth Century* (1910)

Musson, A. E., *Enterprise in Soap and Chemicals, Joseph Crosfield and Sons Ltd, 1815–1965* (Manchester, 1965)

Nash, Robert C., The English and Scottish Tobacco Trades in the Seventeenth and Eighteenth Centuries: Legal and Illegal Trade', *Economic History Review*, XXXV, 3, 1982

Neal, W. Keith and D. H. L. Back, *Great British Gunmakers 1740–1790* (1975)

Nockolds, Harold, *The Coachmakers* (1977)

Oliver, J. L., *The Development and Structure of the Furniture Industry* (Oxford, 1966)

Osbahr, Alan, *Felton's Carriages* (1962)

Owen, Roderic, *Lepard and Smith's Limited 1757–1957* (Crawley, 1957)

Pannell, J. P. M., *An Illustrated History of Civil Engineering* (1964)

Perren, Richard, *The Meat Trade in Britain 1840–1914* (1978)

Perrotts, *A History of 250 Years of Clothworking in London* (1961)

Pollard, S., 'The Decline of Shipbuilding on the Thames', *Economic History Review*, III, 1, 1950

Porter, Roy, *Health for Sale, Quackery in England, 1660–1850* (Manchester, 1989)

Postgate, R. W., *The Builders' History* (1923)

Powell, C. G., *An Economic History of the British Building Industry 1815–1979* (1982)

Price's Patent Candle Co Ltd, *Still the Candle Burns* (1947)

Ramsden, Charles, *London Bookbinders, 1780–1840* (1956)

Redlich, Fritz, 'Some English Stationers of the Seventeenth and Eighteenth Centuries: In the Light of their Autobiographies', *Business History*, 8, 1966

Rees, J. A., *The Grocery Trade, Its History and Romance* (1932)

Rosoman, Treve, *London Wallpapers, Their Manufacture and Use 1690–1840* (1992)

Rothstein, Nathalie, *Silk Designs of the Eighteenth Century* (1980)

— 'The Successful and the Unsuccessful Huguenot, Another Look at the London Silk Industry in the 18th and early 19th Centuries', *Proceedings of the Huguenot Society*, XXV, 5, 1993

Sadler, Arthur, *One Hundred and Seventy Five Years of the House of Christy* (1951)

Seager and Evans, *Mr Seager and Mr Evans, the Story of a Great Partnership* (1963)

Simmons, Douglas A., *Schweppes, the First 200 Years* (1983)

Slinn, Judy, *A History of May and Baker 1834–1984* (Cambridge, 1984)

Smith, D. J., 'Army Clothing Contractors and the Textile Industries in the 18th Century', *Textile History*, 14, 2, 1983

Smith, Raymond, *Sea Coal for London* (1961)

Stern, Walter M., 'The London Sugar Refiners Around 1800', *Guildhall Miscellany*, 3, 1954

— 'Where, Oh Where, are the Cheesemongers of London', *London Journal*, 5, 2, 1979

Sugden, Alan Victor and John Ludlum Edmondson, *A History of English Wallpaper* (1925)

Thomas, E. Wynne, *The House of Yardley 1770–1953* (1953)

Thoms, David W., 'Joseph Travers and Sons and the London Wholesale Grocery Market, 1824–1861', *Guildhall Miscellany*, III, 2, 1970

Travers, Joseph and Sons, *A Few Records of an Old Firm* (1907)

Turvey, Ralph, 'Street Mud, Dust and Noise', *London Journal*, 21, 2, 1996

Tweedale, Geoffrey, *At the Sign of the Plough, 275 Years of Allen and Hanbury and the British Pharmaceutical Industry 1715–1990* (1990)

Twining, Stephen H., *The House of Twining, 1706–1956* (1956)

Wainwright, David, *The Piano Makers* (1975)

Walker, Richard, *The Savile Row Story* (1988)

Whitbourn, Frank, *Mr Lock of St James St* (1971)

Whitbread's, *The Story of Whitbreads* (1947)

Wild, Charles James, *John Wild, 1729–1801* (Harpenden, 1914)

Wilson, Charles, *First With the News, the History of W H Smith 1792–1972* (1985)

Wright, David, *An Index of London Surgical Instrument Makers 1822–65* (1989)

Ziegler, Philip, *The Sixth Great Power, Barings, 1762–1929* (1988)

Index